A Classic Turn of Phrase
Music and the Psychology of Convention

Studies in the Criticism and Theory of Music

Janet M. Levy. *Beethoven's Compositional Choices: The Two Versions of Opus 18, No. 1, First Movement.* 1982
Robert O. Gjerdingen. *A Classic Turn of Phrase: Music and the Psychology of Convention.* 1988

A Classic Turn of Phrase.

Music and the Psychology of Convention

Robert O. Gjerdingen.

University of Pennsylvania Press
Philadelphia

Permission to reprint material in the text is acknowledged from the following sources:

From *Scripts, Plans, Goals and Understanding: An Inquiry into Human Knowledge Structures* (pp. 41, 70, 77, 99) by Roger C. Schank and Robert P. Abelson, 1977. Hillsdale, N.J.: Lawrence Erlbaum Associates. Copyright © 1977 by Lawrence Erlbaum Associates. Reprinted by permission of Lawrence Erlbaum Associates and the authors.

From *Principles of Perceptual Learning and Development* (figure, p. 161) by Eleanor J. Gibson, 1969. Englewood Cliffs, N.J.: Prentice-Hall. Copyright © 1969 by Prentice-Hall, Inc. Used by permission of Prentice-Hall, Inc.

From "Theories of Memory Organization and Human Evolution," (figure, p. 163) by Janet L. Lachman and Roy Lachman, in *Memory Organization and Structure*, ed. C. Richard Puff, 1979. Orlando, Fl.: Academic Press. Copyright © 1979 by Academic Press. Used by permission of Academic Press and the authors.

From "A Model for the Encoding of Experiential Information," (figure, p. 410) by Joseph P. Becker, in *Computer Models of Thought and Language*, ed. Roger C. Schank and Kenneth Mark Colby, 1973. New York: W. H. Freeman. Copyright © 1973 by W. H. Freeman and Co. Used by permission of W. H. Freeman and Co.

Figures 4-4, 5-1, 5-4, 6-2, 9-4, and 12-1; and examples 2-11, 2-19, 4-11, 5-30, 5-33a, 7-23, 7-24c, 7-25, 7-26, 7-27, 7-28, 8-8, 8-10, 8-15, 8-18, 9-1b, 9-3, 9-36, 9-42, 10-27, 10-28, 11-22, 11-23, and 11-35b first appeared in and are reproduced or adapted from Robert O. Gjerdingen, "The Formation and Deformation of Classic/Romantic Phrase Schemata," *Music Theory Spectrum* 8 (1986). Copyright © 1986 by the Society for Music Theory. Used by permission of the Society for Music Theory.

Library of Congress Cataloging-in-Publication Data

Gjerdingen, Robert O.
    A classic turn of phrase.
    (Studies in the criticism and theory of music)
    Bibliography: p.
    Includes index.
    1. Musical analysis—Psychological aspects.
I. Title.   II. Series.
ML3838.G45   1988   781'.15   87-19184
ISBN 0-8122-8075-X

Flawlessness of an analysis, although
it may be taken as the triumph of a method,
is a reason for scholarly, theoretical mistrust.

Carl Dahlhaus

CONTENTS

PREFACE

Once, in a general discussion of the problems of musical research, a friend mentioned the maxim that "when your only tool is a hammer, all your problems look like nails." Though I found this witty, I did not at first see its relevance to my own concerns with the analysis of classical music. After all, it seemed self-evident that the salient problem of musical analysis was to reduce the surface complexities of actual music to orderly progressions of structurally significant tones. And while skilled musical analysts might disagree over which tones were structurally significant, there was little doubt that a hierarchical system of pitch reduction was the tool to use.

At about the same time, my interest in eighteenth-century musical themes and phrases had led me to consider Leonard Meyer's ideas about archetypal musical schemata. These are normative abstractions of basic melodic, harmonic, or formal patterns so common as to constitute part of the very fabric of classical music. Meyer's notion of normative abstractions appealed to my musical intuitions but presented a major technical obstacle to reductive analysis. Simply stated, the rather large patterns identified by Meyer are difficult if not impossible to reduce to uniform, simpler constituents. Apparently the same stumbling block had been encountered by the music theorists Fred Lerdahl and Ray Jackendoff,[1] who, while admitting the intuitive appeal of archetypal musical schemata, nonetheless chose to exclude them from their analytical system in order to preserve its unfettered ability to reduce any musical pattern to a smaller set of constituent tones.

To turn one's back on shared musical institutions merely for the sake of an analytical system seemed, to me at least, unjustified. What profit is there in hammering out a dogmatic analysis of a musical composition if those melodic or formal elements that we perceive to be present must be effaced in the process? Surely it is not the goal of musical analysis to be systematic at all costs. Perhaps this tool of hierarchical pitch reduction was unduly influencing the perceived agenda of musical analysis.

My eventual response to the dilemma of choosing between shared musical intuitions and structural-tone reductionism can be summarized by a rewording of the above-mentioned maxim: "When you suspect that your problems may *not* be nails, don't keep beating them with a hammer—find a better tool!'' The study that follows is an attempt to find a better tool for understanding how knowledgeable listeners perceive many of the sublimely beautiful musical phrases of the eighteenth and nineteenth centuries. I do not propose a universal analytical system based on a few tidy axioms and procedures. Nor do I suggest a grand concept—unity, organicism, perfection—on which to base an exegesis of all great music. My methods are far more modest. I present no more than a framework for examining the musical structures present in classical phrases. To be sure, this framework can yield a detailed and revealing analysis of musical structure, but the framework itself merely guides a simple and straightforward examination of musical patterns and their interactions.

I would like to thank the people who have influenced and assisted this study. Leonard Meyer's work on musical archetypes has been a major influence, as have been Eugene Narmour's theoretical studies on the methodology of musical analysis. Both these scholars contributed greatly to the improvement of this manuscript in its several stages. Thoughtful criticisms or additional musical examples were suggested by Easley Blackwood, William Caplin, Richard Freedman, James Moore, and Lewis Rowell. Because this study frequently addresses the music of many lesser-known eighteenth-century composers, I have been greatly reassured in having been able to consult Eugene Wolf's encyclopedic knowledge of this period and to refer to his own work on the phrase structure of early Classic music. The staff of the Albrecht Music Library of the University of Pennsylvania deserves my thanks, as do the many musicologists who have devoted themselves to making eighteenth- and early nineteenth-century scores available in reliable editions. The musical examples in the text were produced through the artistry of Johanna Baldwin at A-R Editions, Inc. Finally, the financial support of the Mellon Foundation and Carleton College and the editorial assistance of my wife Catherine have helped to bring my good intentions to fruition.

PART I

Theoretical Foundation

CHAPTER 1

What is a Schema?

Hardly a month goes by without the postman delivering yet another ingenious mis-spelling of my last name. In the past few years the following have appeared:

Djaragun	Gijerdingen	Gjirdingen	Jerdigen
Gjerdingla	Ggerdinger	Gjardingen	Gyerdingen
Gjeedingen	Gierdingen	Gjernigen	Gjerdenger
Gjerdinger	Jerdingen	Djerdigan	Gjerdigan
Djardingen	Gjerdingon	Gennigan	Jeridingen
Gerdingen	Gerjerdingen	Gdjernigen	Gjerdengen
Gerdigen	Ggerdingen	Guerdingen	Gjerdingei
Gjerdigen	Yunnigan	Jordinger	Ogjerdingen
Gherdingen	Jernigan	Gjordingen	Gjeroingen
Gjerdmjen	Cjerdingen	Gordine	Djerdingen
Gjerienen	Gjedingen	Gjereingen	Bjerdingen
Sjerdingen	G. J. Erdingen	Fjerdingen	Gjerdignen
Gjerkingen	Gjerdingeu	Cjerdinger	Gjerdingens
Guerdinger	Gjeringen	G. Jerdingen	Gjirendgen

As a mere collection of letters of the alphabet, *Gjerdingen* should be no more per-plexing than, say, *Washington*. After all, both are three-syllable words ten letters long, each with seven consonants and three vowels. They share the morpheme *ing* and the same pattern of accentuation. *Gjerdingen* should perhaps be even easier to spell because whereas *Washington* has three consonants in a row, *Gjerdingen* never has more than two. The reality of the situation is, of course, quite different. *Gjerdingen* is much harder to spell because *gj* does not fit into an English-language con-text. While Scandinavians may find the name unexceptional, speakers of English have difficulty remembering it and, as the above list suggests, have problems even perceiving it accurately.

Perhaps having such a name sensitizes one to the crucial role that an interpretive context can play in memory and perception. Even meaning can depend on a particular context. For example, we have all certainly heard objections to taking a word or phrase out of context. Such objections rightly presume that meaning may be conditional upon a particular interpretive context. Certainly this is the case with music. Whether a tone is dissonant or consonant, for instance, depends entirely on the context in which it is found. So to accurately perceive, understand the significance of, and remember particular musical events, one must in some way understand the contexts in which they occur. But how can one gain other than an intuitive, subjective knowledge of musical context? In other words, is there a theory of context, and if so, are there methods for objectively studying it?

If we conceive of an interpretive context as a psychological entity residing in "that portion of the entire perceptual cycle which is internal to the perceiver, modifiable by experience, and somehow specific to what is being perceived,"[1] then we may study such a context under the technical term of a *schema* (pl. *schemata*). This word gained currency within the psychological vocabulary in the 1930s through its use by Frederick Bartlett in his *Remembering: A Study in Experimental and Serial Psychology:*

> "Schema" refers to an active organization of past reactions, or of past experiences, which must always be supposed to be operating in any well-adapted organic response. That is, whenever there is any order or regularity of behavior, a particular response is possible only because it is related to other similar responses which have been serially organized, yet which operate, not simply as individual members coming one after another, but as a unitary mass.[2]

A concept at once so provocative and yet so vaguely defined has been adopted and reinterpreted by scholars in many fields. For example, an information-theory specialist, Selby Evans, views a schema as "a set of rules which would serve as instructions for producing in essential aspects a population prototype and object typical of the population."[3] A specialist in pattern perception, Stephen Reed, thinks of schemata as "cognitive structures that organize systems of stored information."[4] Some cognitive scientists, Joseph Becker for example, define a schema as "a particular formal structure for representing information."[5] Others, David Rumelhart for example, think of schemata as "active processing elements which can be activated from higher level purposes and expectations, or from input data which must be accounted for."[6] And a contemporary cognitive psychologist, Jean Mandler, defines a schema as a mental structure "formed on the basis of past experience with objects, scenes, or events and consisting of a set of (usually unconscious) expectations about what things look like and/or the order in which they occur."[7]

Of the authors just quoted, David Rumelhart has provided perhaps the most accessible introduction to schema theory. In discussing the general properties or characteristics that all schemata seem to share, he singles out six for special mention.[8] First, "schemata have variables"; since no experience is ever exactly repeated, we must be able to discover intuitively both the dimensions of variation and the range of variation that characterize our generalizations of the world. Second, "schemata can embed, one within another"; a particular schema may be part of a larger network of relationships. Third, "schemata represent knowledge at all levels of abstraction." Fourth, "schemata represent knowledge rather than definitions." In his words, "our schemata *are* our knowledge. All of our generic knowledge is embedded in schemata." Fifth, "schemata are active processes"; through schemata we can make predictions and form expectations. And sixth, "schemata are recognition devices whose processing is aimed at the evaluation of their goodness of fit to the data being processed."

The "input data," "information," "events," or "variables" for which schemata provide interpretive contexts can be discussed under the broad rubric of "features." While our ability to distinguish some features of the world around us appears to be innate, many other features must be learned, especially those defined by culture. To illustrate one theory about how such learning might progress, I reproduce in figure 1-1 a diagram prepared by Eleanor Gibson.[9]

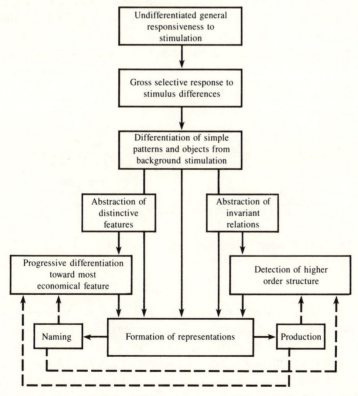

FIGURE 1-1. Feature acquisition (From Eleanor J. Gibson, *Principles of Perceptual Learning and Development* [Englewood Cliffs, N.J.: Prentice-Hall, 1969], p. 161. Copyright © 1969. Reprinted by permission of Prentice-Hall, Inc.)

In specifying a process such as "progressive differentiation toward [the] most economical feature," Gibson rightly implies that our knowledge of features is mutable and capable of refinement. But what governs our selection and refinement of features? Concepts such as need, utility, economy, and function all depend on some larger context. For instance, the phonetic features we learn to perceive in language are intimately tied to the many contexts in which they occur. A full understanding of specific learned features can thus require a careful study of specific contexts, which brings us back to schemata.

In music, we learn to recognize many types of features. Some, such as the tone qualities of instruments, can usually be identified in or out of context. But other features, such as harmonic relationships, are highly context-sensitive. Consider the circled section in example 1-1. The various pitches in this circled section (B♭–C–D–E♭–F) do not together constitute one of the chords—that is, one of the harmonic features—of classical music. Instead, we hear the left-hand accompaniment beginning the Alberti-bass figuration of the dominant seventh chord while the right-hand melody continues the triadic descent of the tonic chord. Two harmonic features—tonic and dominant—are perceived as overlapping, because this is the only interpretation consistent with the larger *context* formed by our schemata for classical phrase structure, melody, and harmonic progression. The type of musical cognition implied by this example requires that a reciprocal relationship exist between features and schemata. Features serve as cues in the selection of schemata, and schemata serve as guides in the detection of features. Schemata can be defined as meaningful sets of features, and features can be defined as meaningful elements in sets of schemata.

EXAMPLE 1-1. Beethoven, Piano Sonata in D Major, Op. 10, No. 3 (1797–98), iv, Allegro, meas. 35–37

When a feature—whether an attribute, quality, figure, relationship, or symbol—is presented to us, we attempt to find a context for it, or, more technically speaking, we take it to be the partial instantiation of one of several possible schemata. As more features are perceived, rival schemata can be eliminated and the most likely schema selected. This process is often called data-driven or bottom-up processing because low-level features select a higher-level schema. This type of processing can be very effective when the incoming features are separate, distinct, and unambiguous. But the torrent of features that is presumed to flood in upon our senses may make exclusively bottom-up processing difficult.

Schema theory asserts, consequently, that once distinctive features of a schema are instantiated, we actively seek out the remaining features. Such a procedure is often called concept-driven or top-down processing, because a higher-level schema directs a search for lower-level features. In those cases where top-down processing locates all but one or two of the expected features, psychologists believe the missing features may be given *default values*. In other words, human cognition may "fill in the blanks" left by perceptions if an overall context seems appropriate. The concurrent top-down and bottom-up processing of noisy, ambiguous features and changing schemata is a fluid, adaptable, and responsive process predictive of the future implications of present events. It represents a sophisticated model of cognition that explains how we relate an outer world of sensations and percepts to our inner world of abstractions and concepts.

The methodologies developed by cognitive psychologists to study various mental processes can be profitably adapted to investigate musical schemata. Several recently reported experiments suggest not only that different types of musical schemata have a psychological reality, but also that the concept of a schema may prove extremely useful in studying the perception of music.[10] Among these experiments, one with special relevance to the study at hand was undertaken by the psychologist Burton S. Rosner in collaboration with the music theorist Leonard B. Meyer.[11] Using what is termed a forced-choice experimental procedure, Rosner and Meyer showed that "ordinary listeners" could abstract two musical schemata shared by two groups of recorded excerpts of classical music. The subjects were given no descriptions or definitions of the schemata (known only as A or B); they had to learn them intuitively through a process of trial and error. Subjects then used this knowledge to identify instances of schema A or schema B in another group of recorded excerpts. Music theorists have always presumed that listeners perform intuitive musical analyses, but Rosner and Meyer seem to be among the first to have demonstrated it for complex structures in actual artworks.

The two schemata used in these experiments are what Meyer has termed gap-fill and changing-note archetypes ("archetypes" being his term for innate or universally valid schemata). The first is characterized by an initial melodic leap, usually upward, followed by a linear descent filling in the space—the gap—created by the leap. "Twinkle, Twinkle Little Star" is such a melody (example 1-2). The second is characterized by two melodic dyads, the first leading away from and the second leading back to tonic harmony (example 1-3).

EXAMPLE 1-2. A gap-fill melody

harmony: I – V   V – I

EXAMPLE 1-3. A changing-note melody

Both these schemata have initial configurations that demand an appropriate terminal configuration for resolution and closure. Thus both schemata have elements of
an antecedent-consequent form, though each is quite a different type of abstraction.
In the style of classical music, the first two schema-relevant notes of a changing-note
melody can be said to imply not only the likely pitches of a second pair of notes but
also their likely metrical placement and harmonization. On the other hand, a gap-fill
schema is not specific in the implications its initial gap creates. We may expect the
melody to descend, but both when and how are largely undetermined.

The differences between these schemata are similar to what Roger C. Schank
and Robert P. Abelson call the differences between scripts and plans.[12] While Rumelhart uses the single term "schemata" for both higher- and lower-level abstractions of
event sequences, Schank and Abelson use different terms. Here is their definition of
a script:

> A script is a structure that describes appropriate sequences of events in a
> particular context. A script is made up of slots and requirements about
> what can fill those slots. The structure is an interconnected whole, and
> what is in one slot affects what can be in another. Scripts handle stylized
> everyday situations. They are not subject to much change, nor do they
> provide the apparatus for handling totally novel situations. Thus, a script
> is a predetermined, stereotyped sequence of actions that defines a well-
> known situation. Scripts allow for new references to objects within them
> just as if these objects had been previously mentioned; objects within a
> script may take 'the' without explicit introduction because the script itself
> has already implicitly introduced them.[13]

Plans are more general:

> A plan is intended to be the repository for general information that will
> connect events that cannot be connected by use of an available script or by
> standard causal chain expansion. A plan is made up of general informa-
> tion about how actors achieve goals. A plan explains how a given state or
> event was prerequisite for, or derivative from, another state or event. . . .
> There is a fine line between the point where scripts leave off and plans
> begin. In a sense it is an unimportant distinction. We are interested
> in predictions. . . . The point here is that plan-based processing is differ-

ent in kind from script-based processing. Script-based processing is a much more top-down operation. Furthermore it is a process which takes precedence over plan-based processing when an appropriate script is available.[14]

The changing-note archetype is a predictable, "stereotyped sequence of actions" and therefore a scriptlike schema. The gap-fill archetype, on the other hand, is a more general, planlike schema.

If Schank and Abelson are correct that we use script-based processing whenever possible and resort to plans only when no script is available, we might use this principle to explain the indication that Rosner and Meyer's subjects, when given the task of sorting gap-fill from changing-note melodies, learned the changing-note schema first and simply labeled everything else a gap-fill schema.[15] They made the lower-level abstraction first and then relied on their script-based knowledge to perform the classificatory task. To circumvent this tendency, Rosner and Meyer devised a new experiment—a gap-fill versus non–gap-fill sorting problem—that forced subjects to abstract this higher-level, planlike schema.

For my own study, the prime significance of Rosner and Meyer's experiments lies in their empirical validation of the concept of complex musical schemata. Lingering doubts about the psychological reality of such schemata can be provisionally set aside and attention focused on the details of specific schemata. In this respect, my differentiation of changing-note and gap-fill structures as scripts and plans promises to shed light on an important aspect of style change. Meyer has suggested, and my own studies confirm, that many of the stereotyped, scriptlike musical phrases of the eighteenth century are transformed into the generalized, planlike musical phrases of the nineteenth century. In the next chapter we will see a transitional example of this process of style change—an excerpt from Schumann's song "Wehmut" in which both changing-note and gap-fill schemata are superimposed upon the same phrase.

Summary

Schema theory affords a promising conceptual framework for the study of musical cognition. But before a general schema theory can be established for music, several issues must be addressed. First of all, because schema theory is a type of structuralism, emphasizing in Bartlett's words "an active organization of past experiences," any consideration of a musical schema must also be a consideration of musical structure. Simply bringing terms like *schema* or *feature* into the vocabulary of musical analysis does not mean that the basic questions of musical structure are displaced. Indeed, questions of how musical structures are perceived and stored in memory become crucial for a psychologically based analysis of music. Even an experimental approach of the kind pioneered by Rosner and Meyer requires an analysis of musical structure not only for the selection of musical examples but also for the evaluation of the final results. For these reasons, a more detailed investigation of musical schemata must be delayed while, in the next chapter, attention is first focused on the subject of musical structure.

CHAPTER 2

A New Look at Musical Structure

Among the central concerns of music theory are the definition, representation, and interpretation of musical structures. I have already intimated a definition of musical structures as cognitive schemata of various degrees of abstraction, and later chapters will broach the subject of interpreting musical schemata in a historical context. In this chapter, I want to discuss a broad range of topics pertaining to the representation of musical structures, both to challenge some prevalent assumptions and to explain my own manner of structural representation. The chapter begins with a general discussion of mental structures from the perspective of George Mandler, followed by a discussion of tree-structures, hierarchies, and networks. I argue that networks afford representations of musical structure that least distort the manifold relationships inherent in even the simplest music. Several examples taken from published analyses of music demonstrate some limitations of tree-structure representations and point out the need to consider structural networks. The chapter concludes with a consideration of how initially to identify musical schemata and how to prove that a musical schema does or did exist.

The Representation of Structure

The diagrams used to represent mental structures—and implicitly the hypotheses that underlie these diagrams—have been much discussed in recent years. The subject is important because, as is becoming evident, there is no visual representation of a structure—whether a memory structure or a musical one—that does not in some way distort or bias the data being represented. Moreover, only by being aware of all the possibilities can a reasonable choice of a representation be made. One might liken the problem to the cartographer's dilemma of representing a spherical world on a flat surface. Each projection creates a different distortion, so that the only sensible course is to choose the projection that causes the least distortion considering both the region being represented and the needs of the map's user. Similar criteria can guide the selection of a representation of mental topography, provided that we understand both the range of mental structures to be represented and the various means of representing them. To that end, this section begins with an examination of three classes of mental structures distinguished by the psychologist George Mandler.[1] Once these have been considered I will discuss how they may be represented, coming to the conclusion that network representations are the optimal choice for complex musical structures.

Mandler's first class, *coordinate structure,* is characterized by elements all directly related to one another. Coordinate structures presume no preferred path through them; if one begins at any one element, one can move directly to any of the other elements (figure 2-1). Notice that an arithmetic increase in the number of elements results in a geometric increase in the number of relationships. A coordinate structure of five elements would have ten relationships, six elements fifteen relationships, and so on. Mandler believes that because of the brain's various processing limitations, mental coordinate structures will likely have only two, three, or four elements.[2]

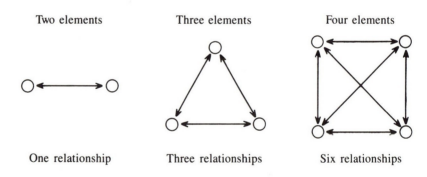

FIGURE 2-1. Coordinate structures

A low-level musical example of a three-element coordinate structure could be an isolated augmented triad, for example, C–E–G♯ (or C–E–A♭ etc.). All three pitches are required for the structure to be perceptible, and no single pitch subordinates or necessarily precedes the other two. In like fashion, certain atonal sets of pitches may be considered low-level coordinate musical structures. For example, a basic notion of musical set theory is that a four-element set such as C–D♯–E♯–F♯ can be presented in any order or spacing, has no reference pitch or "tonic," and gives rise to six intervallic relationships (C–D♯, C–E♯, C–F♯, D♯–E♯, D♯–F♯, E♯–F♯). Higher-level examples of purely coordinate structures are rare in classical music but can sometimes be discerned in the music of the avant-garde when, for example, heterogeneous masses of sound are simultaneously juxtaposed.

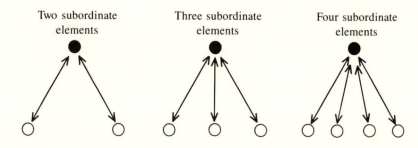

FIGURE 2-2. Subordinate structures

Mandler's second class, *subordinate structure,* is the familiar tree-structure (figure 2-2). A special feature of this structural type, implicit but often ignored, is that its tree-structure representation specifies no direct relationship *between* the subordinate elements; only subordinate, "vertical" relationships are indicated. For example, the white circles in figure 2-2 may have direct, "horizontal" interrelationships, but these relationships cannot be represented by the tree-structures. Tree-structures, as will be shown later, abound in musical analyses. The analysis of an ornamented ascending triad in example 2-1 would be typical.

EXAMPLE 2-1. A musical subordinate structure

Two proordinate   Three proordinate   Four proordinate
    elements   elements   elements

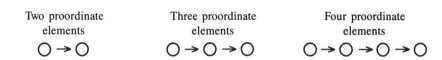

FIGURE 2-3. Proordinate structures

The third class is *proordinate* or *serial structure* (figure 2-3). Here one must move through the elements in a specified order. Proordinate structures are so fundamental to music that they tend to be taken for granted. For instance, a theorist might assume that the tree-structure analysis given in example 2-1 represents the proordinate structure C–E–G–C. But strictly speaking it does not—the essential tree-structure *would be the same* even if the music were played backward.

Obviously our minds must be able to relate dozens of elements in order to accomplish even the simplest tasks of cognition. Most psychologists believe this is possible through the combinations we make of basic structures. Figure 2-4 shows how a multileveled, composite structure utilizing various combinations of Mandler's classes might be organized. This structural complex represents aspects of the opening measure of part 2 of Stravinsky's *Rite of Spring*. Coordinate structures depict the juxtaposition of subordinately structured chords, and proordinate structures indicate the time- and order-dependent nature of melody and rhythm.

The structural complex shown in figure 2-4 is a logical extension of Mandler's premises but atypical of the structural representations people actually use. Scholars and scientists have apparently preferred a cognitive "Mercator projection," which can result in significant distortions but proceeds from a single premise. For instance, the literature of music theory abounds in structural representations consisting solely of subordinate structures; several such analyses are discussed later in this chapter. Clearly, such representations do not imply that proordinate and coordinate structures are absent in music. Rather, it seems obvious that these analyses are a type of short-hand, a culturally sanctioned mode of structural representation where the part is taken as a symbol of the whole.

Inasmuch as Mandler's three modes of relationship are not equally well served by typical structural representations, it may be useful to examine some modes of representation in greater depth, especially considering that with several commonly used modes of structural representation it is possible to convert one mode into another. From the psychological literature, Michael Friendly lists four common "structural frameworks"—ways of representing relationships—that are permutable: a taxonomy, a dimensional representation, a tree-structure, and a network.[3] Assume for the purpose of an illustration that we wish to make a structural representation of the short melody in figure 2-5. The most informal way of graphically representing one aspect of its structure is simply first to draw circles around the pitches that form the two melodic dyads and then to draw a large circle around the entire melody. Friendly terms this approach "taxonomy" (figure 2-5), implying that it is essentially a classification scheme meant to highlight things that seem to "go together."[4]

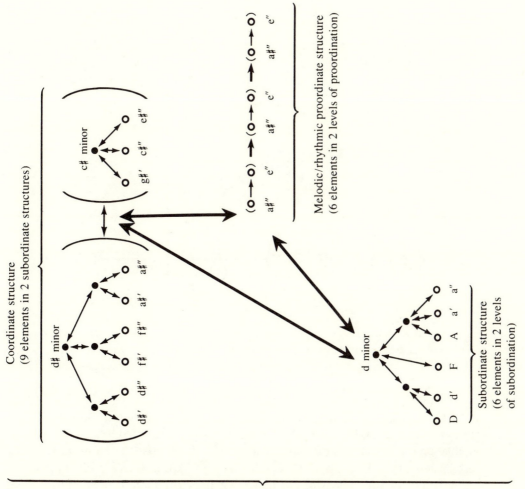

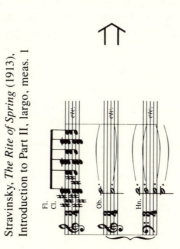

Stravinsky, *The Rite of Spring* (1913).
Introduction to Part II, largo, meas. 1

FIGURE 2-4. A combination of coordinate, subordinate, and proordinate structures

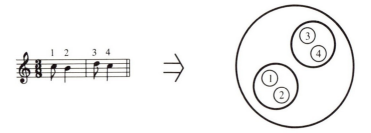

FIGURE 2-5. A taxonony

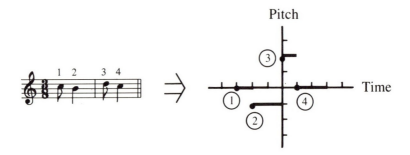

FIGURE 2-6. A dimensional representation

At the opposite extreme from the informality of a loosely defined taxonomy is the almost too precise method of a "dimensional representation" with scaled parameters (figure 2-6). Here aspects of relationship are converted into separate, measurable parameters represented as the axes of a one-, two-, or more dimensional coordinate system. Two dimensions are most often used in such representations, recalling the two basic dimensions of music notation. But there is nothing to prevent representations in more or fewer dimensions. For example, the structure shown above could be presented in only the single dimension of duration (figure 2-7) (in this form it resembles a proordinate structure). These dimensional representations can be transformed back into the taxonomy of figure 2-5 by equating spatial proximity with relatedness.

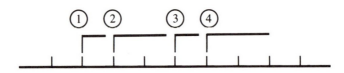

FIGURE 2-7. A dimensional representation reduced to a single dimension

Another alternative to taxonomy is to see the circles surrounding related elements as symbols for a tree-structure (figure 2-8), in effect replacing the defined relation "goes with" by the more formal and narrower "is subordinate to." The tree-structure of figure 2-8 could also have been mathematically derived from the dimensional representations of figures 2-6 and 2-7 by again equating proximity with relatedness. The tree-structure in figure 2-8 associates element 1 with element 2, and 3 with 4, but obscures any possible direct relationship between elements 1 and 4, 2 and 3, 1 and 3, and 2 and 4. To represent all this information we must move from tree-structures to "networks" (figure 2-9). In terms of graph theory, a tree-structure is a restricted case of a network.[5] A network can represent any tree-structure without loss of structural information, but the reverse is not true. For example, the network representation of figure 2-9 shows at one and the same time that, while the melody might imply an ascending continuation to E, it nonetheless ends with a return to the tonic C. The various open and closed aspects of the melody coexist. But a tree-structure representation can accept only one interpretation; the melody is either open or closed, not both. This distinction between tree-structures and networks is discussed at length in the next section.

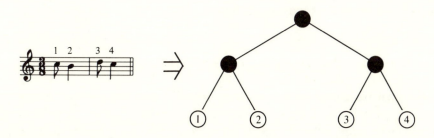

FIGURE 2-8. A tree-structure

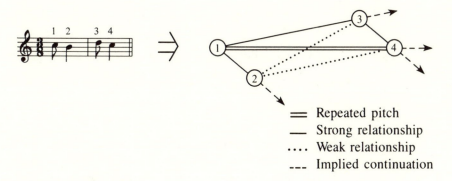

FIGURE 2-9. A network

Not all modes of graphic representation—taxonomy, the use of scaled parameters, tree-structures, and networks—can deal equally well with Mandler's coordinate, subordinate, and proordinate structures. Tree-structures, for instance, are ideal for representing subordinate structures but create gross distortions when used for coordinate or proordinate structures. Scaled parameters are often more appropriate for statistical than structural information and can be difficult to apply to music. Taxonomy—drawing circles around things that belong together—is a rudimentary approach sometimes seen in early analyses of twelve-tone music. The remaining mode of graphic representation, the use of networks, is able both to display all three of Mandler's structural categories and to accommodate Friendly's three other structural frameworks without the loss of structural information. (Though this assertion is demonstrable in terms of graph theory, it may not be intuitively obvious. Subsequent comparisons of tree-structure and network representations of particular musical structures should provide positive evidence of this point.)

What the work of Mandler and Friendly suggests is that network representations have the greatest potential for representing mental structures and, by inclusion, musical structures. Why then are network representations rare in musical analyses? The main reason seems to be that a tradition has been established holding that only tree-structures can represent the hierarchies of typical musical structures. This tradition is considered in the following section.

Hierarchies, Tree-Structures, and Networks

The eight-bar pattern of drum beats in example 2-2 presents a simple hierarchy of strong and weak beats. A long-standing tradition in music theory views this pattern as a nesting of binary subdivisions, today representable as a tree-structure, as in example 2-3 (the left branch of each binary division is assumed to represent the strong beat; the right branch, the weak beat). The question to be addressed in this section is whether this type of tree-structure, especially when composed solely of pitches, is adequate to represent the more complex hierarchies of tonal music.

EXAMPLE 2-2. A hierarchy of strong and weak beats

One belief behind the use of tree-structures of individual pitches is that the same tonal relationships operate on every level—that the relationships are recursive. Structural recursion is attractive because it is conceptually economical. That is, if relationships are recursive, then a small set of relationships is sufficient to describe

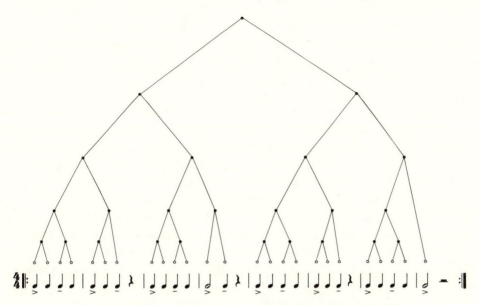

EXAMPLE 2-3. A tree-structure representation of example 2-2

an infinitely complex structure. The negative side of economy is, however, poverty. To say that one set of relationships will describe all structural levels is tantamount to saying that no new relationships are formed in the transition from a lower to a higher level. But such a statement would seem to contradict our intuitive sense that new relationships do emerge as we ascend hierarchical levels. For example, a series of electronically produced clicks, if accelerated from a frequency of one per second to fifty per second, will at some point seem to merge into a low pitch. When we perceive that change we have shifted to a different level of perception. We are aware of the emergent property—pitch—and of a new description needed for this property.

The phrase "emergent properties" and the idea that new descriptions must often accompany new structural levels have wide currency among both humanists and scientists.[6] In relation to musical analysis, one might question whether recursive analytical systems that exclude the possibility of newly emergent properties provide a realistic image of music perception. Consider the melodic fragment in example 2-4.

EXAMPLE 2-4. A hypothetical melody

Two of this melody's salient features are an ascending major triad and a repeated note. In example 2-5 these two features are placed on separate staves. Pitches shared by both features are joined by dotted lines to facilitate their visual alignment. In terms of Mandler's structural categories, this analysis presents two lower-level proordinate structures (the repeated notes and the ascending triad) in a higher-level coordinate structure (i.e., the two lower-level proordinate structures related one to another). And in terms of the idea of emergent properties, each new level requires a new description. For instance, the two lower-level patterns are simple melodic processes and can be so described. But the higher-level coordinate structure is a more closed, formal unit and would need to be described as such. The whole structure of example 2-5 is hierarchical, but not in the same way as example 2-3.

The hierarchical analysis presented by example 2-5, even though it would seem relatively unobjectionable and straightforward, is significantly different from the prevailing types of structural analysis. As mentioned, to a large number of theorists "hierarchy" means a tree-structure in which the many pitches at the bottom level are successively eliminated at higher and higher structural levels. Example 2-6 shows how the melody of example 2-4 might be transformed into such a hierarchy.

The tree-structure of example 2-6 was created by equating metric accent with tonal importance. Many other tree-structure interpretations are possible. But regardless of how the tree-structure is organized, the result remains the same: low-level "surface tones" are transformed into higher-level "structural tones." But what exactly is a structural tone? Is it a new description of other structures or a summary of lower-level events? We can recognize the economy of description and the summary nature of a term such as *Christmas tree;* all manner of subsidiary structures, surfaces, textures, colors, materials, and relationships are entailed by such a high-level term. Does the highest-level pitch in example 2-6 likewise entail or summarize the melody in question? I believe the answer is no, and conclude that an exclusive reliance on models requiring tree-structures of pitches may be incompatible with a flexible approach to musical analysis.[7] This is not to say that structural tones do not exist; not all pitches are of equal importance. But evidence for hierarchic perception and for distinctions between structurally central and ornamental pitches does not in itself provide a compelling reason for analyzing music solely with tree-structures of pitches.

An alternative to tree-structure representation is provided by networks. Whereas a tree-structure has a predictable shape and, more important, a strong influence on how an analysis proceeds, a network is unpredictable and places no initial constraints on an analysis. The differences are evident from a comparison of examples 2-5 and 2-6. Consider example 2-6. Once the tree-structure is chosen as the mode of structural representation, one knows that the melody being analyzed will be reduced to one or more structural tones. The constraints imposed by the tree-structure come to light if one tries to represent relationships that, so to speak, skip over branches of the tree. For instance, all the C's in the melody have a direct relationship to each other as repeated pitches (see example 2-5); but this relationship cannot be included in example 2-6 without deposing E and G from their positions as structural tones.

EXAMPLE 2-5. Two simple features contained in example 2-4

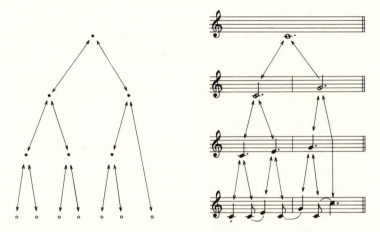

EXAMPLE 2-6. A tree-structure reduction of example 2-4

The case is quite different with a network representation. In example 2-5, a network expressed in musical notation, the ascending triad and the repeated notes coexist; representing the one does not prevent representing the other. And representing these features does not preclude representing still others, such as the several melodic leaps, the implied C-major harmony, or the rhythmic groupings (example 2-7). Of course the task of deciding which features are significant remains, irrespective of what type of representation is chosen. But network representations free an analyst from the graphic constraints of tree-structures and obviate the use of overly systematized methods.

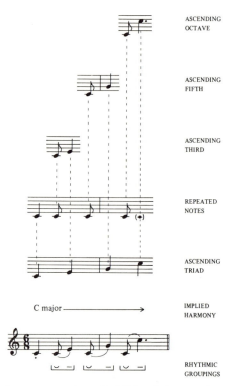

EXAMPLE 2-7. A network representation of additional features in example 2-4

A COMPARISON OF ANALYSES

Thus far I have examined some limitations of strict tree-structures with respect first to psychological theories of memory structure and then to small, hypothetical musical examples. Let us now turn to an examination of how actual artworks—phrases from the standard literature of classical music—fare when analyzed exclusively as tree-structures.

With respect to the harmonic and voice-leading aspects of classical music, an early proponent of a type of schema theory was the great Austrian theorist Heinrich Schenker. He maintained that in the works of the masters the organization of harmony and voice leading was guided by a high-level schema termed the *Ursatz* or "fundamental structure" (see example 2-8).[8] For Schenker, this background schema represented the highest level of structure and summarized the numerous lower-level

EXAMPLE 2-8. A version of the "fundamental structure" as given by Schenker in *Der freie Satz*

voice-leading schemata that provide the temporal expansion or "prolongation" of the abstract background into a perceptible musical foreground. An illustration of this process is provided by two Schenkerian analyses showing how the first four measures of Mozart's G-Major Keyboard Sonata, KV 283 (189h), constitute an initial prolongation of the beginning of the *Ursatz:* voice-leading $\hat{5}$ and harmonic I (examples 2-9 and 2-10). The first analysis, by Felix Salzer,[9] an early proponent of Schenker's theories in the United States, and the second, by Joel Lester,[10] one of the most respected of a younger group of Schenkerian analysts, differ in various details. But overall both concur in presenting Mozart's phrase as the hierarchical expansion of a descending third-progression, d″–c″–b′, with a resulting I–V–I harmonic progression. Since the emphasis in these analyses is on the related subordinate structures of harmony and voice leading, they can be easily represented by the informal tree-structure implicit in the successive analytical reductions. If, however, one tried to include other aspects of music within the same framework, then the limitations of a single tree-structure would become more apparent. In particular, the coordinate and proordinate structures of melody, rhythm, and form would conflict with the subordinate structures of harmony and voice leading. The bipartite form of Mozart's phrase and its paired melodic motives, for example, could not be simultaneously represented on the same tree-structure with the tripartite I–V–I harmony and the

EXAMPLE 2-9. The first four measures of Mozart's Keyboard Sonata in G Major,
KV 283 (189h), as analyzed by Felix Salzer

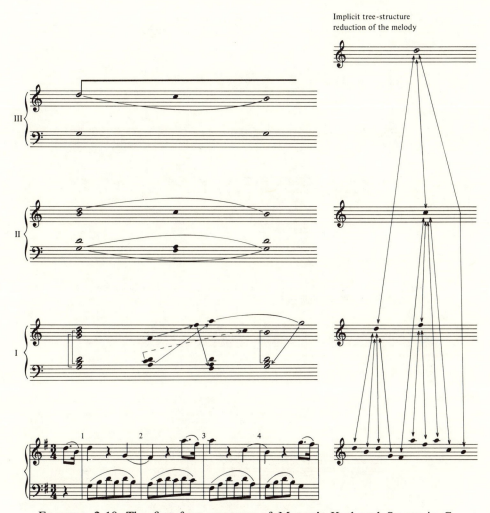

EXAMPLE 2-10. The first four measures of Mozart's Keyboard Sonata in G Major, KV 283 (189h), as analyzed by Joel Lester

EXAMPLE 2-11. A network representation of the first four measures of Mozart's Keyboard Sonata in G Major, KV 283 (189h)

tree-element d″–c″–b′ third-progression. To include these other relationships a more powerful mode of representation is needed—a network representation. I have provided a network analysis of the opening phrase of Mozart's G-Major Keyboard Sonata in example 2-11. Because this analysis is such a departure from the better-known graphic conventions of tree-structures, the following description is in order.

Mozart's phrase occupies the center of example 2-11. Above it lies the network of musical patterns in the melody, and below it lies the network of patterns in the accompaniment. Closest to the center of example 2-11 are the melody, harmony, and bass of the musical schema that this phrase shares with hundreds of other phrases from the eighteenth century. Leonard Meyer calls this schema a "musical archetype," while Leonard Ratner views it as a "structural melody." [11] By whatever name, this schema constitutes a recognized structural type that accounts for the highest level in the loose hierarchy of this network analysis ("highest level" being defined as the largest pattern accounting for the most features). Musical patterns farther from the center of example 2-11 show the subsidiary patterns overlaid upon the schematic framework. The first staff above the schema melody, for example, presents the descending third-progression identified in both the Schenkerian analyses. The network representation not only shows both this descending third-progression and the schema melody, but also shows how these two patterns converge on the pitches c″–b′. Other patterns are self-explanatory, involving for the most part repetitions or transpositions of simple motives.

Just as in the mathematical theory of graphs, in which networks can subsume any information presented by tree-structures, so in musical analysis it can be shown that a network analysis can subsume any information presented by a tree-structure analysis. But whereas anything represented in a tree-structure can be incorporated in a network, the reverse is not true. Thus, while the essential harmonic and voice-leading information found in the Schenkerian analyses is present in the network analysis, few of the many other features represented in the network analysis could be successfully incorporated into a Schenkerian analysis. In part this is because a Schenkerian analysis does not aim to include other features; Schenker's methods were optimized for the analysis of harmony and voice leading. But the exclusion of these features is also in large part due to the fact that whereas a network analysis can include diverse kinds of features and structures (linear progressions, conformant motives, rhythmic patterns, harmonic features, irreducible schemata, contrapuntal combinations, etc.), an analysis focused on a strict tree-structure of structural tones may be forced to exclude everything that cannot be reduced to a smaller set of pitches.

A rather different, more formalized type of tree-structure analysis has been proposed by the music theorist Fred Lerdahl and the linguist Ray Jackendoff. Let us examine their analysis of one phrase from Schumann's song "Wehmut," a phrase comparable in many ways to the Mozart phrase just discussed. [12]

To circumvent the limitations of a single tree-structure, they propose two superimposed tree-structures that converge at upper levels. The first tree-structure represents "grouping, metrical, and time-span analyses" (example 2-12; only the portion of the tree-structure pertaining to this phrase is given). Notice that any trace of the phrase disappears from the upper levels, which pertain to the song as a whole. The second tree-structure is labeled a "prolongational reduction" (example 2-13).[13] It ultimately reduces the whole phrase to a single pitch: G♮ instead of the F♯ produced by the first tree-structure.

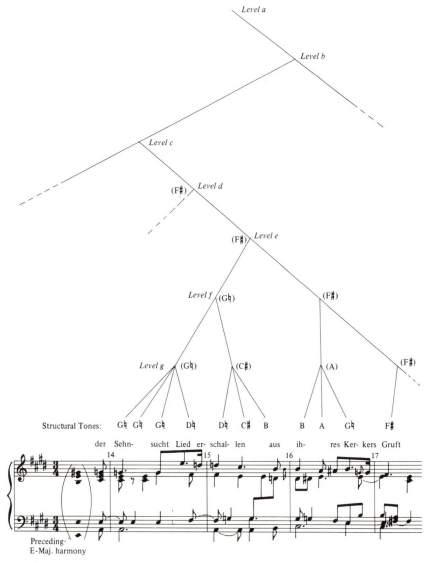

EXAMPLE 2-12. A tree-structure analysis by Lerdahl and Jackendoff of Schumann, *Liederkreis*, Op. 39 (1840), No. 9, "Wehmut," meas. 14–17

These analyses have problems that are perhaps best highlighted with reference to the text that Schumann set. For though Lerdahl and Jackendoff specifically exclude the text from consideration in their analyses, it is still fair to ask what their completed musical analyses might tell us about Schumann's manner of setting a text.[14] Of course the exclusion of a text from the analysis of a song is by itself open to question. Psychologically formulated analyses, as these claim to be, can hardly be justified in prejudging what is and is not significant in the music. More important, the text of "Wehmut" has an acoustical structure of its own. The text set in the

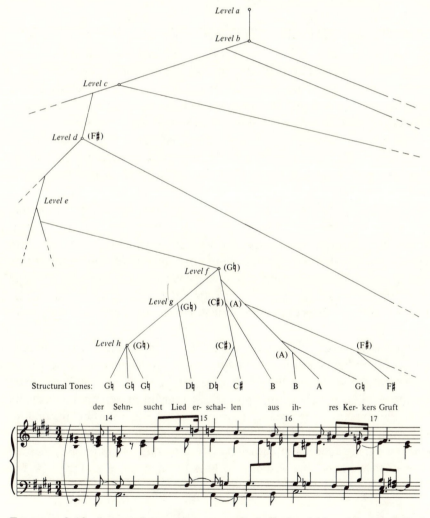

EXAMPLE 2-13. A second tree-structure analysis by Lerdahl and Jackendoff of Schumann, *Liederkreis*, Op. 39 (1840), No. 9, "Wehmut," meas. 14–17

phrase given in examples 2-12 and 2-13 is from the second half of the poem's middle quatrain:

> Es lassen Nachtigallen,
> Spielt draussen Frülingsluft,
> Der Sehnsucht Lied erschallen
> Aus ihres Kerkers Gruft.

(Roughly):   Nightingales,
             A spring breeze playing outside,
             Sound a song of longing
             from their prison's tomb.

One need not understand German to perceive the structure of this text. In particular, there can be little question that the word *Aus* in the fourth line is at the beginning of a structural unit. Yet both of Lerdahl and Jackendoff's analyses place *Aus* as part of the preceding line. In terms of the question, "What do these analyses tell us about Schumann's manner of text setting?" their answer would seem to be that he did not respect the structure of the text. Of course this is erroneous.

These analyses fare no better when dealing with harmony. For instance, one of the psychological attributes of traditional harmony is a sense of tonality. By several criteria, the phrase in question has a D-major tonality. Why, then, is there no trace of D major in either analysis from level *f* upward? The answer is that these analyses have no separate symbols for tonality; they cannot represent tonality, an emergent property requiring a new description, unless it happens to coincide with a root-position triad. Thus the whole phrase is instead analyzed as a subdominant region in E major by virtue of the root-position chord on A (albeit A^7) that begins the phrase. The direct and striking harmonic relationship between E major and D major that occurs before the word *Sehnsucht* (longing) (see end of meas. 13 in example 2-13) is obscured by the analysis because these tonalities reside in different branches of the tree-structures.

Schumann's phrase is distantly related to the phrase already analyzed from Mozart's G-Major Piano Sonata. Two of the many components in that network representation were the schema melody (scale degrees $1-7-4-3$) and a linear descent (see example 2-14). In Schumann's phrase, a larger linear descent connects the two halves of the same schema melody (example 2-15). This particular combination, also shown in examples 2-16 and 2-17, is quite common. In most cases these structures end on a tonic chord. But occasionally, as in Schumann's phrase, they veer toward the relative minor. For instance, a later restatement of example 2-17 moves from D major toward B minor (example 2-18).

EXAMPLE 2-14. Two components in the network representation of example 2-11

EXAMPLE 2-15. The linear descent and schema melody of the phrase from Schumann's "Wehmut"

EXAMPLE 2-16. The linear descent and schema melody from Haydn, Symphony No. 69 in C Major, "Laudon" (?c1775/6), iv, Presto, meas. 27–30

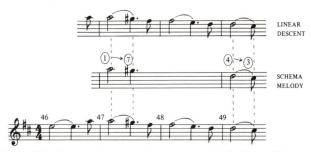

EXAMPLE 2-17. The linear descent and schema melody from Mozart, Serenade in D Major, "Posthorn," KV 320 (1779), i, Allegro con spirito, meas. 46–49

EXAMPLE 2-18. A later restatement (meas. 205–8) of example 2-17

To the extent that Schumann's phrase shares the traditional pattern network of a linear melodic descent and the schema in question, it can be considered, in the jargon of schema theory, a stereotyped *script*.[15] But there is also a Romantic dynamism in Schumann's phrase not accounted for by this script. The effect is explained by Schumann's incorporation of this Classic script into a Romantic *plan*,[16] which Meyer calls the "gap-fill archetype."[17] That is, the more generalized schema of an initial leap or gap (G♮–E in Schumann's phrase) followed by a linear descent or fill is presented simultaneously with the stereotyped schema of the last several examples. The network analysis of example 2-19 displays this complex arrangement.

Now, if one asks what this network analysis tells us about Schumann's manner of text setting, several specific answers present themselves. First, Schumann scrupulously aligns the two halves of the schema melody with the poetic line endings— *erschallen* and *Kerkers Gruft*. Second, he employs word painting: *Lied erschallen* (sound a song) follows a leap to the highest pitch in the entire piece; *Kerkers Gruft* (prison's tomb) is at the bottom of a long melodic descent and is further darkened by a move toward B minor. Third, *Der Sehnsucht Lied erschallen* is the only line in "Wehmut" not followed by some form of punctuation. Schumann recognizes this lack of poetic closure and melodically connects his phrase halves by means of a large linear descent. In other words, he uses an appropriate musical pattern to reflect a fine point of poetic structure. And fourth, note that just as the text incorporates Romantic conceits into a stereotyped form, the music incorporates a Romantic plan into a stereotyped script. This important point cannot be gleaned from either tree-structure.

Mention was made of the same schema melody occurring in the Mozart and Schumann phrases analyzed above. In the Mozart phrase, this schema melody was clearly presented, its two halves conformant in several respects. In the Schumann phrase, however, the schema melody was not at all obvious. What, then, justifies its appearance in this analysis? The answer is that this schema melody is but one feature in a special set of features making up the musical schema associated with this phrase. Without the presence of the other features of the schema, one might *not* be justified in singling out the pitches of the schema melody. Of course, one must first justify the schema being invoked. How this might be done is the subject of the next section.

EXAMPLE 2-19. A network representation of the phrase from Schumann's "Wehmut"[18]

Schema Validation

Knowledge of schema theory is necessary for research on musical schemata, and knowledge of mental structures can suggest ways in which musical schemata might be represented. But how does one acquire knowledge of a particular musical schema, and what evidence would prove it to be a valid abstraction? One approach, which has already been cited, is psychological testing (see chapter 1). Another approach is to make a careful study of musical scores and treatises, looking for evidence of shared sets of features.

Consider the evidence presented in the case of an eighteenth-century cadential schema. Charles Cudworth, working in the 1940s, examined numerous eighteenth-century compositions of the so-called *style galant*. Based on this examination he published an article in which he proposed the cadence in example 2-20 as the *galant* cadence "par excellence"—an irreducible *galant* schema.[19] Cudworth did not specify the extent to which this cadence might be varied, if at all. In this regard it may be better described as a cliché (Cudworth's own term) than as an abstracted schema. But this cliché could serve as a point of departure for the abstraction of a more general schema. Daniel Heartz has observed that in the treatise *Fundamenten des General-Basses* (Berlin: I. G. Siegmeyer, 1822), ascribed posthumously to Mozart and related to his teachings as preserved by Thomas Attwood, a contrapuntal cadence with prepared suspensions is contrasted with the "*modern (gallant)*" cadence in example 2-21.[20] This "*gallant*" cadence is close in several respects to the cadence given by Cudworth. Heartz also points out an intriguing coincidence in Mozart's *Don Giovanni* where, after the cadential figure shown in example 2-22 (Act I, Finale), Leporello exclaims "Che maschere galanti!" (What gallant masqueraders!).

Heartz describes the schema underlying the preceding three cadences as a I–IV (ii^6)–I$_4^6$–V–I harmonic progression in a triple meter. While it is true that the schema *has* this progression, it is nevertheless an oversimplification to say that the schema *is* this progression. A I–IV (ii^6)–I$_4^6$–V–I harmonic progression can be found in all types of musical styles and, even if in a triple meter, may sound very little like these *galant* cadences. A defensible definition of the schema underlying these cadences would require that the norms and interrelationships of meter, harmony, rhythmic groupings, voice leading, melody, and texture all be specified. Of course a consideration of just three cadences could yield only provisional specification of the schema. Many more *galant* cadences would need to be examined before a historically accurate abstraction of a schema could be claimed to have been made.

Examining many individual compositions for the presence of a particular schema creates a type of external, statistical evidence. Internal evidence of a schema is also possible. For instance, the existence of slight variations in repetitions or restatements of a musical phrase can lead to insights concerning what is central or peripheral to its underlying schema. As an example of internal evidence, let us examine the three statements of a theme from an early symphony by Joseph Haydn

EXAMPLE 2-20. The *galant* cadence of Charles Cudworth

EXAMPLE 2-21. A cadence given in *Fundamenten des General-Basses*

EXAMPLE 2-22. Mozart, *Don Giovanni* (1787), Act I, Finale, Minuetto da lontana, meas. 218–19

EXAMPLE 2-23. Haydn, Symphony No. 14 in A Major (1764), iii, Trio, Allegretto, meas. 29–32, 33–36, and 49–52

shown in example 2-23. The differences in melodic contour, rhythm, bass line, and
harmonic detail are such that each statement is easily distinguishable from the
others. Yet the similarities in overall harmonic movement (the second phrase, of
course, being in the relative major), the prominence of the melodic scale degrees
1–7 and 4–3, and the metric placement of these features are obvious enough to
suggest that all three statements share a common schema. As a first approximation
of the central tendencies of this schema, those features shared by all three statements
are shown at the bottom of example 2-23.

The phrases in example 2-23 have more in common than the simple schema
presented at the bottom of the example. But this provisional schema does provide a
point of departure for further studies; it is a hypothesis that can be tested on still
other phrases. For instance, the schema derived from the three Haydn phrases could

EXAMPLE 2-24. Louis Massonneau, Symphony in E♭ Major, Op. 3, Book 1
(c1792), i, Vivace, meas. 19–22, 52–55, and 156–59

be compared with the features shared by three statements of a theme by Louis Massonneau (1766–1848) (example 2-24).

Ultimately every type of evidence supporting the abstraction of a musical
schema is relevant: similarities in phrases that "sound alike," central tendencies in
variations, examples from music treatises, research in the psychology of music, historical music criticism (to the extent that it can be interpreted), and evidence that a
schema has a particular function (cadential, thematic, linking, etc.). But the goal of
uncovering evidence is not simply to compile it. The goal must be to seek evidence
that can be arranged in a coherent pattern that either supports or calls into question a
theory of musical structure. The theoretical and empirical aspects of researching
musical schemata must function together.

SUMMARY

The review of basic mental structures and structural representations given at the beginning of this chapter suggested that network representations offer the most flexible and least constrained means of graphically displaying musical structures. Because tree-structure representations dominate the literature of music theory, several comparisons were made between tree-structure and network representations of the same musical phrases. In each case, the network representation was able to provide a more psychologically defensible analysis by avoiding the graphic and procedural constraints associated with tree-structure representations.

   An important element in each network representation was a musical schema. Several general suggestions were given for how one might abstract and identify a musical schema. But identification is merely a first step; the problems involved in clearly defining a schema raise significant issues that require the extended discussion provided in the following two chapters.

CHAPTER 3

Style Structures and Musical Archetypes

In the first chapter several basic concepts of cognitive psychology were discussed. Special emphasis was given to the concept of schemata—"large, complex units of knowledge."[1] In this chapter I discuss several music-theoretic concepts that can be applied to schema research. Most useful in this regard is Eugene Narmour's threefold categorization of musical structures: style forms, style structures, and idiostructures. These categories provide a necessary terminology for describing the complex interplay of different musical dimensions at various levels of structure. I argue that a style structure, considered as a specific complex of features, is a musical schema. Later in the chapter, I present a different but closely related approach to musical schemata—Leonard Meyer's concept of musical archetypes. I discuss his definitions of form and process—the basic elements in a Meyerian archetype—and introduce his "changing-note archetype," a term encompassing a common group of eighteenth-century musical schemata, one of which will be carefully analyzed in the remainder of this book.

NARMOUR'S STRUCTURAL CATEGORIES

Consider the various meanings of "melodic triad" in examples 3-1a, b, and c. Example 3-1a merely names an abstract concept, example 3-1b presents a stable melodic/durational complex with an implied C-major harmony, and example 3-1c shows a latent, destabilizing aspect of this complex—G–E–C as the beginning of a series of descending thirds—brought out by the effects of a larger context. In each of

EXAMPLE 3-1. Various meanings of *melodic triad*

these three cases, "melodic triad" has a distinct interpretation expressible through theoretical concepts developed by Eugene Narmour—his "style forms," "style structures," and "idiostructures." Narmour writes:

> By style form, I mean those parametric entities[2] . . . which achieve enough closure to enable us to understand their intrinsic functional coherence without reference to the functionally specific, intraopus context from which they come. . . . Combining all the style forms in the various parameters . . . produces a specific functional complex of *style structures* which together create a network of relationships I will call the *idiostructure*.[3]

At first glance Narmour's definitions might appear to describe a hierarchy in which style forms are at the bottom, style structures are in the middle, and an idiostructure is at the top (figure 3-1). Yet a closer reading of *Beyond Schenkerism*[4] reveals that a simple subordinate or superordinate relationship is lacking between any two of these terms. The following attempt at an exegesis of Narmour's terms should clarify the intended interrelationships.

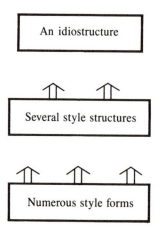

FIGURE 3-1. Oversimplification of Narmour's categories

Style Forms

> Style forms may be defined as those parametric entities which achieve
> enough closure so we can understand their functional coherence without
> reference to the specific intraopus contexts from which they come—all
> those seemingly time-*independent* patterns, large and small, from pa-
> rameter to parameter, which recur with statistically significant frequency.[5]

The collection of all the style forms found in a particular musical style is a "lexicon"
of the "stylistic language"—"an encompassing circle of 'facts' into which all relationships of similarity in the given repertory may be placed."[6] That is, just as the
English word *robin* has a recognized meaning independent of the sentences in which
it may be found, so in classical music the style form *melodic triad* is a recognizable
pattern of pitch succession independent of its occurrence in an individual composition. Narmour cites the ascending tetrachord G–A–B–C as another example of a
style form.[7] Again, this pattern involves only a single musical dimension—pitch
succession—and, like a melodic triad, it can occur at more than one level in a musical hierarchy. The very existence of the terms *melodic triad* and *ascending tetrachord* suggests a prior recognition of the "functional coherence" of the patterns and
reinforces Narmour's contention that style forms are "constructed classes of things."[8]
In addition to melodic style forms, there are style forms in the dimensions of harmony and durational proportion: for example, a *perfect authentic cadence* is a style
form of tonal harmony, and *iteration* (e.g., ♩♩♩ etc.) is a style form of durational
proportion (1 : 1 : 1...).

Style Structures

Narmour's definition of style forms is elaborated by means of the dialectical opposition that he establishes between style forms and style structures:

> In order to avoid creating an ocean of lifeless facts, devoid of operational
> significance, and in order not to deny facts their proper habitat, . . . the
> style analyst will attempt to restore the syntactic function of style forms
> by arranging them in various specific contexts according to their statis-
> tically most common occurrences. The contexts which result from such
> arrangement can be called *style structures* in the sense that they are di-
> rectly tied to and contribute to the structure of real pieces, not just to con-
> structed classes of things, as are style forms. Unlike the description of
> style forms, the identification of style structures involves ascribing time-
> dependent function to patterns.[9]

From the passage above, and from Narmour's further discussion of style structure, it
is possible to construct a table of oppositions (figure 3-2).[10] This table demonstrates

Style Forms	vs.	Style Structures
lexicon		syntax
context free		context specific
extraopus norms		intraopus and interopus norms
constructed classes		parts of actual structures
time-independent		time-dependent
isolated parameters		parameters in combination
mode		code
abstract		concrete

FIGURE 3-2. A contrasting of style forms and style structures

that style forms and style structures are not in a relationship of part to whole but rather in a relationship of antithesis: "The fixed relationship between these two poles at any level in a work will therefore account for that complex of things we call style."[11] As a simple example of a style structure, recall the melodic triad presented earlier as example 3-1b (example 3-2). The constituent style form "melodic triad" participates in a specific structural complex involving harmony (an implied C-major triad) and durational proportion (the pattern *long-short-long:* 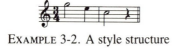). As a more complex example of a style structure, one might place the melodic triad of example 3-2 in the context of the V⁷–I cadence, a harmonic style structure, as in example 3-3. In this case the resulting complex itself is a style structure, and it creates relationships not found in either of its constituent style structures. The E in the melody, for instance, no longer functions purely as part of a C-major descending triad but rather participates in and colors the dominant seventh chord on G.

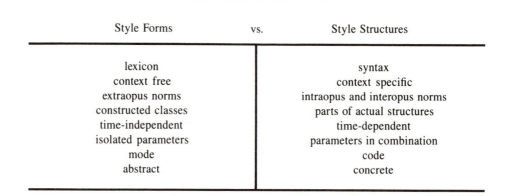

EXAMPLE 3-2. A style structure

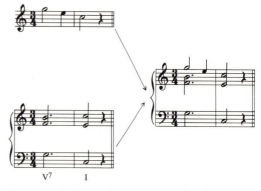

EXAMPLE 3-3. Another meaning of *style structure*

Idiostructures

Both style forms and style structures are classlike concepts abstracted from real pieces; style forms occur with "statistically significant frequency" and style structures are arrangements of style forms "according to their statistically most common occurrences."[12] In contrast, an idiostructure is often unique. It is the "network of relationships"[13] created by the interaction of the closural properties of one or more style structures with the nonclosural implications inherent in any real musical movement. A second table of oppositions can be gleaned from Narmour's discussion of how style structures and idiostructures differ (figure 3-3).[14] Again we see that an antithesis is established—a dialectical opposition between style structure and idiostructure. As an example of an idiostructure, refer back to example 3-1c. There a realization of nonclosural implications inherent in the style structure of example 3-1b creates a unique network—"melodic triad" as both a formal and a processive entity.

Style Structures	vs.	Idiostructures
closural		nonclosural
the signified		the signifying
the formed		formation
structural		structuring
more treelike		heavily networked
form		content
stability		mobility
formal		processive

FIGURE 3-3. A contrasting of style structures and idiostructures

The Interrelationships of Style Forms, Style Structures, and Idiostructures

Just as it would be misleading to consider a style form as the complete opposite of a style structure, or to consider a style structure as the complete opposite of an idiostructure, so it would be misleading to view the three terms as separate levels in a hierarchical system. The key to understanding Narmour's formulation of these terms lies in his distinction between style analysis and critical analysis. The one emphasizes movement from the specific to the general; the other, movement from the general to the specific (figure 3-4).[15] Given the previous definitions of Narmour's terms, a style structure must be more specific than a style form, and an idiostructure must be more specific than a style structure. These two relationships allow the three terms to be ordered along the continuum in figure 3-5.

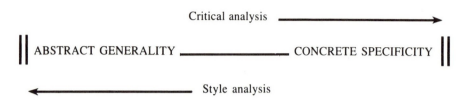

FIGURE 3-4. The domains of critical and style analysis

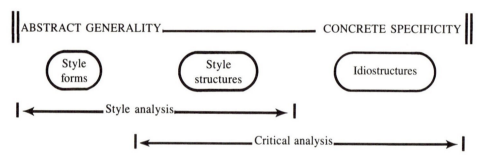

FIGURE 3-5. Narmour's categories in relation to critical and style analysis

In view of this larger context, it should now be possible to understand the way in which a style structure may be both the dynamic "opposite" of a static style form and the static "opposite" of a dynamic idiostructure. The antitheses Narmour develops between these terms are only in relation to his two analytical orientations: the work of the style analyst will fall between the poles of style forms and style structures; the work of the critical analyst will fall between the poles of style structures and idiostructures.

The distinctions between style forms, style structures, and idiostructures need not be actually represented by differences in musical material. Rather, they may depend on the analyst's viewpoint—a viewpoint that depends on the goals of the inquiry. The present study focuses on style structures, though it also constitutes an investigation of style forms and idiostructures. These latter categories receive less emphasis, but the reader should try to keep them in mind, because changes in style structures are often attributable to changes in these other categories.

Narmour and Schemata

There appears to be general agreement among psychologists that feature recognition is a first step in complex pattern recognition. The first term in Narmour's structural typology is the parametric style form. Are style forms therefore distinctive features? They may be—if one restricts style forms to an immediate, low level of structure. But distinctive musical features may also be composed of more than one parameter, or be characterized by timbre, texture, or some other attribute that resists scaling. Style forms then account for some but not all musical features.

The definition of a style form as a purely parametric entity probably also needs to be altered when long time spans are involved. The way people remember things in the immediate past and the more remote past is not the same, a phenomenon usually attributed to differences between *short-term* and *long-term* memory. Researchers have noted that information held in short-term memory must often be transferred to long-term memory within five or six seconds (as a norm) or be forgotten.[16] This transfer almost certainly involves a loss or restructuring of some information. For instance, the minute differences in pitch or duration that can be distinguished between two tones separated by only a few seconds may become indistinguishable over the time periods associated with long-term memory. Inasmuch as high-level structures can have elements widely separated in time, it is questionable whether our conception of them permits the discriminations implied by a parametric analysis. These qualifications notwithstanding, the concept of style forms is still quite useful because there is little doubt that certain patterns do retain something of their identity even though they may be situated in quite different contexts. In this study I will use the term *style form* to signify the relatively abstract, context-free constituents of schemata. These constituents may at times involve more than a single musical parameter.

The idea of style structures is very close to the notion of cognitive schemata. Both concepts emphasize a set of features combined to form a specific structural complex. What Narmour does not emphasize is that if the number of "specific contexts" is not to become infinitely large, the concepts of prototype, ideal, abstraction, or norm—all common to schema theory—must hold for style structures. He does not address this topic in *Beyond Schenkerism,* possibly because he was sensitive about positing privileged structures that were in many ways similar to those of Heinrich Schenker. Narmour's goal was to show the dangers inherent in taking one privileged structure as both an axiom and a goal valid for all analyses. In the jargon of cognitive science, such an approach would be an entirely concept-driven or top-down processing of musical information. On the other hand, Narmour's position in *Beyond Schenkerism* sometimes suggests a thoroughly data-driven or bottom-up method of analysis. Because schema theory, as was discussed in the first chapter, assumes that both types of information processing—top-down and bottom-up—occur together, I enlarge Narmour's concept of a style structure to align it more closely with that of a schema. Concrete examples of a style structure treated as a musical schema will be found in chapters 4 and 5.

Narmour's concept of idiostructures has no single equivalent in the literature of cognitive psychology, though it has close affinities with the term *idiolect* as used in psychological studies of linguistics. The joint closural and nonclosural properties of an idiostructure are not equivalent to the alternate interpretations of the ambiguous figures commonly found in psychological texts. Ambiguous figures present two mutually exclusive possibilities, whereas idiostructures present merged, concurrent meanings. Because the nonclosural properties of an idiostructure extend beyond a schema's boundaries, these nonclosural aspects can be predictive of musical patterns that are likely to follow. This implicative feature of idiostructures will become important later in this study when musical contexts larger than a single schema are considered.

LEONARD MEYER AND ARCHETYPES

Some of the most significant investigations of musical schemata have been carried out by Leonard Meyer. Because his work on musical archetypes (i.e., innate schemata) forms one of the foundations for the present study, I want to discuss what he means by *archetype* and how he defines musical archetypes. Meyer has been influenced by concepts from the fields of psychology, literary theory, the theory of history, and natural science. Although it may be from the field of literary theory, especially the work of Northrop Frye,[17] that Meyer adopted the concept of archetypes, his formulation of the concept is in terms of cognitive psychology. Meyer writes:

> Archetypal patterns and traditional schemata are the classes—the "rules of the game," in Koestler's phrase [Arthur Koestler, *The Ghost in the Machine* (New York: Macmillan, 1968), p. 105]—in terms of which particular musical events are perceived and comprehended.[18]

Meyer uses the terms *archetypal patterns* and *schemata* "more or less interchangeably."[19] Even the hybrid term "archetypal schemata" is employed.[20] He does recognize a theoretical distinction between archetype and schema: an archetype is the result of "physiological and psychological constraints presumed innate in human behavior," while a schema is a norm established as "the result of learning."[21] But he feels that in practice the distinction breaks down. The two categories commingle, because stylistic norms are probably based on innate factors of cognition, and innate factors of cognition are likely to be manifested in stylistic norms. Although innate constraints are presumed to be universal, stylistic change and diversity are accommodated because "different sets of conventional constraints may satisfy such [universal] requirements."[22] In the following discussion I will restrict myself to the term *archetype* when referring to Meyer's concept, in order to emphasize his concern with cognitive universals and to distinguish his concept of archetype from the several related schemata that can be subsumed under it.

Meyer clearly views archetypes as central to the understanding of music:

> [Archetypes] establish fundamental frameworks in terms of which cultur-
> ally competent audiences (not only members of the general public but
> also creators, performers, critics, and scholars) perceive, comprehend,
> and respond to works of art. For what audiences enjoy and appreciate are
> neither the successions of stimuli *per se,* nor general principles *per se,*
> but the relationship between them as actualized in a specific work of art.
> Just as we can delight in the play of a particular football game only if we
> understand the constraints governing the actions down on the field (the
> rules, strategies, physical conditions, etc.), so we can enjoy and appreci-
> ate the playful ingenuity and expressive power of works of art only if we
> know—and such knowledge may be tacit: a matter of ingrained habits
> and dispositions—the constraints that governed the choices made by the
> artist and, consequently, shaped the process and form of the particular
> work of art. Thus, archetypes are, in a sense, embodiments of fundamen-
> tal stylistic constraints. As such, they connect understanding to other as-
> pects of aesthetic experience.[23]

Nevertheless, though archetypes are important, he is unwilling to give them precedence over two concepts that he considers more fundamental—form and process.
Before further examining Meyer's formulation of archetypes it is important to understand exactly what he means by these two terms.

Form

When reading the work of Leonard Meyer one must realize that the word *form* is
being used in a special way—as "form-as-the-complement-of-process." While in
ordinary parlance it may be true that any musical structure *has* some type of form,

> when we say that something *is* a particular form . . . we are referring
> both to its hierarchic structure and to its conformant organization on the
> highest level. When both types of relationship are articulated by clear dif-
> ferentiation, then relationships will be formal. That is, the complex event
> will be said to be a form.[24]

Another way to interpret the phrase "articulated by clear differentiation" is as
"characterized by discontinuity." The special emphasis on discontinuity serves to set
form apart from the continuity that characterizes process.[25] For Meyer, pure repetition (emphasizing the separateness of the repeated entities), the return of earlier material (discontinuous because of the intervention of some contrasting section), and
strong, continuity-breaking closure are the obvious indicators of form. The first two
procedures signal the beginning of a form, the last, closure, the ending of a form.

From the point of view of form alone, the only relationships possible between two entities are varying degrees of conformance or contrast.

Process

"Process continuation is the norm of musical progression."[26] Meyer bases this contention on the Gestalt *law of good continuation:* "A shape or pattern will, other things being equal, tend to be continued in its initial mode of operation."[27] There are, of course, obvious musical embodiments of good continuation: a stepwise melodic progression, the harmonic circle-of-fifths progression, and the truly continuous processes of accelerando or ritardando and crescendo or decrescendo. But Meyer, whose name is closely associated with the application of Gestalt laws to musical analysis, was one of the first to point to the limitations of Gestalt laws:

> The vital role occupied by learning in conditioning the operation of Gestalt laws and concepts indicates at the outset that any generalized Gestalt account of musical perception is out of the question. Each style system and style will form figures in a different way, depending upon the melodic materials drawn upon, their interrelationships, the norms of rhythmic organization, the attitudes toward texture, and so forth. . . . Nor does it seem that, even within the confined limits of a particular style, a precise and systematic account of musical perception solely in Gestalt terms is possible. . . . Although there is ample reason for believing that the laws developed by Gestalt psychologists, largely in connection with visual experience, are applicable in a general way to aural perception, they cannot be made the basis of a thoroughgoing system for the analysis of musical perception and experience.[28]

To explain those syntactic relationships that seemed inexplicable by reference to Gestalt laws, Meyer turned to the notion of probability. He made the quite reasonable assumption that learning and general musical experience condition listeners to expect likely successions of musical events. "Any aspect of musical progress governed by probability relationships, whether these relationships are products of learning or the result of relationships created within the context of the particular work, establishes preferred modes of continuation."[29] "Modes of continuation" are obviously not discontinuous, that is, formal, but rather continuous and therefore processive. Consequently, the word *process* is extended to describe all relationships that initiate or resolve some expectation. As a further extension, the word *process* approaches the meaning of *syntax* to the extent that musical syntax, in the view of Meyer and many other theorists, involves the interplay of musical implications and their suitable realizations.

Form, Process, and the Tertium Quid

The dichotomous exposition of form and process presented in *Emotion and Meaning in Music* is tempered in *Explaining Music*. Even in the latter work it is true that hierarchical musical structure is outlined as an alternation of form and process across structural levels (figure 3-6).[30] Yet there appears in *Explaining Music* a *tertium quid*, a third category that falls outside of the form-versus-process dichotomy. For the present discussion the most important structural type within this new category is that of "symmetrical patterns."[31]

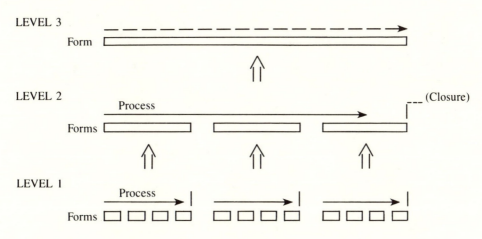

FIGURE 3-6. The alternation of form and process across structural levels

    While the definition of form can be used to explain musical structures charac-
terized by immediate repetition, or return after contrast, and the definition of process can be used to explain musical structures characterized by continuation, or
implication and realization, symmetrical patterns seem to require a different approach. "In symmetrical melodies, the relationship between successive events is
such that one event *mirrors* the patterning of another. In other words, there is a balance of motion and countermotion."[32] In music, balance is, of course, a concept
difficult to define by recourse to notions of conformance, continuation, implication,
or probability. At the same time, a balanced, mirrored relationship is neither uncom-
mon nor unnatural.
    In response to this problem, Meyer takes a different approach to each of the
three musical structures he labels as symmetrical. The first type, complementary
melodies—melodic structures that ascend and then descend, or vice versa—resists
simple explanation in terms of pure form or process; a complementary melody need
be neither discontinuous nor implied. Instead, Meyer concentrates on explaining the
possible higher-level implications that the linear vectors of the separate halves may

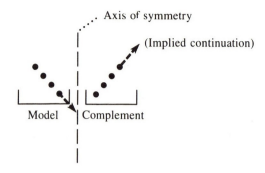

For instance:

Brahms, Symphony No. 1 in C Minor, Op. 68 (1876), iii Un poco allegretto e grazioso, meas. 1–9

FIGURE 3-7. Complementary melodies

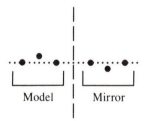

For instance:

Antonin Dvořák, Symphony No. 9 in E Minor, "From the New World," Op. 95 (1893), iv, Allegro con fuoco, meas. 10–12

FIGURE 3-8. Axial melodies

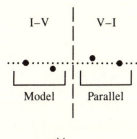

For instance:

Johann Georg Albrechtsberger, Symphony in D Major (1770), iii, meas. 1–3

FIGURE 3-9. Changing-note melodies

engender (figure 3-7). The second type, axial melodies—melodic structures that oscillate about a central axis—is characterized in negative terms. Because a clear ascending or descending line is not realized within the structure, "a true syntactic process is not generated,"[33] and "implication [on the highest level] is absent."[34] If the structure is not a process, then "the relationship between model and mirror is primarily formal."[35] (See figure 3-8.) Changing-note melodies, Meyer's third type of symmetrical pattern, "are superficially similar to axial ones."[36] (See figure 3-9.) But Meyer feels that the changing-note structure is more implicative than an axial pattern because it involves "motion away from and back to stability."[37]

What is important for the study of musical schemata is Meyer's identification of historically valid structural abstractions that are specific to only one or two hierarchical levels and that tie specific patterns of melodic structure to specific formal plans. These entities are neither purely formal nor purely processive; rather, they are form-process amalgams, one of which Meyer identifies as an archetype.

Archetypes

In Meyer's general discussion of archetypes in *Explaining Music*,[38] he employs the word *archetype* almost as a synonym for *ideal:* "Such norms are abstractions. One

cannot find an archetypal gap-fill melody or an ideal cadential schema in the literature of tonal music." [39] It is only much later, in the article "Exploiting Limits," that
his definition of archetype becomes specific:

> There are cases . . . in which fundamental similarities of form or process
> transcend traditional stylistic boundaries. Some kinds of patterning seem,
> if not universal, at least archetypal within one of the major cultural tradi-
> tions. . . . The most patently archetypal patternings are, one suspects,
> those that couple compellingly coherent processive relationships with pa-
> tently ordered formal plans. There are both archetypal processes . . . and
> archetypal forms. . . . An archetypal *pattern,* as I intend the term, com-
> bines such a process with such a form. [40]

In Narmour's terms, the emphasis has shifted from constituent style forms to composite style structures.

Archetypes, as form-process amalgams, become historical and cognitive entities in their own right. If, as Meyer states, they "help listeners to comprehend and
remember the particular patterns in which they are actualized," [41] then archetypes are
central to music perception and must be given serious consideration in musical
analysis. In an idealized scenario, archetypes would be identified through rigorous
stylistic analysis and then form the starting points of serious critical analysis. Employing an archetype in musical criticism must, of course, involve the assumption
that the archetype used is both historically and cognitively a valid entity. But this is
not to say that every archetype must be actually derivable from one or more general
principles. Meyer appears to have considered it necessary to refute the implication
that an archetype might serve critical analysis better if simply taken as a stylistic
given rather than as a specific form or process:

> It may occasionally seem that archetypes have been given a kind of Pla-
> tonic reality or have been reified in some way. Thus it should be empha-
> sized that, in my view, archetypes are cognitive constructs abstracted
> from particular patternings that are grouped together because of their
> similar syntactic shapes [= processes] and/or formal plans. That is, ar-
> chetypes are classlike patterns that are specially compelling because they
> result from the consonant conjoining of prevalent stylistic conventions
> with the neuro/cognitive proclivities of the human mind. [42]

His defense—that an archetype (the reified whole) is a composite or "consonant conjoining" of stylistic conventions and cognitive proclivities (the more fundamental parts)—is probably unnecessary. After all, a description of an archetype
specifying, for example, precise interactions of structural tones, rhythmic groupings, metrical placements, and harmonic progressions would be far less reified and
idealized than a description of a basic form or process.

The Changing-Note Archetype

For review, figure 3-10 shows my representation of the changing-note melodic structure as specified in *Explaining Music* (Meyer also included its inversion under the same rubric).[43] Although Meyer suggested that this melodic structure "might be thought of as [an] archetypal pattern,"[44] it was only several years later, in his article "Exploiting Limits," that he specifically discussed this structure as an archetype.

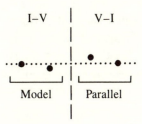

FIGURE 3-10. Changing-note melodies

Indicative of this change in orientation is the fact that instead of the abstract configuration shown in figure 3-10, he now presents the archetype as a detailed polyphonic complex with hierarchical formal levels (example 3-4).[45] If this complex pattern is an archetype, as Meyer persuasively argues, then it cannot simply be a combination of one archetypal form with one archetypal process. Rather, it must be a complex of structures and features, many of which Meyer does not make explicit. For example, in the text of the article in question, references are frequently made to rhythmic groupings and metrical placement. Yet an abstraction of these elements is not transferred to Meyer's analytical model. This and other analytical problems are taken up in the next chapter, where the relationship between an archetype and a schema is explored.

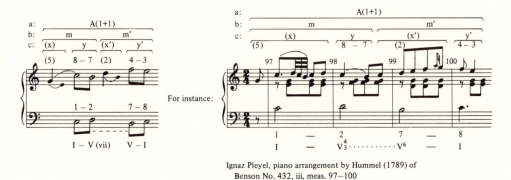

Ignaz Pleyel, piano arrangement by Hummel (1789) of
Benson No. 432, iii, meas. 97–100

EXAMPLE 3-4. Meyer's specification of a particular changing-note archetype

SUMMARY

Schema theory, as presented in the first chapter, is abstract in order to be applicable to diverse cognitive tasks. Once a specific cognitive task is identified—for example, listening to music—general schema theory can be supplemented by additional concepts of more limited applicability. In this chapter, the general notion of musical schemata has been supplemented with the more specific concepts of style structures and archetypes; the terms *style structure, form,* and *process* have been added to the general category of distinctive features; and, under the concept of idiostructures, the principle has been introduced that musical patterns have latent destabilizing features. An understanding of these special terms, all taken from the work of Narmour and Meyer, helps to provide a background for the type of detailed musical analysis that follows. The specific object of this analysis will be Meyer's changing-note archetype, a "symmetrical" pattern with a bipartite, mirrored structure.

CHAPTER 4

Defining the Changing-Note Archetype

Several criteria guided the selection of a musical schema for this study. The chosen schema had to be common enough that anyone familiar with classical music would recognize it; it had to be simple enough that its smallest detail could be studied in depth; and it had to avoid being so abstract that its features and relationships could not be clearly defined. Lastly, the schema had to be a type of structure recognized by other scholars but not as yet fully investigated.

Leonard Meyer's changing-note archetype seemed a good choice; it is common, simple, not too abstract, and recognized by other scholars.[1] Furthermore, an investigation of this archetype promised to provide an interesting case study of a style structure and its component style forms.

CHANGING-NOTE PATTERNS

In Meyer's book *Explaining Music*, the term changing-note archetype refers to a structural melody with scale degrees 1–7...2–1 (or 1–2...7–1, its inversion). In his later articles the same term also refers to the structural melodies with scale degrees 3–2...4–3, 3–4...2–3, and 1–7...4–3.[2] Hypothetical versions of all these patterns are given in example 4-1.

What set of features do these patterns have in common? Obviously they all have a bipartite, AA′ form and a I–V–V–I harmonic progression, but then so do many other patterns. For instance, example 4-2 combines such a form and harmonic pattern with an ascending melody.

If the changing-note archetype is to be distinguished from example 4-2, then some definition of the group of possible core melodies is necessary. Inasmuch as the patterns variously begin on different scale degrees, end on different scale degrees, or progress by different intervals in different directions, the only thing common to all is an S-like contour. But even the set of features comprising an AA′ form, a I–V–V–I

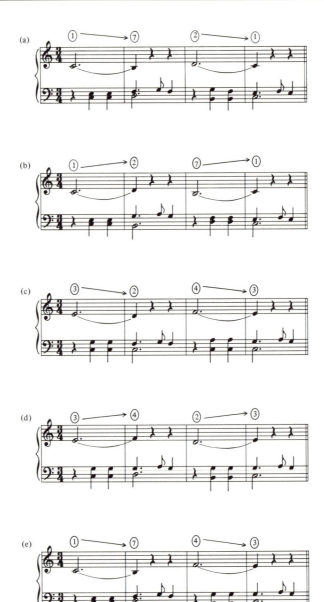

EXAMPLE 4-1. Changing-note archetypes

EXAMPLE 4-2. AA′ form and I–V–V–I harmony without a changing-note melody

harmonic progression, and an S-like contour for the structural melody is not sufficiently discriminating. This feature set would include a rather rare type of phrase
not mentioned by Meyer—5–4...6–5 (example 4-3).[3] This same set of features
would exclude the very common I–ii⁶–V–I harmonic progression often heard with
changing-note melodies, as in example 4-4. Also excluded would be the common
ABA′ form of many changing-note melodies (example 4-5).

EXAMPLE 4-3. The changing-note pattern 5–4...6–5

EXAMPLE 4-4. Changing-note archetype with I–ii⁶–V⁷–I harmony

EXAMPLE 4-5. Miniature ABA′ form

The only feature common to all these phrases is a changing-note melodic contour, but to argue that one criterion alone determines class membership subverts the whole concept of complex musical schemata. Such an approach would represent a reversion to the methods of taxonomy. The complete specification of a complex musical schema thus must involve more than a categorization of one of its salient features. According to Rumelhart, "A schema contains, as part of its specification, the network of interrelations that is believed to normally hold among the constituents of the concept in question."[4] A polyphonic schema, hierarchically structured in both musical space and time, is above all a relational complex, and the relationships between elements of *different* parameters may be as significant as the relationships between elements of the same parameter.

A different approach to the problem of defining the overall changing-note archetype is to view each of Meyer's specific patterns as a separate schema. After all, Meyer does not present these patterns as actual four-note melodies but rather as classlike structural melodies abstracted from hundreds of phrases. Viewed in this way, the particulars of each pattern take on significance. For instance, example 4-1c above—the 3–2...4–3 pattern—is distinguished by a tonic pedal and the parallel motion of imperfect consonances. Generations of composers have preserved these central features of the schema. Even in Shostakovich the "network of interrelations" remains largely intact (example 4-6).

EXAMPLE 4-6. An example of a 3–2...4–3 schema in Shostakovich, 24 Preludes and Fugues, Op. 87[1] (1951), Prelude 7, meas. 19

Besides having individual structural characteristics, the various changing-note schemata react quite differently to standard musical transformations. For example, the 1–7...4–3 schema is frequently heard with the 4–3 melodic dyad lower than the 1–7 dyad and thus without an S-like melodic contour (example 4-7). On the other hand, a corresponding version of a simple 1–7...2–1 schema (example 4-8) would be rare. When the 1–7...2–1 or 3–2...4–3 structural melodies are inverted, the closely related 1–2...7–1 or 3–4...2–3 patterns result. But an inversion of the 1–7...4–3 pattern would not produce any recognized structural melody (e.g., 1–2...5–6?).

EXAMPLE 4-7. The 4–7 dyad placed below the 1–7 dyad

EXAMPLE 4-8. The 2–1 dyad placed below the 1–7 dyad

These distinctions, coupled with the similarities already mentioned, suggest that the changing-note archetype is really a complex network of associated schemata. In this network the schemata bear a family resemblance to each other based on their sharing of features, even though no single set of features defines each and every member of the family. The structure of this associative network may be comparable to those structures psychologists have formulated for other complex mental concepts. So in the next section we examine how associative networks are presumed to be organized, in order to better conceptualize how several unique schemata might together form a larger construct—Meyer's changing-note archetype.

ASSOCIATIVE NETWORKS

Endel Tulving proposed two basic kinds of memory: episodic memory, roughly equivalent to memory of events, and semantic memory.[5] Jean Mandler makes a similar distinction between schematic and categorical memory.[6] By the terms *semantic* or *categorical* memory these authors mean our internal organization of concepts. (In music, concepts might include, among other things, abstract style forms such as *S-like contour* or *binary form*.)

The prevailing representation of this organization is not in terms of schemata but rather in terms of memory nodes and a network of simple interconnections. Figure 4-1 is an example of a network associated with the concepts *bird, animal, fish,* and so on.[7] The length of each arrow in this network is significant; for example, people associate *canary* more closely than *ostrich* with the concept *bird*. The direction of each arrow only clarifies a relationship (e.g., "[a] bird [has] wings," not "wings [have] bird") and does not imply that associations move in any particular direction; the strings of association "(a) bat (can) fly (as can a) bird (like a) canary" and "(a) bat (is a) mammal (as is a) cow" are equally valid. One can easily imagine a comparable string of music-theoretic associations connected with various changing-note schemata. For example, "(a) 1–7…2–1 schema (has an) S-like contour (and has a) binary form."

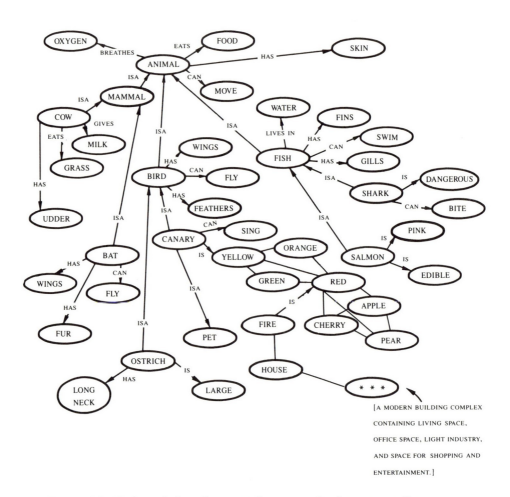

FIGURE 4-1. The association of concepts by a network of memory nodes (From Janet L. Lachman and Roy Lachman, "Theories of Memory Organization and Human Evolution," in *Memory Organization and Structure*, ed. C. Richard Puff [Orlando, Fla.: Academic Press, 1979], p. 163. Copyright © 1979. Reprinted by permission of Academic Press and the authors.)

Unlike a network of associations, a schema of related events—an *event schema*—has determinable beginning and ending points. These two types of memory organization commingle if we allow the term *feature* for event schemata to coincide with the term *concept* for semantic networks. *Bird*, for example, can be both a concept linked to the memory nodes *wings, canary, animal,* and so on, and a feature in the schemata *bird-eating-a-worm, flying,* or *nest-building.* Similarly in music, *dominant seventh chord,* for example, can be both a concept linked to the memory nodes *instability, dissonance,* and so on, and a feature in the schemata *perfect authentic cadence* and *1–7...4–3 changing-note.* Figure 4-2 suggests an abstract representation of how two memory nodes—i.e., concepts—might participate as features in four schemata,[8] thus creating an associative network of schemata.

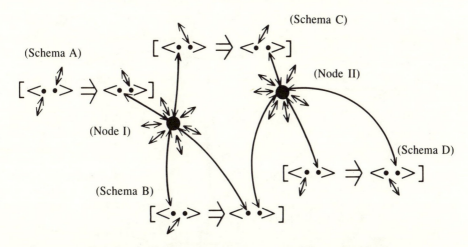

FIGURE 4-2. The association of schemata by memory nodes. (Adapted from Joseph P. Becker, "A Model for the Encoding of Experiential Information," in *Computer Models of Thought and Language,* ed. Roger C. Schank and Kenneth (Mark Colby [New York: W. H. Freeman, 1973], p. 410. Copyright © 1973 by W. H. Freeman and Co. Used by permission.)

In this hypothetical case, schema *A* relates two states or events, the sign "⇒" between them showing that one precedes the other. Each event has two features—the dots connected to arrows—and each feature is connected to some memory node. Schema *A* is related to schema *C* because a feature in the terminal event of schema *A* is connected to the same memory node (node *I*) as is a feature in the initial event of schema *C*. In a similar fashion, every schema in figure 4-2 is related to every other schema, even though a simple definition of these relationships may be difficult to put into words. If the abstract schemata of figure 4-2 are replaced by specific types of changing-note schemata, and the abstract memory nodes are replaced by specific musical style forms, then a rough image begins to take shape of part of the network of associated schemata that defines Meyer's changing-note archetype (figure 4-3).

The concept of rival schemata, that is, of event schemata that share initial events but later diverge, can obviously relate event sequences only on the restricted basis of initial events or cues. The complementary concept of memory nodes can associate features or events irrespective of their order in a schema. It is this latter type of memory organization that allows us at least to suggest explanations for some forms of analogy in music.

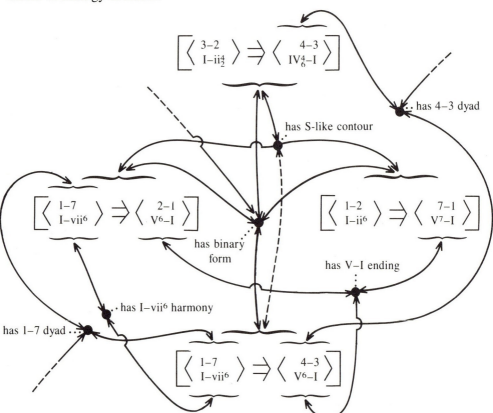

FIGURE 4-3. An associative network of changing-note schemata

A musical example from Mozart's early Symphony in G Major, KV 124 (example 4-9), may clarify what relevance memory nodes have for analysis. This 1–7...4–3 schema is quite simple and not far removed from the hypothetical example 4-1e. In the recapitulation of this Andante, example 4-9 is modified to suggest the 3–2...4–3 pattern in example 4-10, now in the tonic. As before, with the examples from Haydn and Massonneau (see examples 2-23 and 2-24), these Mozart examples challenge our ability to precisely define thematic identity in eighteenth-century music. Schema theory, as outlined in chapter 1, can accommodate the divergence from a norm as seen in Haydn and Massonneau. But the two Mozart examples would, in isolation, derive from slightly different schemata.

Examples 4-9 and 4-10 seem to lend support to Meyer's concept of the changing-note archetype. In effect, Mozart made an implicit equation of two related schemata, both within the scope of Meyer's archetype. Some aspects in which the schemata are similar pertain to time-independent style forms, particularly the S-like melodic contour. Other aspects—the similar endings of each example, for instance—are perceived retrospectively. The relationship between the phrases, then, is not one of rival schemata but more one of closely related nodes in an associative network. The two structures are not synonymous but analogous.

EXAMPLE 4-9. Mozart, Symphony in G Major, KV 124 (1772), ii, Andante, meas. 11–12

EXAMPLE 4-10. Mozart, Symphony in G Major, KV 124 (1772), ii, Andante, meas. 43–44

THE 1–7...4–3 SCHEMA

This study will concentrate on the schema represented by example 4-1e: 1–7...4–3. This schema's melodic pattern is unique among changing-note patterns in having different beginning and ending pitches. But another reason for selecting this schema becomes important for the second, historical, portion of this study. A simple melodic style form such as 1–7–2–1 can be found in a wide variety of historical styles. Indeed, the pattern is so basic to Western music as to be almost stylistically neutral. But this is not the case with the melodic style form 1–7–4–3; this style form is peculiar to the eighteenth and early nineteenth centuries. That is, placing this style form in the context of a single style structure further narrows its historical range and creates a clearly defined time frame within which to study one type of musical structure.

The aim of this section is to provide a basic definition of the 1–7...4–3 schema. My definition entails the same features mentioned by Meyer but views them as features in an event schema. I have adopted Joseph P. Becker's notational conventions (seen above in figures 4-2 and 4-3).[9] These are: (1) square brackets, [   ], to enclose the schema; (2) canted brackets, ⟨   ⟩, to enclose each event; (3) the sign

"⇒" to indicate the order of events; and (4) various special signs representing features. These special signs are the roman numerals referring to harmonic categories, circled numbers referring to scale degrees in the melody and bass, and broken vertical lines referring to metric boundaries (i.e., a bar line or some fraction of a measure). The result is shown in figure 4-4.

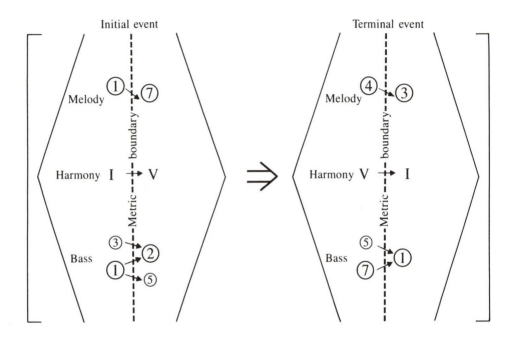

FIGURE 4-4. The 1–7...4–3 schema

The exact placement of the metric boundary in the first event is usually repeated in the second event. Across these boundaries occur coordinated sets of movements. For example, across the first metric boundary there is movement from the melodic scale degree ① to degree ⑦, movement in the bass from ① to ② (or occasionally 3 → 2 or 1 → 5), and harmonic movement to the dominant, usually but not always from the tonic. *It is such a coordinated set of movements and not the presence or absence of any single feature that characterizes each schema event.* Furthermore, the initial and terminal schema events need not be adjacent; they may be separated by other music. This separation, however, rarely if ever exceeds the time limit of short-term memory—perhaps about six seconds in the complex contexts of eighteenth-century music.

The schema outlined in figure 4-4 is applicable to a wide range of musical phrases. One of the simplest examples is from Mozart's Symphony in A Major, KV 114 (example 4-11). (In this and subsequent examples the square brackets delimiting the schema and the arrow sign connecting the schema events are omitted whenever these indications would be superfluous.) A slightly more complex example from Mozart's G-Major Keyboard Sonata, KV 283 (189h) (example 4-12) has already been analyzed to show its network of melodic relationships (see chapter 2 and example 2-11).

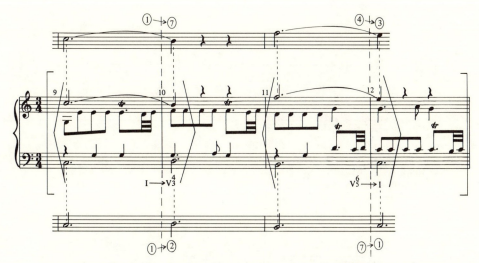

EXAMPLE 4-11. Mozart, Symphony in A Major, KV 114 (1771), iii, Trio, meas. 9–12

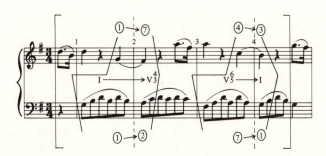

EXAMPLE 4-12. Mozart, Keyboard Sonata in G Major, KV 283 (189h) (early 1775), i, Allegro, meas. 1–4

While the melodic dyads 1–7 and 4–3 are important features, they are easily obscured by other melodic patterns. One way in which these dyads can be given added prominence is through dissonance. In example 4-13, from Mozart's C-Minor Keyboard Sonata, KV 457, notice how the initial notes of each dyad are held across the metric boundaries to create suspensions. Still further melodic variation is possible and indeed common, at times departing from the simple norm of figure 4-4. If, for example, Mozart had used unprepared appoggiaturas in place of suspensions (see example 4-14), the melodic dyads would no longer straddle the metric boundaries. Would example 4-14 then be based on a different schema? No, it would merely represent another possible realization of the underlying 1−7...4−3 schema, a realization with less typical melodic features.

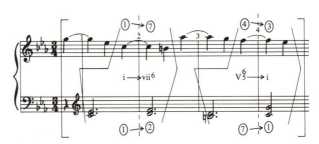

EXAMPLE 4-13. Mozart, Keyboard Sonata in C Minor, KV 457 (1784), iii, Molto allegro, meas. 1–4

EXAMPLE 4-14. A hypothetical version of example 4-13

It is important to bear in mind that a schema is an abstracted norm and not a fixed definition; in other words, it is an inherently psychological phenomenon. To reinforce this point it may be prudent first to briefly review Rumelhart's six characteristics of a schema with reference to the 1−7...4−3 structure and then to present a final example in which Mozart cleverly exploits important aspects of schematic perception.

Rumelhart's first point is that "schemata have variables." A few melodic variations of the 1−7...4−3 schema have already been presented, and the next chapter takes variations of this and other features as its central topic. Rumelhart's second point is that "schemata can embed, one within another." As we shall see, low-level melodic, harmonic, or rhythmic schemata can be embedded within the 1−7...4−3 schema, which itself can be embedded within larger schemata that organize extended phrases or periods. His third and fourth points, "schemata represent knowledge at all levels of abstraction" and "schemata represent knowledge rather than definitions," speak to the differences between a simple definitional list of attributes and more sophisticated, holistic forms of human cognition. While at a low level of structure a schema might be approximated by an if-then type of definition (e.g., If conditions *x, y,* and *z* are met, then the phenomenon in question is a passing tone), at higher levels a schema is better conceived as a unique gestalt. How the mind might use this type of gestalt is suggested by Rumelhart's last two points—"schemata are active processes" and "schemata are recognition devices." By "active process" he means, for instance, that when we hear the initial event of a 1–7...4–3 schema we form an expectation of probable terminal events and actively listen for them. By "recognition device" he means that we first evaluate a phenomenon in terms of the schemata we know and then interpret the phenomenon according to the schema that fits it best. In doing this we weigh evidence for and against various schemata and make a choice based on an overall pattern of features. Since this evaluation takes place as music unfolds, our prospective estimation of an event's significance can in retrospect change as new evidence presents itself. One might, for example, perceive what sounds like a small half-cadence, only to reinterpret it a moment later as the initial event in a 1–7...4–3 schema because the later interpretation better accounts for the overall pattern of features.

A phrase that well exemplifies this fluid view of a schema can be found in the first movement of Mozart's Keyboard Sonata in B♭ Major, KV 333 (315c), where the theme modulates from the tonic to the dominant (example 4-15). In initiating the move toward the dominant, the first event is somewhat ambiguous; the 1–7 melody, the move to the dominant, and the ascending step in the bass are all present, but the event lacks a tonic F harmony and uses the less typical unprepared appoggiatura form of melodic dyad. It is only with the clear and quite regular terminal event that we can reinterpret the first event more securely as the beginning of a 1–7...4–3 schema. Overall, this schema best accounts for the many features and relationships, even though the phrase begins most atypically. By a sleight of hand made possible by schema-based perception, Mozart modulates without obviously modulating and creates the unexpected while still fulfilling our expectations.

EXAMPLE 4-15. Mozart, Keyboard Sonata in B♭ Major, KV 333 (315c) (1778), i, (Allegro), meas. 11–14

CHAPTER 5

Schematic Norms and Variations

The preceding chapters developed concepts of musical schemata in general and the 1–7...4–3 schema in particular. It would be possible now to leave theoretical matters behind and proceed with the chronologically ordered discussion of Part II, but to do so would slight one of the most interesting, if nonetheless problematic, areas of schema research. I refer to the nature of norms, limits of variation, and the effects of the simultaneous variation of several component features.

Because these topics are difficult to address in the abstract, I will present a sizable group of musical examples with which to illustrate the discussion. Some examples are used to show the effects of changes in a single feature, say the harmony or bass line. Others demonstrate how combined changes in several features may so deform a phrase that we no longer feel confident in calling it, for instance, a 1–7...4–3 style structure.[1] As will be seen, the framework that schema theory provides for dealing with the inevitable doubts and uncertainties of schematic categorization is one of its most important contributions.

The idea of variation, as in a theme-and-variations movement, is familiar to all musicians. An analogy can be drawn between a theme with its variations and a schema with its various instantiations. For example, the Finale of Haydn's Keyboard Sonata in G Major, Hob. XVI/27—a theme-and-variations movement—has a theme (example 5-1a) that begins with a 1–7...4–3 style structure. This phrase and each of its subsequent variations (example 5-1, b–f) are also instantiations of the 1–7... 4–3 schema. And just as each variation alters one or more features of the theme, each instantiation (including the theme) alters one or more norms of the schema.

Judging the psychological distance of an instantiation from the norms of a

EXAMPLE 5-1 (facing page). Haydn, Keyboard Sonata in G Major, Hob. XVI/27 (?1776), iii, Presto: (*a*) meas. 1–4; (*b*) meas. 25–28; (*c*) meas. 49–52; (*d*) meas. 81–84; (*e*) meas. 105–8; (*f*) meas. 113–16

(a)

(b)

(c)

(d)

(e)

(f)

schema can be a difficult task, especially when fine discriminations are required. For instance, while it might be taken for granted that examples 5-2 and 5-3 (phrases from other Haydn finales) are instantiations comparable to the phrases of example 5-1, it would not be easy to say which is closer to the norms of the schema. Still more difficult would be an attempt to rank all eight of the aforementioned phrases by their proximity to the schema.

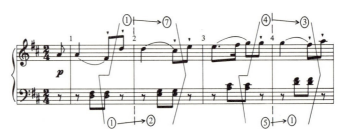

EXAMPLE 5-2. Haydn, Keyboard Sonata in D Major, Hob. XVI/37 (−1780), iii, Presto ma non troppo, meas. 1–4

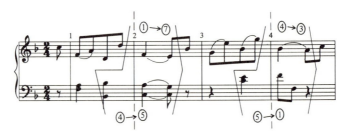

EXAMPLE 5-3. Haydn, Keyboard Sonata in F Major, Hob. XVI/23 (1773), iii, Presto, meas. 1–4

In light of these difficulties a systematic analysis of schema variation would be premature. But an orderly discussion is nevertheless possible. This discussion will proceed by hierarchical levels, beginning with the variation of individual features, moving to the variation of the two schema events, and concluding with the variation of the schema as a whole. At each level we will see that even if fine distinctions prove elusive, gross distinctions can be made that still illuminate important aspects of musical style.

Variation of Individual Features

Bass Line

The most common bass line used with the 1–7...4–3 schema is 1–2...7–1, that is, tonic to supertonic and then leading tone to tonic. Almost all the examples thus far presented use this pattern in the bass. Still, even within the restricted context of the typical I–V–V–I harmony other basses are possible. The three phrases by Haydn in example 5-4 have 1–5...5–1 basses. The 1–5...5–1 bass can be further simplified by omitting or attenuating its first and third pitches, that is, (1)–5...(5)–1 (example 5-5). Hybrid crosses of the 1–2...7–1 and 1–5...5–1 basses will also be seen from time to time in this study. Of the two possibilities, the 1–2...5–1 bass is more common than the 1–5...7–1 bass owing perhaps to a preference for movement toward, rather than away from, the root-position dominant.

EXAMPLE 5-4. (a) Haydn(?),[2] Keyboard Sonata in A Major, Hob. XVI/5 (−1763), i, Allegro, meas. 38–41; (b) Haydn, Keyboard Sonata in B♭ Major, Hob. XVI/41 (−1784), i, Allegro, meas. 8–11; (c) Haydn, Keyboard Sonata in E♭ Major, Hob. XVI/49 (1789–90), i, Allegro, meas. 81–84

(a)

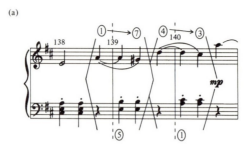

(b)

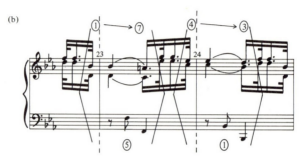

EXAMPLE 5-5. (*a*) Beethoven, Piano Sonata in D Major, "Pastoral," Op. 28 (1801), i, Allegro, meas. 138–40; (*b*) Haydn, Keyboard Sonata No. 18 in E♭ Major in Wiener Urtext Ed. (?c1764), i, Allegro, meas. 23–24

All the basses so far discussed begin with or imply a beginning on a root-position triad. An alternative to such a tonally secure beginning is provided by a 3–2...7–1 bass. In examples 5-6a and 5-6b, Haydn uses this bass to modulate from tonic major to relative minor.

(a)

(b)

EXAMPLE 5-6. Haydn: (*a*) Keyboard Sonata in A♭ Major, Hob. XVI/46 (c1767–70), i, Allegro moderato, meas. 9–10; (*b*) Keyboard Sonata in F Major, Hob. XVI/23 (1773), i, (Moderato), meas. 12–15

Many of these basses could theoretically be used in other related schemata. There would be no part-writing rules violated were the 3–2...7–1 bass used, for example, with a 1–7...2–1 melody. But there is an important distinction to be made between theoretical combinations of eighteenth-century style forms and the actual conventions of eighteenth-century style structures.

When Haydn rewrites example 5-6b as a 1–7...2–1 style structure later in the same movement, he provides the 1–2...2–3 bass belonging to the conventions of that style structure (example 5-7). The same distinction is observed in the two phrases from a Haydn Adagio in example 5-8.

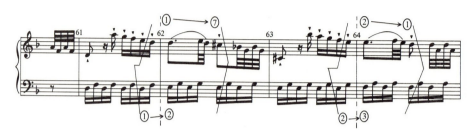

EXAMPLE 5-7. Haydn, Keyboard Sonata in F Major, Hob. XVI/23 (1773), i, (Moderato), meas. 61–64

EXAMPLE 5-8. Haydn, Keyboard Sonata in E♭ Major, Hob. XVI/38 (−1780), ii, Adagio: (a) meas. 1–2; (b) meas. 5–6

Without this distinction, 1–7...4–3 and 1–7...2–1 schemata would differ only in their terminal melodic dyads. With this distinction, composers were able to provide early clues as to which schema was being used. For example, when ② remains in the bass in measure 23 of example 5-9, a 1–7...2–1 style structure can be predicted, even though confirmation must wait until measure 26. It is interesting to speculate that the 1–5...5–1 bass may be less common for the 1–7...4–3 schema because it does not help to differentiate this schema from 1–7...2–1 style structures (see also example 7-15 and the accompanying discussion).

EXAMPLE 5-9. Beethoven, Piano Sonata in F Major, Op. 10, No. 2 (1796–97), i, Allegro, meas. 19–26

Harmony

Variations in the bass lines of 1–7...4–3 style structures concomitantly produce slight variations in harmony; root-position triads are replaced by inverted triads, and vice versa. More extensive harmonic variation is also possible. For example, instead of forming a stable area of tonic harmony at the beginning of a 1–7...4–3 style structure, the harmony can progress toward the dominant chord that closes the first event. This permits modulations (see, for instance, example 4-15) and allows more complex harmonic design. A simple example of a harmonic progression to the dominant chord has already been presented in example 5-3 (i.e., I–IV–I$_4^6$–V). The limits of this type of variation are difficult to fix. For instance, the Scherzo of Schumann's Piano Sonata Op. 11 (example 5-10) opens in F♯ minor, but the tenuous 1–7...4–3 style structure embedded in the first phrase is in A major!

EXAMPLE 5-10. Schumann, Piano Sonata, Op. 11 (1832–35), Scherzo, meas. 1–8

Within the more traditional confines of the 1–7...4–3 schema, one of the standard harmonic variations involves a deceptive cadence at the close of the second event. Frequently this variation occurs in conjunction with a melodic complex that links the two melodic dyads with a linear melodic descent. Example 5-11 presents a simple version of this melodic complex. The phrase from Schumann's "Wehmut" analyzed in chapter 2 is also of this type. In Beethoven's Piano Sonata Op. 111 this same 1–7...4–3 complex is presented first with a tonic cadence (albeit over a dominant pedal) and then with a deceptive cadence (example 5-12).

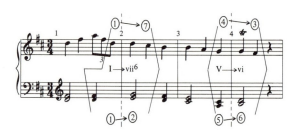

EXAMPLE 5-11. Haydn, Keyboard Sonata in D Major, Hob. XVI/4 (?c1765), ii, Menuet, meas. 1–4

EXAMPLE 5-12. Beethoven, Piano Sonata in C Minor, Op. 111 (1821–22), i, Allegro con brio ed appassionato, meas. 50–54

When the bass line of a 1–7…4–3 style structure first moves up from ① to ② and then descends to the dominant, it sometimes happens that the tonic chord is prematurely touched upon. This does not negate the schema as long as the tonic chord is brief and clearly in passing, as in example 5-13.

EXAMPLE 5-13. Beethoven, Piano Sonata in Eb Major, Op. 31, No. 3 (1802), iii, Minuetto, Moderato e grazioso, meas. 1–4

Melodic Dyads

The possible extent of variation in the harmony or bass line of a 1–7...4–3 style structure depends to a degree on the compensating clarity of the melody. Similarly, against a simple background even florid melodic variations can be accommodated. Example 5-12 has already presented a 1–7...4–3 style structure with a melodically ornamented restatement. Example 5-14 presents a similar pair of phrases. Notice how the 4–3 dyad is obscured by the intervening D♯. The 1–7 dyad is less often thus obscured, perhaps because without a clear initial event the schema itself might be obscured. Three more examples of ornamented 4–3 dyads, all taken from Haydn keyboard sonatas, are given in example 5-15.

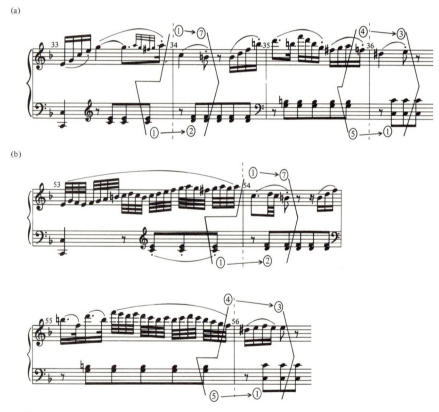

EXAMPLE 5-14. Mozart, Keyboard Sonata in C Major, KV 309 (284b) (1777), ii,
Andante con poco adagio: (a) meas. 33–36; (b) meas. 53–56

EXAMPLE 5-15 (facing page). Haydn: (a) Keyboard Sonata in B♭ Major, Hob.
XVI/2 (−?1760), ii, Largo, meas. 1–4; (b) Keyboard Sonata in D Major,
Hob. XVI/24 (?1773), ii, Adagio, meas. 9–12; (c) Keyboard Sonata in G
Major, Hob. XVI/39 (−1780), ii, Adagio, meas. 8–11

(a)

(b)

(c)

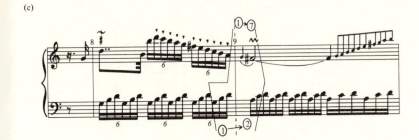

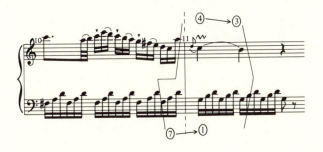

In several of the examples thus far presented, the ① and ④ of the 1–7 and 4–3 dyads have only a fleeting presence. Often the sense of these pitches is reinforced by their earlier, more prominent appearances, as in example 5-16. But the question arises as to whether these pitches can be forfeited to default values:[3] that is, can the melodic pattern be reduced to → 7 ... → 3, much as the 1–5...5–1 bass can be reduced to → 5 ... → 1? For instance, in the two statements of the phrase in example 5-17, is the first phrase a 1–7...4–3 style structure even though it lacks a melodic ④? And is the phrase in example 5-18 also a 1–7...4–3 style structure?

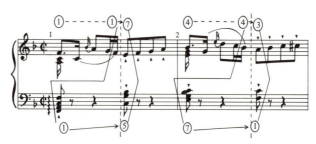

EXAMPLE 5-16. Haydn, Keyboard Sonata in C Major, Hob. XVI/35 (−1780), ii, Adagio, meas. 1–2

EXAMPLE 5-17. Mozart, Keyboard Sonata in F Major, KV A135 (547a) (?1788), i, Allegro, meas. 17–24

EXAMPLE 5-18. A. E. Müller?, once attributed to Mozart as KV³ 498a (1786),
Keyboard Sonata in B♭ Major, iv, Allegro, meas. 110–13

From a historical perspective, these phrases were written just after the heyday
of the 1–7...4–3 schema and were heard and performed by people conditioned to
expect such a schema in this type of thematic role. And from a psychological perspective, these phrases have very clear 1–7 dyads and standard 1–2...7–1 bass
lines, so that an expectation of a 1–7...4–3 style structure may well be formed and
default values for the 4–3 dyad generated. It is still a real question, however, whether
these default values are strong enough to supply a pitch that is not there. Default
values may help us to interpret ornate or obscured 4–3 dyads, yet examples 5-17 and
5-18 have clearly defined patterns *in lieu of* the 4–3 dyads (a descending triad in the
first phrase of example 5-17, a chromatic ascent in example 5-18). With this in
mind, my policy for this study is to exclude from consideration those phrases that
lack either of the two crucial melodic dyads. I hope that this admittedly arbitrary
restriction will eventually be proven to have been unnecessarily conservative.

Though the presence of 1–7 and 4–3 dyads will be considered a necessary
condition for a 1–7...4–3 schema, it is in no way a sufficient condition. In Narmour's terms, the 1–7...4–3 style structure involves more than just the presence of a
1–7...4–3 melodic style form. Not only must other features in the structural complex be present, but there must also be enough rhythmic-harmonic-melodic closure
to establish the two schema events as perceptible points of articulation.

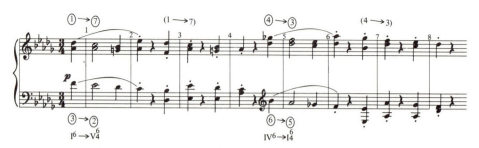

EXAMPLE 5-19. Beethoven, Piano Sonata in C♯ Minor, "Moonlight," Op. 27, No. 2 (1801), ii, Allegretto, meas. 1–8

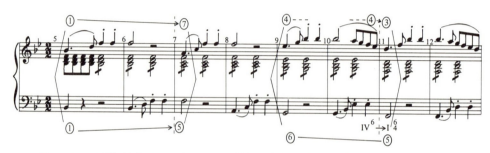

EXAMPLE 5-20. Schubert, Symphony No. 5 in B♭ Major, D485 (1816), i, Allegro, meas. 5–12

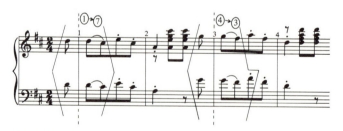

EXAMPLE 5-21. Haydn, Overture in D Major, Hob. Ia:4 (?1782–84), i, Presto, meas. 1–4

In example 5-19 the phrase by Beethoven has 1–7 and 4–3 dyads, harmonic movement to the dominant and then to the tonic, a clear bipartite form, and other features of the 1–7...4–3 schema. But the two schema events are deformed by a lack of harmonic and melodic closure. None of the deforming features of example 5-19 by itself would prevent a phrase from being perceived as a 1–7...4–3 style structure. For instance, the harmonically open tonic six-four chord under the melodic ③ in example 5-19 has already been seen in example 5-12. Likewise, the less closed IV⁶–I₄⁶ progression at this same point in example 5-19 can be found in a 1–7...4–3 style structure by Schubert (example 5-20). By placing the 1–7 and 4–3 melodic dyads at the beginning of phrase halves in example 5-19, Beethoven made them harder to perceive. But again, as is seen in example 5-21, this feature alone does not *prevent* these dyads from being perceived. And finally, the downward melodic continuation of the 1–7 and 4–3 dyads in example 5-19 lessens the closure of the dyads but need not deform them beyond recognition.

The problem with example 5-19 is that a number of deforming features *converge* in a single phrase. The normative structures are not strong enough to compensate for the several variations. Rather than say that example 5-19 is or is not a 1–7...4–3 style structure, I would call it an idiostructure with affinities to the 1–7...4–3 schema. Though anathema to highly systematized analytic methods, this type of description need not be excluded from psychologically based analyses.

Perhaps a simpler example may demonstrate why "fuzzy" categorizations need to be recognized in music theory. Example 5-22, up to the vertical line of dashes, is a fine case of a small 1–7...4–3 style structure. The 1–7 dyad is slightly deformed by the ensuing melodic descent (a′–g♯′–f♯′–e′), but this is compensated by the normative bass, the repeat of the a′, and the appoggiatura a′–g♯′. The 4–3 dyad occurs precisely where expected and is also accompanied by the normative bass—7–1. Yet the phrase continues beyond the closing bracket to a half cadence on the dominant. The melodic descent past the 4–3 dyad (e″–d″–c″–b′), the failure to echo the appoggiatura heard earlier on 1–7, and the suggestion of the very different I–V–I–V harmonic progression, all deform the 1–7...4–3 schema. The evidence for the 1–7...4–3 schema that accumulates before the line of dashes is retrospectively called into question. A doctrinaire assertion that this phrase is or is not a 1–7...4–3 style structure would be entirely out of place and would slight the important interplay of positive and negative evidence. The concept of a *deformed style structure* provides a useful alternative to the contention that a musical structure must either be, or not be, a member of a particular structural category.

EXAMPLE 5-22. Haydn, Keyboard Sonata in C♯ Minor, Hob. XVI/36 (?c1770–75), ii, Allegro con brio, meas. 17–18

As a last example of variations that affect the melodic dyads of $1-7...4-3$ style structures, I present two phrases that have the relative positions of melody and accompaniment inverted. In the first phrase, by Beethoven, only the inversion of melody and accompaniment distinguishes this structure from standard $1-7...4-3$ style structures (see example 5-23). In the following phrase by Schumann, however, a number of variations converge to place this structure either beyond the $1-7...4-3$ schema or at its very fringe (example 5-24); much would depend on how the performer interpreted the accents indicated for the left hand.

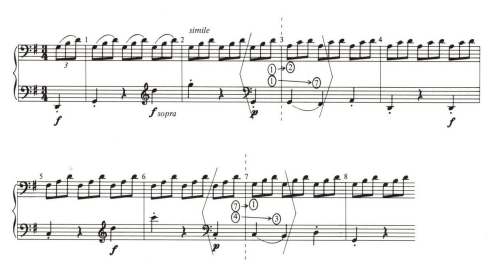

EXAMPLE 5-23. Beethoven, Piano Sonata in D Major, Op. 10, No. 3 (1797–98),
iii, Trio, Allegro, meas. 1–8

EXAMPLE 5-24. Schumann, Faschingsschwank aus Wien, No. 1 (1839–40),
meas. 1–8

VARIATION OF THE TWO SCHEMA EVENTS

There are different ways of viewing schema events. From the top down—that is, from the point of view of the schema as a whole—the two events are high-level features. From the bottom up—that is, from the point of view of individual features—the two events are low-level schemata. Some aspects of variation of the two schema events might thus be described by the same terms used to describe features and schemata. But, to the extent that schema events are different from the schema as a whole or from individual features, a discussion of their variation might require a new and different terminology.

Such a discussion would, first of all, require a way of accurately describing the perception of a schema event. Ideally, one could specify such event qualities as clarity, distinctness, vividness, or prominence. Unfortunately, no satisfactory method for doing this as yet exists. Looking back over the many 1–7…4–3 style structures shown in this chapter, one sees that some undeniably have more prominent, clearly perceptible schema events than others. But merely recognizing that such distinctions exist is not the same as knowing how to discuss them.

Although some central characteristics of schema events and their possible variation must, for the present, remain unspecified, a few peripheral features can be addressed. One of these is metric placement. Whereas all the examples shown thus far have their metric boundaries immediately prior to downbeats, a few other examples shift these boundaries over to just before weak beats. In example 5-25, from one of the late Haydn keyboard sonatas, the schema events close on very weak parts of the meter and are further weakened by the upbeat leaps in the melody that tend to disassociate ① from ⑦ and ④ from ③. Nearly the same metric placement is used in the slow movement of Beethoven's "Waldstein" Sonata (example 5-26). In a very few

EXAMPLE 5-25. Haydn, Keyboard Sonata in E♭ Major, Hob. XVI/49 (1789–90), i, Allegro, meas. 13–14

EXAMPLE 5-26. Beethoven, Piano Sonata in C Major, "Waldstein," Op. 53 (1803–04), iii, Adagio molto, meas. 14

cases the first metric boundary precedes a downbeat and the second precedes a weak beat (example 5-27). This pattern is usually found in minuets and may suggest a type of hemiola.

EXAMPLE 5-27. Haydn, Keyboard Sonata in G Major, Hob. XVI/27 (?1776), ii, Menuet, meas. 1–2

In any 1–7...4–3 style structure, the two schema events account for only two moments. All the other music that precedes, intervenes between, or follows the two moments can effect how the schema events are perceived. For example, if a small phrase is expanded by prefacing each schema event with important melodic material, the schema events may seem to recede into the background. This effect can be demonstrated with three phrases, each of which may be considered, for purposes of illustration, an expansion of the previous one. The first phrase, introduced in the previous chapter, has a melody limited to the two melodic dyads (example 5-28). The second phrase, analyzed in chapter 2, places implied melodic triads before each schema dyad (example 5-29). The third phrase condenses the content of example 5-29 and then precedes it with more triadic figurations (example 5-30), resulting in a greatly expanded type of 1–7...4–3 style structure in which the two schema events make up but a small fraction of the entire phrase. The two schema dyads that were perceived as *the* melody in example 5-28 appeared as part melody, part cadence in example 5-29 and may seem mostly cadential in example 5-30, though they remain more than just perfunctory marks of punctuation.

EXAMPLE 5-28. Mozart, Symphony in A Major, KV 114 (1771), iii, Trio, meas. 9–12

EXAMPLE 5-29. Mozart, Keyboard Sonata in G Major, KV 283 (189h) (early
1775), i, Allegro, meas. 1–4

EXAMPLE 5-30. Beethoven, Piano Sonata in E♭ Major, Op. 27, No. 1 (1800–
1801), i, Allegro, meas. 37–40

In the preceding two examples, conformant enlargements were made to each
phrase half. One-sided enlargements are also possible, though unusual. Enlargements of only the first half of a 1–7...4–3 style structure have a tendency to subsume or subordinate the schema itself. In example 5-31, the impression is not that of
a two-measure schema with extra material preceding it, but rather of a four-measure
phrase with an embedded, subordinate two-measure 1–7...4–3 style structure.

EXAMPLE 5-31. Haydn, Keyboard Sonata in C Major, Hob. XVI/21 (–?1765), i,
Allegro, meas. 1–4

Placing extra material between the two schema events can suggest an extension or interpolation. In example 5-32, notice how the viola's cadenzalike passage stretches the time between the two schema events. Mozart distinguishes the extension from the schema through differences in texture: solo viola for the extension, full quartet for the schema events.

EXAMPLE 5-32. Mozart, String Quartet in G Major, KV 387 (1782), i, Allegro vivace assai, meas. 68–72

In examples 5-25 through 5-32, I have tried to illustrate some of the variations that occur in positioning the two schema events in relation to the prevailing meter. Variations also occur in positioning the two schema events in relation to conformant subphrases.[4] The norm is for the two schema events to be appended to the *ends* of conformant subphrases, as in figure 5-1. Most of the examples in this study are of this type. Less common is for the schema events to begin or to be in the middle of conformant subphrases, as in figures 5-2 and 5-3. A musical example of figure 5-2 has already been given in example 5-21, and one of figure 5-3 in example 5-23.

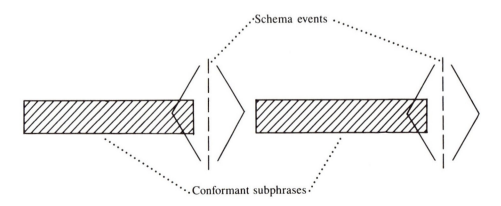

FIGURE 5-1. Schema events following conformant subphrases

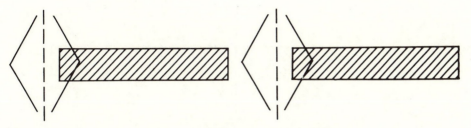

FIGURE 5-2. Schema events preceding conformant subphrases

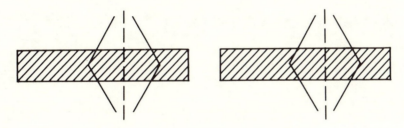

FIGURE 5-3. Schema events within conformant subphrases

In the three types of phrases just presented, each schema event is part of only one subphrase. A slightly different phrase type has a schema event *connecting* two conformant subphrases, as in figure 5-4. The phrase type of figure 5-4 may be considered an elision or enjambment of the phrase type in figure 5-1. The following phrase by Beethoven (example 5-33a) demonstrates how closely related the two phrase types are. Removing the first measure of Beethoven's phrase (see example 5-33b) or inserting a new fourth measure (example 5-33c) would transform this phrase into an ordinary 1−7...4−3 style structure. To indicate the differences between this new phrase type and standard 1−7...4−3 style structures, I label it the x̄ 1̄−7̄...4̄−3 style structure, using brackets to symbolize the conformant subphrases.

In both the 1−7...4−3 and x̄ 1̄−7̄...4̄−3 style structures we have seen that there is almost always a strong melodic connection across each dyad (1 → 7, 4 → 3) and often little direct connection between the scale degrees ⑦ and ④. This situation, normative by virtue of the Gestalt principle of the association of proximate

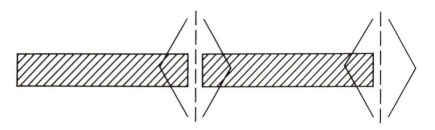

FIGURE 5-4. Schema events linking conformant subphrases

(a)

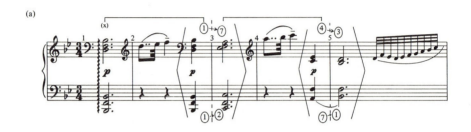

(b)

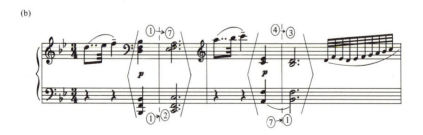

(c)

EXAMPLE 5-33. (*a*) Beethoven, Piano Sonata in D Minor, "Tempest," Op. 31, No. 2 (1802), ii, Adagio, meas. 1–5; (*b*) and (*c*) are altered versions of (*a*)

stimuli, can nevertheless be reversed or at least made ambiguous by a variety of means. For example, in a passage from Haydn's last keyboard sonata, the temporal proximity of ⑦ and ④ overrides (or at least counterbalances—much depends on performance) the spatial (i.e., pitch) proximity of ① and ⑦, ④ and ③ (example 5-34). The melodic connection of ⑦ and ④ in example 5-34 is reinforced by the subsequent conformant leap from ③ to ⑥.

EXAMPLE 5-34. Haydn, Keyboard Sonata in E♭ Major, Hob. XVI/52 (1794), ii, Adagio, meas. 3

Were the 1−7...4−3 schema nothing more than a particular melodic-harmonic succession of pitches, example 5-34 would be such a structure par excellence. But the 1−7...4−3 schema is defined by many more attributes than pitch alone; meter, rhythm, melodic conformance, preceding and succeeding contexts, rests, and articulations must all be considered. In view of these additional considerations, I believe that, while example 5-34 has the nominal pitch structure of a 1−7...4−3 schema, it is deformed into what I label a 1...7−4...3 style structure (the dash between the 7 and 4 referring to the direct melodic connection between these scale degrees). A clearer, more typical case of the 1...7−4...3 style structure appears in the Beethoven excerpt shown in example 5-35.

EXAMPLE 5-35. Beethoven, Piano Sonata in E♭ Major, "Lebewohl," Op. 81a (1809−10), iii, Vivacissimamente, meas. 53−55

Note how the 7–4 interval forms one unit (with a single bass and harmony) while the 1–3 interval forms another unit. Unlike the conformant subphrases of the typical 1–7...4–3 style structure, 1...7–4...3 style structures like example 5-35 often have complementary or antithetical sections. In example 5-35 this is manifested simply as the 3–1 descent versus the 7–4 ascent. In other examples, not only is melodic direction reversed, but contrasting figurations set apart the 7–4 interval (examples 5-36 and 5-37).

EXAMPLE 5-36. Haydn, Keyboard Sonata in E♭ Major, Hob. XVI/49 (1789–90), i, Allegro, meas. 84–85

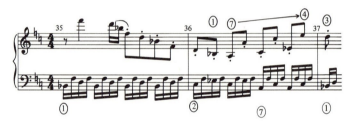

EXAMPLE 5-37. Beethoven, Piano Sonata in D Major, Op. 10, No. 3 (1797–98), iv, Allegro, meas. 35–37

It is not always easy to distinguish between the 1–7...4–3 and 1...7–4...3 style structures. Example 5-38, for instance, has features of both style structures. But a reasonable classification can usually be made on the basis of melodic conformance or contrast and on whether or not the 7–4 interval is a direct, or at least directly connected, interval. Thus, I consider example 5-38 a 1...7–4...3 style structure, although were the melody only slightly changed, as in example 5-39, I would classify the phrase a 1–7...4–3 style structure.

The distinctions between examples 5-38 and 5-39 may seem slight and insignificant, but this is only because such distinctions are greatly attenuated by the simple, four-note melody.[5] In general, composers clearly differentiated between 1–7...4–3 and 1...7–4...3 style structures. Their differentiation of these structures may be rooted in historical factors, or it may also be attributable to differences in the perception of what constitutes the relevant schema events. That is, in the absence of any psychological testing, it may be presumptuous to assume that people perceive the same schema events in a 1...7–4...3 style structure that are perceived in 1–7... 4–3 or x̄ 1–7̄...4̄–3 style structures. Because of this reservation, I have excluded 1...7–4...3 style structures from the historical portion of this study.

EXAMPLE 5-38. Beethoven, Piano Sonata in E Minor, Op. 90 (1814), ii, Nicht zu geschwind und sehr Singbar vorgetragen, meas. 9–10

EXAMPLE 5-39. An alteration of example 5-38

VARIATION OF THE SCHEMA AS A WHOLE

Variation of the schema as a whole must be discussed in holistic terms. That is, the discussion requires concepts and terms distinct from those applied to lower-level features or events. For example, consider two 1–7...4–3 style structures alike in every respect except that one of them cadences on a submediant rather than on a tonic chord. This distinction, when described in terms of chords, pertains to the lower-level feature *harmony*. If it were described as "a slight departure from the norms of the schema as a whole," however, then the reference would be to a higher level.

A terminology for discussing high-level commonness or uncommonness has been provided by cognitive psychologists.[6] Perhaps the most important term is *typicality*—a subjective measure of how typical an example is of a particular schema. Though a typicality judgment is by definition subjective, this does not mean that it is necessarily capricious or inexplicable. For instance, to most Americans *robin* is more typical of the visual schema *bird* than is *ostrich* or *penguin* (see figure 4-1); in large part this is because Americans have had demonstrably greater experience with robins and because robins share features with other well-known birds (starlings, jays, wrens, etc.). In music, carefully reasoned typicality judgments are also frequently made. For example, in describing the first movement of a symphony a scholar might say, "Composition X is highly typical of sonata form."

Two additional terms may help to refine the concept of typicality. The first is *prototype*. There are many related definitions of prototype, such as an experimental model, a perfect example of a type, and the most typical example of a category. We may dismiss the definition of a prototype as an experimental model; this usage is not directly related to perception and cognition. The other two definitions overlap and are not always easy to distinguish. The perfect example is probably what judges of diving contests or dog shows seek. They rate performance or appearance against an abstracted ideal prototype. On the other hand, the most typical example is probably what casting directors seek in extras and character actors—the prototypical widow, gangster, shopkeeper, policeman, and so on. These two aspects of the term *prototype* can become inextricably intertwined in evaluating complex phenomena such as musical compositions. The notion of the "prototypical sonata," for instance, usually involves aspects of being both most typical and a perfect example. Likewise, the identification of prototypical 1–7...4–3 style structures will be unavoidably influenced by both meanings of prototype, even though my intention is to emphasize the more empirically defensible aspect of the most typical example.

One way to view the high-level mental topography of schema variation is as a target with the schema prototype at the bull's-eye. Given this image, the question naturally arises, "How is the target delimited? That is, since each concentric circle moving away from the bull's-eye carries a lower typicality judgment, shouldn't a point be reached where typicality approaches zero?"

To address this question a second, additional term needs to be introduced—*confidence*. Confidence, often expressed on a scale of one to ten, indicates the degree of certainty a person places on a specific example's being an instance of a particular schema. Thus typicality and confidence are slightly different expressions of the same type of evaluation. A schema prototype, for instance, could be expected to have maximum confidence as well as the required maximum typicality. And an instance of a schema near the fringe of our target would have both low confidence and low typicality. But low confidence better implies the doubt felt by a person than does the more abstract concept of low typicality. In fact, low confidence may lead to the reinterpretation of an example in terms of an alternate schema. Thus, a point of zero typicality can rarely be reached, because diminishing confidence will prompt selection of an alternate schema. In this light, our target represents what is often called a fuzzy set—a category whose boundaries merge with the boundaries of other categories.

Following this line of reasoning, a complete knowledge of the limits of variation of a schema requires a knowledge of all other possible schemata. Let me provide a musicological example of this principle. Suppose that a musicologist were attempting to determine the limits of variation—that is, the minima of typicality—for the schema *sonata form*. If this were the only large-scale musical schema known to this researcher, then he or she might easily be led to identify many aria forms, minuets, double-reprise forms, concertos, and rondos as sonata forms of very low typicality. These forms often do have some points in common with sonata form, but that is not the issue. A rondo is not an atypical sonata but rather a schema in its own right. While this may seem obvious in relation to large-scale forms, similar principles are frequently overlooked in relation to smaller musical schemata. For example, the Schenkerian analyses shown in chapter 2 (see examples 2-9 and 2-10) represent the theme of Mozart's G-Major Keyboard Sonata, KV 283 (189h), as a descending linear pattern of low typicality rather than as a 1–7...4–3 style structure of high typicality, because that system of analysis emphasizes quite a small set of schemata.

If the theme of Mozart's G-Major Keyboard Sonata is a 1–7...4–3 style structure with high typicality, the phrase from Schumann's "Wehmut," also analyzed in chapter 2, is an example of the same schema with much lower typicality. Likewise the phrase by Beethoven in example 5-40 is of low typicality. (Notice how the initial schema event is reiterated, the terminal event delayed half a measure, and the harmony diverted toward the relative minor.) Though it is an overstatement, one could say that Mozart's phrase reveals the schema while Beethoven's and Schumann's phrases conceal it. These phrases span nearly seventy years, suggesting that there may also be a historical dimension to typicality. This topic is addressed in the second half of this study.

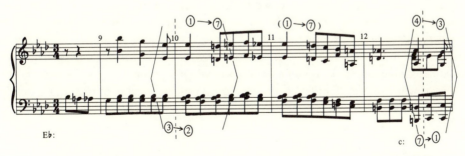

EXAMPLE 5-40. Beethoven, Piano Sonata in E♭ Major, Op. 27, No. 1 (1800–1801), ii, Adagio con espressione, meas. 9–12

SUMMARY

The many examples of variation in harmony, melody, bass line, and other features presented in this chapter indicate that the widest range of variation is permitted to a single feature when the other features are near their norms. For example, the melodically most elaborate style structures are often found to have the simplest, most conventional accompaniments. When many features are jointly varied, the 1–7...4–3 schema can easily be obscured. Examples were presented where each feature, by itself, was within an acceptable range of variation but where the convergence of many variations produced phrases that only vaguely resembled the 1–7...4–3 schema.

Features can be described in relatively concrete terms. Schema events are more abstract and, inasmuch as they have been little studied, present problems of terminology and approach. Two factors that demonstrably affect the perception of schema events are metric placement and the disposition of conformant, complementary, or contrasting subphrases. Normally, the two events of the 1–7...4–3 schema are coincident with metric bar lines. Shifting one or both events to other parts of a measure, or even to other measures, can create qualitative changes in how the events are perceived. Likewise, departures from the normal melodic design of two conformant subphrases can alter the perception of the schema events. One such variant, the x‾ 1–7‾...4–3 style structure, is more processive and open-ended than the 1–7...4–3 style structure. Another variant, the 1...7–4...3 style structure, so deforms the schema events that their perceptual integrity is put into question.

Variations of features and schema events have an effect on the typicality of a phrase as a whole. At least in theory one can place all phrases that are instances of a schema on a measured scale of typicality. At the one end of the scale would be the most typical example of a schema (called the schema prototype). But at the other end of the scale, where the least typical example supposedly resides, the situation would be much less clear because as typicality diminishes, so does one's confidence in the applicability of the chosen schema. Thus an alternative schema will probably present itself when typicality becomes very low.

If, following Rumelhart, we conceive of a schema as knowledge abstracted from experience, then for each listener the knowledge of a musical schema will be somewhat different. The many examples presented in the last two chapters summarize a general knowledge of the 1–7...4–3 schema that is probably shared by listeners with a broad experience of the so-called standard repertory. But this experience is not at all what Mozart's experience was, nor was Mozart's experience anything like Schumann's. To understand the knowledge of the 1–7...4–3 schema held by those who created its most beautiful realizations we must examine it as a historical phenomenon.

PART II

Historical Survey

CHAPTER 6

A Schema Across Time

Complex musical schemata often seem to share similar histories. That is, they appear to have in common periods of experimentation, consolidation, maturity, decline, and obsolescence. Scholars born in the nineteenth century were prone to attribute these similar histories to a spiritual life cycle. They felt that artistic forms shared phases of birth, growth, flowering, aging, and death because all living things shared these phases. While today scholars may be less inclined to view music as a living product of nature, they still frequently employ this life-cycle model of musical structure because no more plausible model has been proposed.

In this chapter a new model is sketched to explain the perceived common histories of musical schemata. I argue that the apparent rise and fall of musical schemata is due to the way in which human intelligence abstracts stable categories from what is usually a continuum of historical change. In other words, musical schemata appear to have similar histories because we who perceive them have similar minds.

The historical environment in which a musical schema exists can be generalized as an infinitely complex array of events (economic events, political events, artistic events, etc.), composers' lives, and various trends. Figure 6-1 is an abstract representation of this environment in relation to a time line.

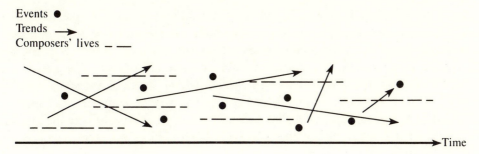

FIGURE 6-1. An abstract historical environment

Several problems arise if one tries to delimit the place in time of a musical schema. Take sonata form as an example. First, how one defines sonata form affects which pieces will be called a sonata form. Second, there were more sonata forms written in some years than in others. Third, some compositions are textbook examples of sonata form, while others are more dubious. And fourth, sonata form was a slightly different thing for the composers who inherited it than it was for those who developed it. These problems are, of course, not peculiar to music. They are general problems of cognition that confront us whenever an attempt is made to categorize some commonality from the manifest diversity of experience.

To surmount the problems associated with the quantitative and qualitative variations among instances of a musical schema I propose two related hypotheses. The first is: *The variation across time in the number of instances of a musical schema approximates a normal, bell-curved statistical distribution.* This means that the "population" of a musical schema rises, peaks, and then falls during the course of the schema's history. Such a rise and fall is idealized and depicted by a special type of symmetrical curve known as a *normal* or *Gaussian* distribution (a mathematical entity that, like the number π or the Fibonacci series, is frequently encountered in the world around us). A normal distribution is shown in figure 6-2. The horizontal axis represents the movement of time, and the vertical axis represents the number of instances of a musical structure per unit of time. Combining the left-to-right movement of time and the up-then-down change in a structure's population produces a normal distribution.

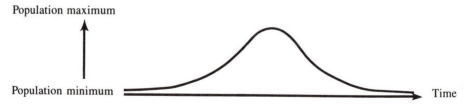

FIGURE 6-2. Hypothetical normal distribution

One important feature of a normal distribution is its lack of specificity concerning where the very first and last instances of a musical structure are to be found. Notice, in figure 6-2, how on either side of the population peak the curve approaches but never quite reaches the absolute population minimum—zero. This means that although the probability of increasingly early or late instances of a structure steadily decreases, the possibility of such additional instances never completely disappears. Even though this concept has its basis in statistics, it is consistent with the practice of musicologists who, for example, would be loath to label any single composition as "the world's first sonata."

The normal distribution curve shown in figure 6-2 is but one possibility chosen from a large set of such curves. From a theoretical point of view there is only one normal distribution, with a single mathematical formula. But in practice the choice of scalings for the horizontal and vertical axes affects the contour of the curve. A distinguishing feature among these curves is the degree of pointedness in the population peak: some curves have gently sloping sides with a rounded peak, while others have steep sides with a peak resembling the point of a spike. A correlation between the general shape of a musical schema's population curve and the nature of its definition can be summarized as follows: The degree of pointedness in the population curve of a musical schema varies directly with the number of constraints specified in the schema's definition.

The most elementary musical schemata would appear to be context-free style forms. Some of these structures are so little constrained by their definitions that they can be identified with equal frequency in all historical periods. For instance, the basic durational grouping *short-long* (e.g. ♪ ♩) is present in practically every composition from Perotin to Crumb. A graph of this omnipresent relationship would approximate a horizontal line—a uniform, "flat" distribution (figure 6-3). Figure 6-3 represents a negative extreme of both defined constraint and population-curve slope. A positive extreme of defined constraint and population-curve slope would be reached by a schema's definition so completely constrained that only a single composition could meet its specifications. For instance, the exact musical structure represented by Beethoven's Fifth Symphony was created in 1807 and at no other time before or since. A graph of this circumstance would approximate a vertical line—a single, sharp spike (figure 6-4).

FIGURE 6-3. A uniform distribution

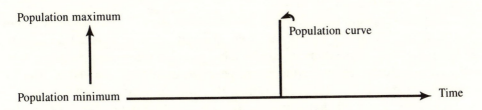

FIGURE 6-4. A population restricted to one point in time

Somewhere between these two extremes lie all the remaining population curves. For example, a simple, though not universal, style form would have a gently sloping population curve reflective of its broad distribution (figure 6-5). On the other hand, a highly constrained structural complex would have a much more pointed population curve reflective of its special conjoining of subsidiary elements (figure 6-6).

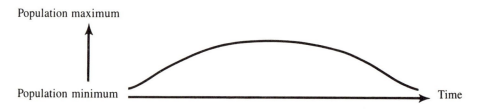

FIGURE 6-5. Possible population distribution of a common style form

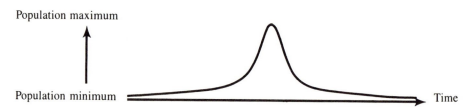

FIGURE 6-6. Possible population distribution of a structural complex

Because there is no way to quantify constraint, it is impossible to predict either the exact contour of a population curve or the exact breadth of a historical distribution. But the first hypothesis does allow relative estimations of constraint to be translated into predictions of a relative nature. For example, it can predict that the constituent style forms in a composite style structure should all have broader historical distributions and less pointed population curves than the style structure itself, because the definition of the style structure stipulates additional constraints of context and interrelationship.

As a case in point, the constituent style forms of the 1–7...4–3 style structure have historical frames of two, three, four hundred years or more. The melodic grouping 1–7–4–3, for instance, can be found across a three-century period from the mid-seventeenth century to the recent past (see examples 6-1a and b). On the other hand, the 1–7...4–3 schema itself, with all its specified interrelationships, is restricted to little more than a century—from the 1730s to the mid-nineteenth century—and, as will be demonstrated, appears to peak sharply around the early 1770s.

EXAMPLE 6-1. (*a*) Froberger, Suite No. 3 for Harpsichord (?1649), Allemande, meas. 6–7; (*b*) Poulenc, Flute Sonata (1956), i, meas. 5–7

The synchronic model implied by the arguments so far presented can account for the diachronic quantitative changes assumed by more traditional music histories. That is, with respect to the numerical rise and fall of a musical schema's population, positing a statistically based population curve has an explanatory force equal to that of invoking an organic metaphor of growth and decay. But more is implied in the typical use of this metaphor than changes solely in population. When Henri Focillon, the great French art historian and a spokesman for the organic view of art, writes of the birth, growth, maturity, aging, and death of an artistic form, he is referring to stages that are qualitatively, not just quantitatively, different.[1] In order for the present model to account for this type of diachronic, qualitative change, a second hypothesis must be introduced: *A musical schema will exhibit a curve of typicality similar to its population curve.*

As discussed in the previous chapter, every instantiation of a schema has a greater or lesser degree of typicality, the schema prototype having the maximum. As mentioned earlier, a robin is more typical of the schema *bird* than is an ostrich, even though both are perfectly legitimate instantiations of the same schema. The dominant factor in most judgments of typicality appears to be a comparison of the instantiation at hand with a central tendency abstracted from previously encountered examples of the same schema. The most obvious, though not the only, mechanism for this process of abstraction is an averaging of all the features of the set of known examples.[2] If averaging features is a major mechanism of abstracting a central tendency, and if musical structures emanating from a narrow time period are more similar than structures from disparate times, then the typicality of a musical structure will follow the structure's population curve. The prototype of the structure will be found at the population peak, and increasingly atypical examples of the structure will be found farther and farther down either slope of the population curve. Think again of the high-level schema *sonata form*. At the peak of its population in the late eighteenth century we find the compositions by Haydn or Mozart that have always been regarded as the prototypical sonata forms, while much earlier (say with Monn or Sammartini) or much later (with Liszt or Bruckner) we find sonata forms that are usually of low typicality.

In psychological experiments designed to study typicality, the population distribution of a schema can be fixed. In music history, however, this controlled relationship of typicality and population is lacking: population affects typicality, and typicality affects population. For example, should a composer become aware of a schema underlying similar musical phrases in the works of his contemporaries, not only could he produce his own instances of this schema—adding to its population—but he could also fashion instances of the schema more (or less) consistent with the central tendency he has abstracted, thereby adding to (or subtracting from) the schema's typicality. In certain situations, typicality and population may become locked in a feedback loop, changes in the one accelerating changes in the other. A similar feedback loop confronts the musicologist who, in cataloging instances of a specific schema, may be hesitant to cite examples of low typicality, with the result that the reported population becomes a function of typicality, even though it was some sample of the population that defined typicality in the first place.

The model thus far introduced—essentially a psychologically based prediction of the formation and deformation of stable categories in a historical context of continual change—has been presumed to be symmetrical. There is, however, an important element in schema theory that, with respect to time, is decidedly asymmetrical—memory. Memory is conservative; it provides schemata derived from past experience to interpret present conditions. The result of this conservatism is a tendency to cling to an old schema beyond the point where a new schema might be more appropriate.

The net effect of memory—whether one composer's memory or the mnemonic force of a culture's exemplary masterpieces—should be to make a structure's population and typicality curves slightly asymmetrical. For instance, the retention of older, established schemata will inhibit the recognition of early examples of a schema. A subsequent realization of the new structure's schema should include a reevaluation of earlier examples, with the effect of a sudden increase in perceived population. This increased population will trigger an acceleration in the population-typicality feedback loop beyond that predicted by the normal distribution. Figure 6-7 shows the effect of memory on the first half of a normal distribution. The descent from the peaks of population and typicality will be the reverse of figure 6-7—an early inhibition of the descent, followed by a subsequent acceleration (figure 6-8). This new descending curve results from the same process as the ascending curve; the schema

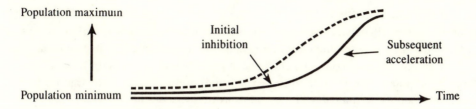

FIGURE 6-7. Probable deviations from normal distribution—population rise

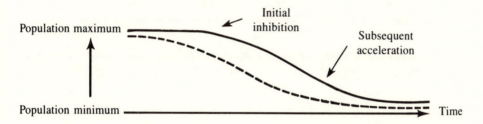

FIGURE 6-8. Probable deviations from normal distribution—population fall

in question is retained until subsequent realizations of new schemata accelerate the decline in population and typicality.

The above deviations in both the typicality and population curves have the related effect of making the peaks of population and typicality appear closer to the left or early side of the overall curves (figure 6-9). Thus, if a certain schema had a one-hundred-year history, one might expect its peaks of population and typicality to occur perhaps in the fortieth, and not the fiftieth, year of that history.

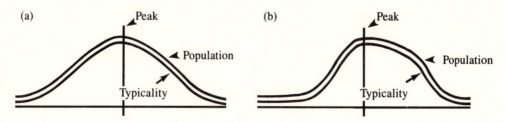

FIGURE 6-9. (*a*) Normal distribution; (*b*) normal distribution plus effect of memory

A "historical context of continual change" has been presumed for both the hypotheses of this chapter. Western polyphonic art music certainly qualifies as such a context; not only is continual change apparent, but it has generally been encouraged and rewarded. Whether continual change characterizes the histories of musical structures from quite different cultural contexts—oriental hieratic or court traditions, for instance—is open to question. Such traditions may discourage innovation and place great emphasis on the faithful replication of established repertories. It is possible, of course, that these conditions merely retard, and do not fundamentally alter, changes in musical schemata. In any case, no attempt is here made to claim validity for the two main hypotheses outside of the context of Western music. Likewise, excluded from this model are consciously historical usages of obsolescent musical structures (actual cases of complex schemata reused unchanged in a different era are quite rare—*sonata* was not the same schema for Hindemith or Stravinsky that it was for Haydn and Mozart).

The model presented in this chapter is admittedly abstract. Yet the predictions it makes are sufficiently specific to be either confirmed or disproved. In the next several chapters I will attempt to demonstrate that, in the single case of the history of the 1–7...4–3 schema, this model is largely confirmed.

CHAPTER 7

1720–1754: Scattered Examples

The period 1720 to 1754[1] was a time during which examples of the 1–7...4–3 schema were rare, of generally low typicality, and frequently interpretable in terms of other schemata. From the many analyses presented it will become apparent that there was no "protophrase," no unadorned pure version of the schema from which all subsequent, more complicated versions were descended. Quite to the contrary, early examples of the 1–7...4–3 schema will be shown to be complicated, often ambiguous structures from which later composers abstracted the simpler schematic constituents.

The twenty-two examples in this period are distributed in such a way that no clear population trend is discernible—the first five-year segment contains as many examples as the last (see figure 7-1). There is, however, a gradual increase in typicality during this period. For example, the 1–5...5–1 and 1–5...7–1 basses of the 1720s begin to give way, in the 1730s, to the more characteristic 1–2...7–1 bass. If

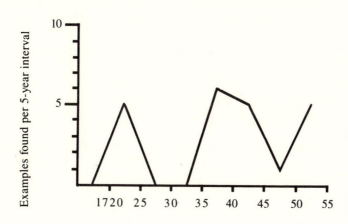

FIGURE 7-1. Population of 1–7...4–3 style structures, 1720–1754

typicality and population are linked, as predicted in the preceding chapter, the population curve should also have an upward slope. The fact that it does not suggests two different possibilities. On the one hand, the underlying hypotheses may be flawed or erroneous. On the other hand, twenty-two examples spaced over thirty-five years in which thousands of pieces were written may be too small a sample to accurately reflect any increase in the structure's population. The much better statistics available for later periods will strongly suggest that the latter inference is correct.

THE EARLY HISTORY OF THE 1−7...4−3 SCHEMA

In the previous chapter I tried to explain in abstract terms how the low typicality of early examples of a schema might contribute to their being interpreted in terms of other patterns. An example from Domenico Scarlatti's opera *Narciso* illustrates this possibility. Line *E* of example 7-1, along with the bass pattern shown in lines *F, G,* and *H,* does indicate a 1−7...4−3 schema (the more typical 1−2...7−1 bass will not appear until the following decade). But lines *A, B, C,* and *D* present other patterns that could easily subsume all or part of the small 1−7...4−3 structure. The weight of additional evidence—the textural, rhythmic, and harmonic features that set apart this 1−7...4−3 structure—does seem sufficient to assert that line *E* presents a primary patterning. Yet sufficient evidence for someone with prior knowledge of this eighteenth-century schema might have been insufficient for someone with extensive seventeenth-century musical experiences. In other words, while the 1−7...4−3 style structure from *Narciso* may be perceptible to us in spite of its low typicality, it could easily have been overlooked by its contemporary audience.

EXAMPLE 7-1. Domenico Scarlatti, *Narciso* (1720), Overture, i, Allegro, meas. 98–101

There is no indication that Scarlatti was the very first composer to utilize a 1–7...4–3 schema. Given the preexistence of the structure's style forms and the potential recombinations of older schemata, almost any composer from the early decades of the eighteenth century could have produced the pattern. Some idea of a general early limit for the structure can be gathered from examining the historical frames of its constituent style forms. Of course, concepts such as "tonality" or "binary form" are too abstract to be of any use in this endeavor. But other, more constrained, constituents of the 1–7...4–3 style structure provide good indications. For example, the melodic style form 1–7–4–3 appears, to my knowledge, with no marked frequency earlier than the mid-seventeenth century. The passage by Froberger in example 7-2 first approaches this style form through the technique known as *Freistimmigkeit* (i.e., varying at will the number of voices in a keyboard texture) (example 7-2, line *B*). The second and third measures of the example then create a sequence of 4–3 cadences. Notice that out of context the three dyads of line *A* in example 7-2 could form two different 1–7–4–3 patterns (G–F♯–C–B, C–B–F–E). But in context they function only as consecutive units in a repetitive sequence.

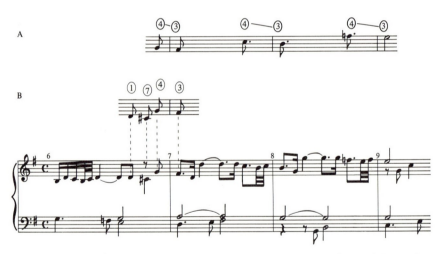

EXAMPLE 7-2. Froberger, Suite No. 3 for Harpsichord (?1649), Allemande, meas. 6–9

Missing from Froberger's music is the harmonic-formal unit I–V...V–I found in prototypical examples of the 1–7...4–3 style structure. This style form appears later in the century, as shown in example 7-3 by Corelli. Example 7-3 of course presents this style form in conjunction with a 5–4...4–3, not a 1–7...4–3, melodic structure.

EXAMPLE 7-3. Corelli, Trio Sonata, Op. 3, No. 2 (1689), Allegro, meas. 95–96

Examples 7-2 and 7-3 suggest that instances of 1–7...4–3 style structures were possible as early as the 1680s or 1690s. If the range of structures found in any musical period were simply all the combinations of the available style forms, then good examples of the 1–7...4–3 style structure should be found well before 1720. But after examining dozens of compositions written in this early period I was unable to find a single 1–7...4–3 style structure. Perhaps this structure was in some way incompatible with the prevailing set of seventeenth-century musical schemata (see the discussion accompanying example 7-5). This might explain why for as long as forty years (1680–1720) the 1–7...4–3 schema was an option not exercised by an entire generation of composers.

My initial speculations about the origin of the 1–7...4–3 schema concerned Italian vocal music. For instance, a prototypical 1–7...4–3 melody with the rhythmic pattern $\frac{2}{4}$ | ♪ ♫♫ | ♩ ♩ ♪ | ♪ ♫♫ | ♩ ♩ ♪ ‖ would be ideal for setting a couplet of seven-syllable Italian verse. I surmised that if Italian prosody were indeed a major influence in the development of the 1–7...4–3 schema, then the best early examples of the structure would be found in Italian opera arias. This assumption seemed all the more credible, since the Italian opera composers of the early eighteenth century (such as Pergolesi, Leo, Vinci, etc.) have often been credited with introducing important elements of the later Classic style. But my search of the early operatic repertory failed to uncover a single unequivocal example. There were, to be sure, excellent examples of other Classic schemata. The excerpt from Orlandini's *Ormisda* in example 7-4 presents a seven-syllable verse set to a very clear 1–7...2–1 schema. Nevertheless, the 1–7...4–3 structure appears not to have developed directly from operatic models.

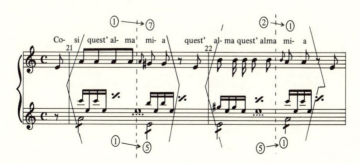

EXAMPLE 7-4. Orlandini, *Ormisda,* in Reinhard Strohm,[2] ex. 101 (1722), meas. 21–22

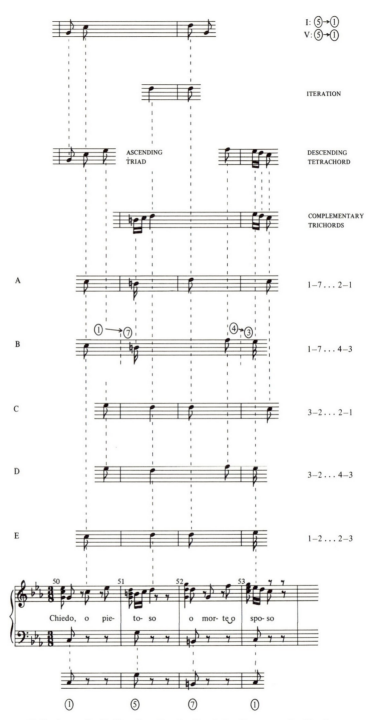

EXAMPLE 7-5. Antonio Pollarolo, *Lucio Papirio dittatore,* in Strohm, ex. 102 (1721), Andante, meas. 50–53

As an interesting example of how seventeenth-century traits interfered with the early development of the 1–7...4–3 schema, consider the excerpt from Pollarolo's *Lucio Papirio dittatore* in example 7-5. This four-bar structure weakly presents at least five potential Classic schemata (lines *A, B, C, D*, and *E*), all of which are irregular in terms of metric placement. A composer of the mid-eighteenth century might have regularized this melody by the simple device of switching the second and third pitches (example 7-6). Such a change would have clarified a 1–7...4–3 style structure and strengthened the sense of complementarity between the two con-tours of the melody. But this same slight alteration would have destroyed a prized seventeenth-century example of affective text setting—the use of the descending di-minished fourth E♭–B♮ for the word *pietoso* (pitiful). Pollarolo maintained the low-level gesture so important to the seventeenth century at the expense of the higher-level clarity so dear to the eighteenth century.

EXAMPLE 7-6. A hypothetical version of example 7-5 in which the
1–7...4–3 style structure is more evident

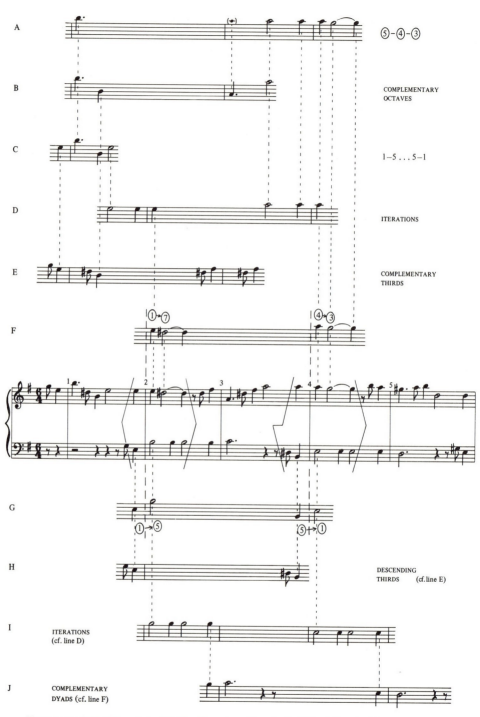

EXAMPLE 7-7. Veracini, Violin Sonata, Op. 1 (1721), No. 6, iii, Pastorale, Adagio, meas. 1–5

The clearest early examples of the 1−7...4−3 schema are all found in Italian or Italian-influenced instrumental music. The opening of Veracini's Pastorale in example 7-7 has the breadth, clarity, and surface simplicity characteristic of much later examples. Yet the surface simplicity demanded by the pastoral genre conceals a very complex network of motivic relationships. For instance, having the bass echo the opening of the melody forces the bass "out of phase"; the two halves of the melody close a measure ahead of the respective halves of the bass (compare lines *F* and *J*). Because the bass moves in both its halves to close on dissonant chords, the overall effect of the phrase is much less closed, more contrapuntal than comparable mid-century examples. A modern performer, raised on Haydn and Mozart, needs to suppress the tendency to articulate the bass with the melody, as shown in example 7-8. A more defensible performance, shown in example 7-9, is to emphasize the ongoing process of the repeated bass notes and the formal nature of the terminal bass dyads (see example 7-7, lines *I* and *J*).

EXAMPLE 7-8. A hypothetical phrasing of example 7-7 in which the melody alone determines the articulations

EXAMPLE 7-9. A hypothetical phrasing of example 7-7 in which melody and bass are independently articulated

In the slightly later excerpt from Sammartini's Symphony No. 3, almost all traces of melody-against-bass counterpoint have disappeared (example 7-10). Sammartini's playful unison strumming of the tonic and dominant triads is far closer to the style of Vivaldi than of Haydn. But his unequivocal presentation of the 1–7...4–3 style structure is characteristic of the later Classic style.

EXAMPLE 7-10. Sammartini, Symphony in D Major, Jenkins/Churgin No. 14 (1739), i, Allegro, meas. 29–36

The model of chapter 6 rightly predicted that the probability of finding very early examples of the 1−7...4−3 schema would be low indeed. Whereas perhaps half of the compositions written in the 1770s contain this structure, dozens of pieces from the 1720s and 1730s have to be examined before even a questionable example can be located. Because the difficulty of finding early examples was compounded by the unavailability of many compositions, especially early Italian symphonies, a satisfactory account of the origin of the 1−7...4−3 schema is not possible. One area of inquiry, however, did raise an interesting question that further biographical and archival study might someday answer. That is, how did Gregor Joseph Werner acquire the type of highly characteristic 1−7...4−3 style structures heard in his *Symphoniae sex senaeque sonatae* (Six Symphonies Paired with Six Sonatas) (1735)?

Werner was Haydn's predecessor and nominal supervisor at the Esterházy court. His reputation was quickly eclipsed by Haydn's, and he has been dismissed as a merely competent, conservative court composer. Such a judgment is no doubt predicated on Werner's retention, even beyond mid-century, of many archaic musical traits. For example, he chose to continue writing simple binary-form movements and maintained the Baroque traditions of rhythmic uniformity and trio-sonata texture— two high, equal voices over a basso continuo. Yet, as the present study is at pains to demonstrate, there is an important area of musical style midway between high-level form and low-level rhythm or texture. In terms of the mid-level 1−7...4−3 schema, Werner produced some phrases that were not to become common for another twenty years.

Werner is by no means a neglected musical visionary. The following two phrases in examples 7-11 and 7-12 show the type of questionable 1−7...4−3 structures already discussed in connection with Pollarolo (example 7-5). Notice in particular how example 7-11, written fourteen years after *Lucio Papirio dittatore,* still does not use melodic conformance to reinforce a higher-level melodic style form (1−7...4−3 or 3−2...4−3 or 1−2...2−3).

EXAMPLE 7-11. Werner, *Symphoniae sex senaeque sonatae* (1735), No. 4, i, Spirituoso, meas. 1–4

EXAMPLE 7-12. Werner, *Symphoniae sex senaeque sonatae* (1735), No. 5, iii,
Allegro assai, meas. 1–4

Yet some of Werner's phrases are quite close to prototypical examples. In example 7-13, notice how, in spite of numerous Baroque traits, Werner composes a structurally clear 1–7...4–3 phrase. When he begins the second half of his binary form with this phrase, he varies only those elements not part of the 1–7...4–3 style structure. In other words, to recognize both phrases as the subject or theme of the movement requires an abstraction of the common schema (example 7-14).

EXAMPLE 7-13. Werner, *Symphoniae sex senaeque sonatae* (1735), No. 2, iii, Allegro ma non troppo, meas. 1–4

EXAMPLE 7-14. Werner, *Symphoniae sex senaeque sonatae* (1735), No. 2, iii, Allegro ma non troppo, meas. 10–13

The bass of example 7-14 is the earliest instance I have found of the more typical 1–2…7–1 pattern. All of the earlier examples use 1–5…7–1 or 1–5…5–1 basses. The difference may seem slight, but it has stylistic significance. In the first place, 1–2…7–1 is a pattern far less mobile than the norm for Baroque basses. Instead of skipping about, this pattern remains closely tethered to the tonic. The second aspect of the 1–2…7–1 bass is that it differentiates the two schema events and thus reduces the likelihood of a 1–7…4–3 style structure's being perceived as the first two units of a continuing process (example 7-15). Similarly Baroque in texture and Classic in structure is the phrase by Werner in example 7-16. Note the chain of descending thirds in the melody, a particularly Classic pattern.[3]

In light of the Italian provenance of all the 1–7…4–3 examples prior to Werner, it would hardly be surprising if he had used Italian models in the construction of his own works. I have been unable to ascertain whether this was actually the case, but given the advanced state of his mid-level structures as presented in examples 7-13, 7-14, and 7-16, two possibilities suggest themselves. Either Werner had access to some body of Italian or Italian-influenced instrumental music with more typical instances of the 1–7…4–3 structure than those yet presented in this discussion, or he was in fact a significant innovator in at least one mid-level structure of the early Classic style. At any rate, with Werner the protohistory of the 1–7…4–3 schema may be said to conclude.

EXAMPLE 7-15. The 1–5…5–1 and 1–2…7–1 basses contrasted with respect to sequential continuation

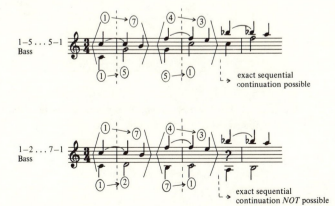

EXAMPLE 7-16. Werner, *Symphoniae sex senaeque sonatae* (1735), No. 6, iii, Allegro assai, meas. 5–8

Two Common Melodic Complexes

A nineteenth-century historical model still prominent in contemporary music theory assumes a preexisting fund of simple, pure patterns that became successively more complex and diversified. The metaphors employed in the description of this model often imply that these basic patterns are, in a genetic sense, the ancestors of later music. By placing the prototype of a structure near the center of the structure's history, and by positing a process of schema abstraction as the means of arriving at that prototype, the historical model proposed in this study presumes that the early examples of a structure are *more* complex than the prototype. The phrases so far presented in this chapter show this: all are more complex than the prototypical realizations first presented in chapters 4 and 5.

The four, five, or more staves presented above many of the examples analyzed in this chapter indicate various networks of melodic relationships. Some of these networks clearly exhibit family resemblances beyond the simple sharing of the 1–7...4–3 pattern. They appear, in fact, to have been preferred 1–7...4–3 networks—shared melodic complexes—that preceded the appearance of 1–7...4–3 prototypes. Two of these are discussed below.

The first melodic complex is easily defined: a descending stepwise connection of 1–7 with 4–3. The potentially deforming effect of this combination was mentioned in chapter 5 (see the discussion of example 5-19). The composer's problem is to create a balance between the formal 1–7...4–3 pattern and the processive linear pattern. One solution, by Carl Heinrich Graun, is shown in example 7-17. Graun articulates the first dyad (1–7) by the reversal of melodic direction, by the small embellishment, and by means of the following rest. The terminal dyad (4–3) is articulated by its closing off of eleven consecutive sixteenth-notes, by another reversal of melodic direction, by its embellished rhyme with the first dyad, and by the disjunction of G and the following D♭. His phrase works so well that the premature return to the tonic triad (I⁶) midway through the phrase is scarcely noticed. The balance achieved by Graun is easily upset. To illustrate this, I have altered his melody (example 7-18), bringing out both the medial I⁶ chord and the descending linear progression, while suppressing the 1–7...4–3 style structure (the bass line remains the same).

EXAMPLE 7-17. Graun, Trio Sonata in E♭ Major (?1750), ii, Adagio, meas. 1–2 [in *Hortus musicus* No. 211]

EXAMPLE 7-18. Hypothetical alteration of example 7-17

A different solution to the problems inherent in this melodic complex is provided by Matthias Monn. In example 7-19, from his Symphony in B Major, the linear connection of 1–7 with 4–3 is minimized in three ways. First, he articulates the six-note descent from B to D♯ as three separate dyads: B–A♯, G♯–F♯, E–D♯. Second, he places the second of these dyads an octave lower than the others. And third, by beginning the phrase with the same G♯–F♯ dyad used in the linear descent, he allows its second appearance to function more as a formal return or restatement than as a processive continuation.

EXAMPLE 7-19. Matthias Monn, Symphony in B Major, DTÖ XV.2 (?1742), ii,
    Andante, meas. 9

EXAMPLE 7-20. A small resultant 1...7–4...3 pattern

EXAMPLE 7-21. Ordonez, Symphony in C Major, Brown I:C1 (?1753), iii, Andante, meas. 8

Monn's technique of breaking the linear descent into separate dyads is employed by numerous later composers. Nevertheless, example 7-19 is itself of very low typicality. Unlike the bass of the Graun example, Monn's bass line makes no concessions toward distinguishing the 1–7...4–3 structure. Where the 1–7...4–3 schema calls for a move to the dominant chord (over the F♯ in the bass), there is instead the mediant chord resulting from the process of descending sixth chords. Furthermore, the metric boundaries of the schema are atypical in their placement before weak beats of the measure. As a result, the potential for the first half of the phrase to serve as a cue for the 1–7...4–3 schema is so low that the schema must be understood retrospectively, if it is to be understood at all. The existence of revised or retrospective understanding is, of course, well established in cognitive psychology. Although schema theory has clearly emphasized the predictive, anticipatory character of cues and distinctive features, there is no reason why it should exclude the role of retrospection.

There is one final point that I wish to make concerning example 7-19. Notice that the large yet weak 1–7...4–3 structure coexists and is probably strengthened by association with a small, direct 1...7–4...3 pattern produced by the combination of the two upper voices (see example 7-20). The low-level, older 1...7–4...3 pattern, already seen in Froberger (example 7-2), is integrated with the more modern, higher-level 1–7...4–3 structure. It would be erroneous to conclude that the larger pattern grew from the smaller through some organic process of elaboration and differentiation. The two structures are related psychologically through an association of shared features, but there is no historical evidence of a genetic link.

The second melodic complex to be discussed in this section features a descending melodic leap from ② to ④, as can be seen in the excerpt by Ordonez in example 7-21. Leonard Meyer has noticed that ② (fifth of the dominant chord) preceding the 4–3 dyad often answers ⑤ (fifth of the tonic chord) preceding the 1–7 dyad, and that both ⑤ and ② are associated with the basic 1–7...4–3 schema.[4] To be sure, the Ordonez example does begin with a high G, ⑤ of C major. But the immediate repetition of the pattern omits the initial ⑤. The musical examples with which Meyer worked were composed by men one or two generations removed from the period here in question. So while the conformant relationship between ⑤ and ② may be evident in a 1–7...4–3 structure by Mozart (see example 7-22), this relationship alone constitutes only a weak explanation for the much earlier examples presented in this chapter. The fact is that during the early eighteenth century, ⑤ is not often part of this melodic complex.

EXAMPLE 7-22. Mozart, Symphony in A Major, KV 114 (1771), iv, Allegro molto, meas. 82–88

EXAMPLE 7-23. Bach, *The Well-Tempered Clavier,* Book I, Prelude No. 8 in E♭ Minor (1722), Lento moderato, meas. 1–4

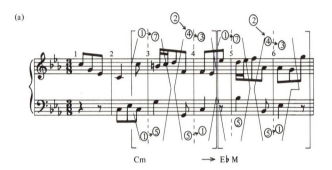

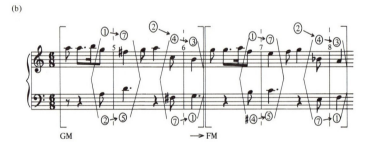

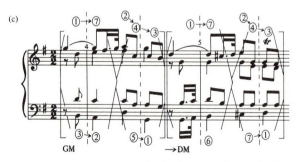

EXAMPLE 7-24. (*a*) Veracini, Violin Sonata, Op. 1 (1721), No. 4, iv, Allegro, meas. 1–6; (*b*) Veracini, Violin Sonata, Op. 1 (1721), No. 2, iii, Siciliana, Cantabile, meas. 5–8; (*c*) Sammartini, Symphony in G Major, Jenkins/Churgin No. 39 (1740), i, Allegro ma non tanto, meas. 4–5

In discussing the origin of the 1−7...4−3 style structure I emphasized that its earliest constituents antedate the structure itself. Two parts of the Ordonez excerpt (example 7-21), with their 2−4−3 melody and V–I harmony, appear to contain one such preexistent element. For example, instances of this small structure abound in Italian opera from the 1720s, while the 1−7...4−3 style structure is rare. Likewise, in Bach's first book of *The Well-Tempered Clavier* (1722), which does not contain any obvious 1−7...4−3 style structures, there are several good examples of this older pattern. Example 7-23 presents one from the E♭-Minor Prelude.

This small cadential pattern, when preceded by an initial 1−7, formed a melodic complex that became a cliché often used to confirm a modulation or to effect a sequential tonicization. Example 7-24 shows this stock pattern in three common shifts of key.

Example 7-24c, by Sammartini, provides an insight into the dual nature of this melodic complex. The first time the pattern appears, in G major, the initial three pitches might be considered (1) the preparatory tone of a suspension, (2) its resolution, and (3) a passing tone (example 7-25). Yet with e″ in the alto of the first full measure, the melodic F♯ might be a lower neighbor rather than a chordal tone. This implication is realized in the second measure. The new bass line accompanying the modulation to D major allows the first three notes of the corresponding melody to be interpreted as (1) a simple chordal tone, (2) a lower neighbor, and (3) a return of the chordal tone (example 7-26). The original interpretation would support the 1−7...4−3 structure by emphasizing the paired suspensions 1−7 and 4−3. The second interpretation suggests a 1−2−3 pattern. Composers can emphasize one or the other aspect of this complex by subtle shifts in rhythmic grouping or by changes in the metrical position of ②. For instance, in my opinion, examples 7-24a, b, and c are arranged in ascending order of emphasis on the 1−2−3 pattern and in descending order of emphasis on the 1−7...4−3 pattern. No version of this convention, however, can be arranged to completely negate either aspect of the melodic complex. In future references to this pattern, I will call it the "high-②" complex, taking note of the fact that ② is usually the highest pitch.

EXAMPLE 7-25. One interpretation of example 7-24c

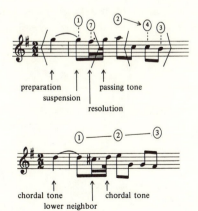

EXAMPLE 7-26. A different interpretation of example 7-24c

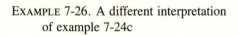

J. S. BACH

The 1–7...4–3 style structure is comparatively rare in the works of J. S. Bach, and his influence on the structure's early period may have been minimal. Yet given the great interest shown in his work by later generations of composers and the universal distribution of his best-known compositions, some discussion is warranted.

One example illustrative of the place of the 1–7...4–3 style structure in early eighteenth-century music is found in the first book of *The Well-Tempered Clavier* (1722), Prelude No. 13 in F♯ Major (example 7-27). This phrase is *not* a 1–7...4–3 style structure. Nonetheless, many features of this structure are present. The dotted lines in example 7-27 show that one could construe an initial schema event in the middle of measure 22. At that point the melody reverses direction and the harmony shifts from the sequential pattern that began the phrase toward a consolidation of the dominant chord. But no terminal schema event confirms the initial event. The closure provided by the tonic chord in the middle of measure 23 is not supported by the melody, which avoids cadencing until the middle of measure 24. Thus the effect of the phrase as a whole is of a rhythmically uniform and unbroken succession of small motives that cadences only when the head motive of the prelude reappears in the bass midway through measure 24.

Inasmuch as the 1–7...4–3 schema was not part of the common currency of mid-level forms in 1722, it is possible that Bach had no sense of the latent two-measure schema in his phrase. By the 1740s, however, the 1–7...4–3 schema was in increasingly wide circulation—a fact that may shed light on a variant that crept into manuscripts of this prelude. Example 7-28 shows the central part of Bach's phrase as copied out by his onetime student Kirnberger. Notice how by altering one note (g♯′ is changed to a♯′) Kirnberger supplied the 4–3 dyad needed to bring out the 1–7...4–3 style structure. Of course, it can never be established whether the alteration was a conscious or unconscious act. But in many respects it does not matter. The significance lies in Kirnberger's supplying a clearer mid-level context more consistent with the structures of his own experience. This alteration became *the* eighteenth-century version of the phrase and, in Czerny's edition, can still be purchased today. Only in the later nineteenth century (when the 1–7...4–3 schema had begun to fade from view) was the original version reinstated.[5]

EXAMPLE 7-27. Bach, *The Well-Tempered Clavier,* Book I, Prelude No. 13 in F♯ Major (1722), meas. 21–24

EXAMPLE 7-28. Kirnberger's version of meas. 22–23 of example 7-27

EXAMPLE 7-29. Bach, *The Well-Tempered Clavier*, Book II, Fugue No. 12 in F Minor (?1744), meas. 1–4

EXAMPLE 7-30. (*a*) Hypothetical version of meas. 25–28 of Bach's Fugue in F Minor, *The Well-Tempered Clavier*, Book II, intended to emphasize the 1–7...4–3 schema; (*b*) actual version of meas. 25–28

The much later second book of *The Well-Tempered Clavier* (1744?) suggests that Bach had become more aware of the 1–7...4–3 schema. The three-voice Fugue No. 12 in F Minor has a 1–7...4–3 style structure implied by its opening subject (example 7-29) and confirmed by the several contrapuntal contexts in which the subject participates.[6] To illustrate how just a few melodic alterations would bring the fugue's subject still closer toward the schema prototype, I have taken the liberty of rewriting the fugue's A♭-major section in example 7-30.

Freed of the constraints of fugal technique, Prelude No. 7 in E♭ Major opens with the most characteristic example of a 1–7...4–3 style structure in the entire "Forty-eight" (example 7-31). The intricate second half of this structure creates unrealized implications for its own continuation, which are discussed in the next section.

EXAMPLE 7-31. Bach, *The Well-Tempered Clavier,* Book II, Prelude No. 7 in E♭
    Major (?1744), meas. 1–4

INTERCONNECTION WITH PRECEDING AND SUCCEEDING PASSAGES

Examples of the 1–7...4–3 schema from the earlier part of the eighteenth century are generally well integrated into their larger contexts. As a good illustration of various ways in which this integration is effected, example 7-32 gives the closing restatement of the Bach theme analyzed in example 7-31. In lines *B* and *C* of example 7-32, a process of parallel ascending tenths terminates on the downbeat of the theme. I call this type of interconnection *linkage;*[7] the ascending linear process is directly joined to the 1–7...4–3 structure but does not extend beyond the structure's outer boundaries. Often, however, ongoing processes continue right through the structure's boundaries. For instance, the iterative processes of lines *A* and *D* (repetitions of neighbor-note figures and the pedal-like B♭ bass) continue to the middle of the 1–7...4–3 structure. In lines *E* through *I,* processes implied by the second half of the 1–7...4–3 structure—the stream of eighth-notes, the circle-of-fifths harmonic progression, and the descending linear progressions—are extended for several measures.

Notice that in continuing these last-mentioned processes Bach sacrificed the small but formally significant appoggiatura a♭'–g' found in the earlier statement of the theme (example 7-31). This tradeoff is typical; the more interconnected a structure is with its larger context, the more obscured are its formal boundaries. As a general trend, 1–7...4–3 style structures during this period move away from the complex interconnections of overlapping forms and processes, and toward the simpler relationships of linkage or even plain juxtaposition. This trend is reflected in other musical examples in this chapter. For instance the earliest structure, by Scarlatti, is highly interconnected with various preceding and succeeding processes (example 7-1), while the latest structure, by Ordonez, employs simple linkages and the juxtaposition brought about by repetition (example 7-21). In a sense, the trend is already implied by the model of chapter 6. That is, since abstracting the schema prototype involves being able to partition it off from some larger context, it is possible that in the eighteenth century this mental partitioning influenced subsequent compositions, eventually resulting in a less highly interconnected style.

SUMMARY

Relatively few examples of the 1–7...4–3 schema were found to have been composed during the first half of the eighteenth century. The earliest of these make it clear that this schema was not produced out of thin air. Instead, it resulted from a particular arrangement of preexistent elements. The possibility of such an arrangement, based on the wider historical frames of these elements, exists from perhaps the 1680s or 1690s. But the probability of such an arrangement becomes significant only in the 1720s, apparently first in Italian instrumental music.

EXAMPLE 7-32. Bach, *The Well-Tempered Clavier*, Book II, Prelude No. 7 in E♭ Major (?1744), meas. 57–65

The complex melodic networks from which the 1−7...4−3 structure begins to stand out can occasionally be grouped according to certain family resemblances. Of the two melodic complexes discussed in this chapter, the first combined a 1−7...4−3 pattern with a stepwise descending melody. The second involved the participation of a 1−7...4−3 pattern, a descending leap from ② to ④ (over the leading tone in the bass), and the weak impression of a 1−2−3 melodic structure. The point was emphasized that these complexes did not derive from some basic 1−7...4−3 style structure; rather, the 1−7...4−3 schema was abstracted from these and other related melodic networks.

Given the low population and generally low typicality of examples in the first two-thirds of this period, it is entirely possible that early eighteenth-century composers interpreted 1−7...4−3 style structures as no more than convenient but chance associations of lower-level schemata. Indeed, the emphasis many of these composers placed on proximate and affective melodic conventions worked against larger-scale schemata, as was seen in the example by Pollarolo. Near the end of this period, however, the increasingly characteristic realizations of Ordonez, Graun, and others provided examples from which composers ought to have abstracted the schema. If this abstraction did occur in the later 1740s and early 1750s, then it should be followed by a noticeable upturn in the population curve. As the next chapter will show, this upturn was dramatic.

CHAPTER 8

1755–1769: Sharp Increases in Population and Typicality

During the period discussed in this chapter (1755–1769) the population curve of 1–7...4–3 style structures rose steeply. As the graph in figure 8-1 shows, the number of examples per five-year interval more than quadruples from earlier levels. Whereas examples in the previous chapter were drawn from several different vocal and instrumental genres, the examples in this chapter are, with the exception of a few arias, restricted to a single genre—the symphony.[1] Had all the genres of Classic music been surveyed, the population increase would no doubt have been far steeper.

The chapter begins with a look at several 1–7...4–3 structures from Carl Heinrich Graun's opera *Montezuma*. These examples introduce a variant of the high-② melodic complex discussed in the previous chapter and present additional evidence for the correlation between typicality and isolation from a larger context. This is followed by a discussion of Haydn—specifically his use of the 1–7...4–3 structure in his early symphonies. The more than thirty examples found in just this narrow segment of Haydn's output testify to this structure's status as a commonplace after mid-century. Of particular interest is the manner in which Haydn simplifies the high-② melodic complex. He slightly separates its two halves and makes the first half conformant with the second half by affixing to it a descending melodic leap. Thus an asymmetrical complex with multiple interpretations is reduced to a simpler antecedent-consequent form.

The latter part of the chapter is devoted to examining the appearance after 1765 of scattered examples by Haydn, Mozart, and Dittersdorf that approach the schema prototype and to a discussion of schema variants; I present a bass line commonly used by Gassmann and a technique evident in works by Gossec, Ruge, and Haydn for expanding the middle portion of a 1–7...4–3 style structure.

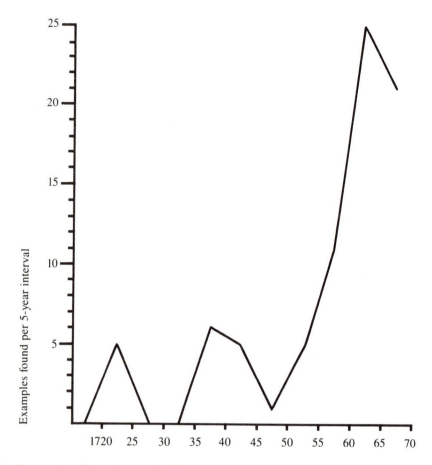

FIGURE 8-1. Population of 1–7...4–3 style structures, 1720–1769

GRAUN'S *MONTEZUMA*

In the discussion of Bach in the previous chapter, I pointed out that the typicality of an example depends not only on its specific internal structure but also on how it is interconnected with its external context. The examples compared were from quite different periods in Bach's life, and it might be argued that the proposed correlation between high internal typicality and relative autonomy from an external context— or, conversely, low internal typicality and integration within an external context—is somehow accidental. In *Montezuma*, Graun's most famous opera for the court of Frederick the Great, the use of a broad range of 1–7...4–3 structures permits this correlation to be tested among phrases written at the same place and time.

Example 8-1 comes from the opening Allegro of the opera's three-movement Sinfonia (the $1-7\ldots4-3$ structure in question is enclosed in square brackets). The main $1-7\ldots4-3$ structure is at some distance from the prototype[2] and is obscured by several overlapping processes. Graun could easily have made the phrase more prominent, more characteristic. But as the hypothetical version in example 8-2 shows, such changes would have been at the expense of the structure's integration with its larger context.

EXAMPLE 8-1. Graun, *Montezuma* (1755), Sinfonia, i, Allegro, meas. 43–48

EXAMPLE 8-2. A hypothetical version of example 8-1 with greater typicality

EXAMPLE 8-3. A suspension implied by the high-② complex

EXAMPLE 8-4. Graun, *Montezuma* (1755), Aria di Narvès (DDT ed., p. 54), Allegro, meas. 9–10

Midway between the maximum interconnection of overlapping processes and the minimum interconnection of a simple juxtaposition lies the procedure of linkage. One way to link two larger contexts is through a small contrapuntal device such as a suspension. In example 8-3, a descending leap from ② to ④, characteristic of what I have called the high-② melodic complex, creates the potential for an implied suspension and resolution. Graun exploits this potential in example 8-4. Although the specific high-② melodic complex shown in example 8-2 has, by this time, had a rather long history, Graun provides it with a modern 1−2...7−1 bass. Such a joining of the old with the new is a hallmark of *Montezuma*—a "reform" opera still firmly set in the venerable tradition of Hasse and Jommelli.

In example 8-5, the links connecting example 8-4 with the preceding and succeeding passages are circled. The second link consists of the above-mentioned suspension and of the 1−7...4−3 structure ending on the same beat that begins an ascending linear progression. The first link can be largely explained as a common-chord modulation, though on a higher level the two-measure 1−7...4−3 style structure functions as the consequent phrase of a four-measure unit.[3] Neither link deforms the internal relationships of the 1−7...4−3 structure.

EXAMPLE 8-5. Example 8-4 with its links to a larger context

The 1–7...4–3 style structure closest to the prototype is, as might be predicted, clearly separated from the passages that precede and follow it (see example 8-6). The separation of the 1–7...4–3 structure from the preceding passage is unequivocal, representing as it does the formal division between the first ritornello and the first quatrain of text. The separation from the succeeding passage is equally clear for the voice, although the accompaniment does provide two low-level connections (the iterated D in the bass and the ascending D-major triad in the violins).

EXAMPLE 8-6. Graun, *Montezuma* (1755), Aria di Eupaforice (DDT ed., p. 156), Allegro, meas. 20–24

I do not mean to imply that a 1–7...4–3 style structure isolated from other passages is, in an aesthetic sense, intrinsically any better or worse than a structure crisscrossed by overlapping processes. Likewise, for a composer such as Graun, the distinction between a semiautonomous and a highly interconnected style structure need not indicate modernism or archaism. I do believe, however, that the more compartmentalized, modular style of example 8-6 is closer to the schema prototype than are the interconnected or linked styles of examples 8-1 and 8-5, because typicality is not just the presence of schema-relevant patterns but also the absence of schema-extraneous ones.[4]

HAYDN'S EARLY SYMPHONIES

Haydn's earliest symphonies date from the end of the 1750s. The precise chronology of these works has not been established, so it is impossible to say which ones contain the earliest 1–7...4–3 style structures. Still, a few generalizations can be made about Haydn's early use of this pattern. First, among those symphonies that may date from 1760 or before, 1–7...4–3 style structures tend to be very small. In symphonies 15 and 19 (–?1761 and ?c1759/60 respectively), Haydn miniaturizes this structure to the point where the entire schema, if indeed it is still recognizable as such, is presented in about one second (example 8-7).

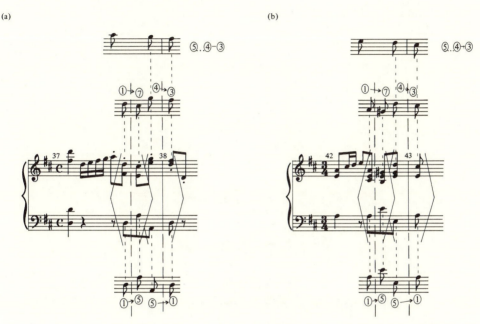

EXAMPLE 8-7. Haydn: (*a*) Symphony No. 15 in D Major (−?1761), i, Presto, meas. 37–38; (*b*) Symphony No. 19 in D Major (?c1759–60), i, Allegro, meas. 42–43

Had Haydn's use of the 1–7...4–3 schema been traced back from his mature works to these early symphonies, the contrast between the tiny structures of example 8-7 and the four- and eight-measure structures of his later years might have suggested that the small structures "grew" into the larger ones. But, as I hope is evident from this and the preceding chapter, large 1–7...4–3 style structures were widespread long before Haydn's early symphonies. If anything, the tiny structures of example 8-7 are near the end of a stylistic development stretching from C.P.E. Bach back to the seventeenth-century clavecinists.

More in line with Haydn's later style is the following modified high-② complex from his Symphony "B" (i.e., the second of two early works outside the main list of Haydn symphonies) (example 8-8). Two features distinguish this high-② complex from the earlier type seen in Veracini, Sammartini, or Graun (examples 7-24 and 8-4). First, the stepwise connection of ⑦ with ② has been abandoned (example 8-9). In the earlier type, the ② is quite prominent as both the terminus of the ascending third progression and the end of the small rhythmic grouping ♪♪. . This complex, as mentioned earlier, permits interpretation as both 1–7...4–3 and 1–2–3. Haydn's usage diminishes the prominence of ②, making it serve as an upbeat to the following 4–3 dyad. The significance of this small alteration is that a structure carried over from a period of greater complexity has been simplified in such a way as to suppress one of its former relationships.

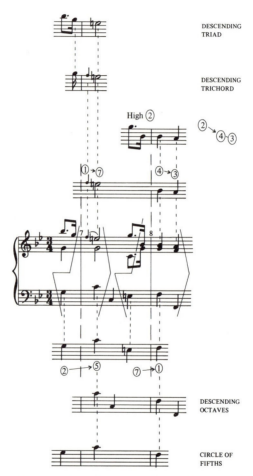

EXAMPLE 8-8. Haydn, Symphony B in B♭ Major, Hob. I:108 (1759), ii, Allegretto, meas. 7–8

EXAMPLE 8-9. A change in the high-② melodic complex

The second new feature in example 8-8 is the addition of a descending motive prior to the 1–7 dyad. This appears to be a type of "back-formation." That is, to the original high-② melodic complex is prefixed a descending motive (the first two notes of example 8-8's melody, B♭–G), which, after the fact, makes the 2–4 descending leap seem like a derivative, answering motive. Back-formations are common in colloquial speech. For instance, colloquial verbs like *orientate* and *connotate* are back-formations derived from *orientation* and *connotation*. In a similar sense, the historically antecedent 2–4 leap becomes, in the 1–7...4–3 style structures of the Classic style, an apparent consequence of a preceding motive, most frequently 5–1 (see example 8-10). The conformance of these two motives strengthens the bipartite form characteristic of the 1–7...4–3 prototype.

EXAMPLE 8-10. Changes in the high-② complex

If example 8-8 demonstrates a method of balancing the asymmetrical, older high-② complex by transferring a motive from the structure's second half back to its first half, then example 8-11 demonstrates the reverse procedure. That is, the ascending third 7–2 (see line *E* of example 8-11), which is an important feature of the older high-② melodic complex, is balanced by the addition of another ascending third, 3–5, to the end of the structure. The implications of this small addition are

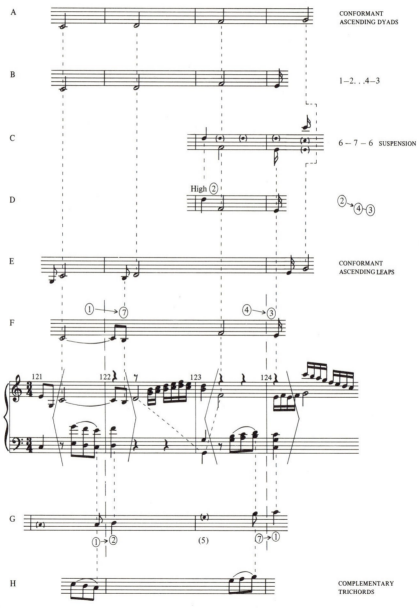

EXAMPLE 8-11. Haydn, Symphony No. 7 in C Major, "Le midi" (1761), i, Allegro, meas. 121–24

twofold: new ways—often involving conformant relationships—of limiting the closure of 1–7…4–3 style structures and creating connections with subsequent passages are developed; and 1–7…4–3 structures are created wherein the boundary
dyads are no longer always phrase endings, but sometimes in the middle or even at
the beginning of conformant phrases.

　　The last example is, of course, much longer than the minute examples 8-7 and
8-8. Four-measure 1–7…4–3 structures are, within the limits of presumption af-
forded by an uncertain chronology, present in all but the very earliest of Haydn's symphonies. Example 8-12 shows a four-measure phrase probably derived from the
older high-② complex. An archaic feature of this phrase is the active, skipping bass
line. A more modern feature is the mirror or complementary contours of the descending sixteenth-notes in the bass and the ascending sixteenth-notes in the melody.

EXAMPLE 8-12. Haydn, Symphony No.
　　　20 in C Major (?c1757–63), iv,
　　　Presto, meas. 45–48

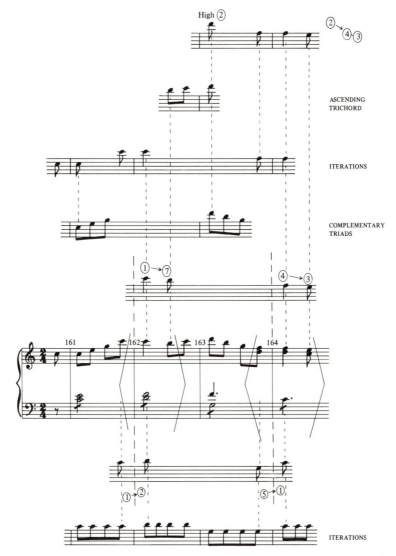

EXAMPLE 8-13. Haydn, Symphony No. 32 in C Major (−?1760), i, Allegro
molto, meas. 161–64

In the slightly later example 8-13 the tendency toward complementary contours is
still more evident.

Although complementary contours are common in the Classic style, the more
common 1–7...4–3 style structures generally employ the simpler relationship of
ordinary conformance. For example, the two-measure 1–7...4–3 style structure
embedded in the four-measure I⁶–II⁶–V–I schema in example 8-14 (and slightly deformed by it; see the discussion of example 4-15) uses conformant descending triads
prior to each dyad.

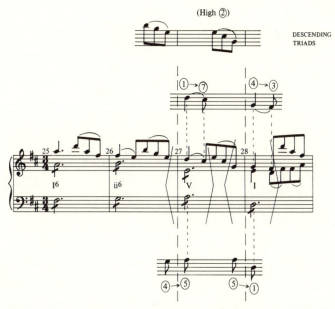

EXAMPLE 8-14. Haydn, Symphony No. 31 in D Major, "Hornsignal" (1765), i, Allegro, meas. 25–28

It is interesting to observe that all the Haydn examples presented in this section have continuous melodies. In other words, no notated rest intervenes between the 1–7 and 4–3 dyads. This small feature appears to distinguish most of Haydn's 1–7...4–3 style structures written before 1765 or 1766 from those written later. A rest or obvious articulation after the first half of the 1–7...4–3 structure helps to facilitate perception of the schema in several ways. First, silence closes off the first half of the form. Second, silence provides a ground against which the beginning of the second half of the form can be detected. Third, the temporary cessation of new melodic information allows a listener to more fully process the first half of the form. This last point is important, because the mental processing of a continuous string of melodic information is of necessity largely retrospective. Only when the brain is given opportunities to "catch up" with the flow of stimuli can the prospective or implicative force of musical schemata be fully developed. As an illustration of this phenomenon, notice how much more implied the second half of example 8-15 (1767) seems than the corresponding segment of the more continuous example 8-14 (1765).

The typicality of example 8-15 and several other phrases written after 1765 approaches that of the schema prototype. These near prototypes produced by Haydn and others during the later 1760s are the topic of the following section.

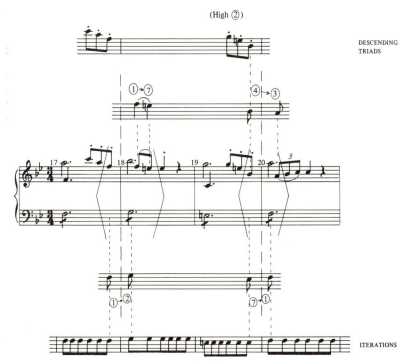

EXAMPLE 8-15. Haydn, Symphony No. 35 in B♭ Major (1767), i, Allegro di molto, meas. 17–20

NEAR PROTOTYPES

Though historically backwards, the procedure adopted in discussing the three phrases presented in this section is to view them as complications of a later and simpler prototype. The advantage of this approach is evident from a consideration of example 8-16 by Dittersdorf. Since this phrase was written by 1766 at the latest, only in a comparative and not a historical sense can it be considered an alteration of a prototype by Mozart written in late 1771 (example 8-17). Yet this comparison quickly reveals two important features of the Dittersdorf example—its lack of a rest between the two halves of the structure, and the presence of many repeated notes in the melody.

Closely related to the Dittersdorf example is a phrase by the eleven-year-old Mozart (example 8-18). The first half of this example is quite near the prototype, but the second half, with the large presence of ②, creates some complications.

The phrases by Mozart and Dittersdorf are surprisingly similar. Inasmuch as Mozart wrote his example in Vienna, we cannot exclude the possibility of a direct influence from one composer to the other. In fact, one traditional approach to explaining this similarity would be to determine if there was actual contact between the composers. Another approach would be to claim that these phrases are similar only

EXAMPLE 8-16. Dittersdorf, Symphony in C Major, Krebs 1 (1766), i, Allegro
moderato, meas. 1–4

EXAMPLE 8-17. Mozart, Symphony in A Major, KV 114 (1771), iii, Trio, meas.
9–12

EXAMPLE 8-18. Mozart, Symphony in F Major, KV 43 (1767), ii, Andante, meas. 1–4

because the numerous stylistic constraints of Classic music inevitably result in like productions.

Because proof of direct influence is very difficult to establish and an appeal to the uniformity of the Classic style would seem to posit a cause incommensurate with such a restricted musical effect, I would argue that consideration must first be given to a corollary derived from the model of chapter 6. Specifically, since there is tremendous variation among 1–7...4–3 style structures at the extremes of the structure's historical frame, and since there should be only slight variation among structures identifiable as 1−7…4−3 prototypes, it follows that the structure's range of variation ought to change inversely with the structure's curves of population and typicality. The similarity of the two phrases mentioned above may be due to a very specific set of historical and psychological constraints that converge in the later 1760s. Taken to its extreme, this corollary implies the existence of identical melodies at the peak of population and typicality. Surprising as it may seem, this occurs and will be discussed in the next chapter.

As should be expected, Haydn also made a contribution to the category of near prototypes. In the Trio of his Symphony No. 32 (written no later than 1766) he wrote a phrase that eliminates all schema-extraneous patterns until the fourth measure (example 8-19). It should be noted once again that this phrase has no written indication of an articulation between its first and second halves. Only this small feature and the deformation of the 4−3 dyad caused by the triplet descent to the tonic separate example 8-19 from the prototypes of the 1770s.

EXAMPLE 8-19. Haydn, Symphony No. 32 in C Major (−?1760), ii, Trio, meas. 1−4

SCHEMA VARIANTS

A composer's unique experiences and individual style can lead him to favor some variant form of a musical schema. Such may be the case with Florian Gassmann. His Italian training and Viennese employment gave him access to a broad range of important stylistic influences that, as an examination of his many symphonies reveals, must have included contact with characteristic examples of the 1–7...4–3 schema. For instance, example 8-20a (from 1765) is, in terms of its particular incorporation of a large 5...4–3 pattern, closer to the polished manner of Cambini (example 8-20b) or Mozart (example 8-20c) in the mid- to late 1770s than to the contemporary structures of Haydn.

EXAMPLE 8-20. (*a*) Gassmann, Symphony in C Minor, Hill No. 23 (1765), iv, Allegro molto, meas. 37–40; (*b*) Cambini, Symphonie concertante No. 6 in F Major, Brook II, p. 144 (1776), i, Allegro, meas. 1–4; (*c*) Mozart, Serenade in D Major, "Posthorn," KV 320 (1779), i, Allegro con spirito, meas. 197–200

The variant feature of Gassmann's personal approach to the 1–7...4–3 style structure seems to be a preference for a 3–2...7–1 bass instead of the prototypical 1–2...7–1 pattern. This variant, already suggested in example 8-3 by Graun, creates an implied descending bass line and slightly shifts the structure's balance toward its second half (example 8-21). A fine example of this bass is found in the gavotte-like finale of Gassmann's Symphony No. 85 (example 8-22). Another example confirms a modulation to the dominant, using the standard high-② melodic complex, in the opening movement of Gassmann's Symphony No. 26 (example 8-23).

EXAMPLE 8-21. The 1–2...7–1 bass compared with the 3–2...7–1 bass

EXAMPLE 8-22. Gassmann, Symphony in E♭ Major, Hill No. 85 (?1769), iv, Allegro molto all'Eclips, meas. 1–2

EXAMPLE 8-23. Gassmann, Symphony in E♭ Major, Hill No. 26 (1765), i, Allegro assai, meas. 19–20

Gassmann's apparent preference for a certain bass line is a small matter and not prominent in the perception of the overall schema. He is simply varying a standard type. A much more drastic variation is found in the next three examples. In each, the middle of the schema is expanded, or, viewed differently, the arrival of the 4–3 dyad is delayed. Perhaps the best way to illustrate the techniques involved is first to present each example in a hypothetical normal form and then to present the actual phrase.

Example 8-24 is the presumed normal form of a phrase by Gossec. The rhetorical contrast between the brusque unison writing and the delicate, more leisurely cadence is heightened when Gossec extends the second half of the structure. This extension is abetted by the B♭ in the bass, which indicates a return to low A in the next measure. By retaining this A in the bass, Gossec weakens the effect of the momentary return of the tonic in the middle of the extension (example 8-25).

EXAMPLE 8-24. A hypothetical normal form of example 8-25

EXAMPLE 8-25. Gossec, Symphony in G Major, Op. 12, No. 2 (1766), ii, Andante moderato, meas. 40–44

Example 8-27 is by Filipo Ruge, an Italian composer working in France. One can envision as his starting point the hypothetical structure in example 8-26. Ruge interpolates two additional measures into this basic form (example 8-27). The similarities to the Gossec phrase are numerous, in particular the *forte* unison beginning followed by a *piano* extension and cadence and the use of the ♭6 degree in the bass to embellish the dominant. In the third full measure of this example, Ruge repeats the 1–7 dyad before presenting the corresponding 4–3 dyad. This detail illustrates an interesting facet of schema theory, namely, that there is no rule preventing a cue from being given more than once.

The last example of an expanded 1–7…4–3 style structure is from the Adagio of Haydn's Symphony No. 12 (example 8-28). Most of the techniques employed here by Haydn are common to both of the previous examples and should be evident from the comparison of a hypothetical normal form and the actual phrase. Notice, however, that Haydn (unlike Ruge or Gossec) uses the change in texture to differentiate the extension from the schema.

EXAMPLE 8-26. A hypothetical normal form of example 8-27

EXAMPLE 8-27. Ruge, Symphony in D Major, Brook III, p. 49 (1757), iii, Allegro ma non troppo, meas. 44–47

(a)

(b)

EXAMPLE 8-28. (*a*) A hypothetical normal form of example 8-28b; (*b*) Haydn, Symphony No. 12 in E Major (1763), ii, Adagio, meas. 1–5

SUMMARY

In the fifteen years prior to 1770 the rise in the population of $1-7...4-3$ style structures was sufficient to establish this structure as a commonplace, and the concomitant rise in typicality brought examples from the later part of the period very near to the schema prototype. Characteristic of the changes occurring during this period was Haydn's simplification and structural clarification of the high-② melodic complex. By breaking the direct melodic connection between the two halves of the melodic complex, and by prefixing a descending melodic motif to the beginning of the structure, Haydn reduced an asymmetrical complex with multiple interpretations to a simpler $1-7...4-3$ structure with conformant subphrases. In cases where he split the melody into two halves by means of a rest or indicated articulation, he facilitated perception of the schema and allowed the predictive or implicative aspects of schematic cognition to come more fully into play.

CHAPTER 9

1770–1779: The Peak

In terms of the traditional historical metaphor, the 1770s are the "golden age" of the 1–7...4–3 schema. Not only does the decade contain prototypical examples in which the central features of the schema are presented as clearly and directly as one could imagine, but during this period the number of all types of 1–7...4–3 structures is extremely high. The population peak is clearly evident in figure 9-1. Because of the particular averaging and graphing techniques adopted, the peak of population appears midway between 1770 and 1775. A closer examination of all the examples within this interval revealed that the actual peak of population occurs between 1771 and 1773. Inasmuch as the largest cluster of prototypical examples is found within this same three-year period, it seems that typicality does in fact follow population very closely.

Much of this chapter is devoted to an examination of a large number of 1–7...4–3 prototypes and near prototypes. I will also discuss the common "descending-triads" melodic complex, a possible descendant of late forms of the high-② complex. The descending-triads complex highlights melodic conformance, unlike the earlier high-② and "linear-descent" complexes. While the first part of the chapter emphasizes this period as one of arrival—the attainment of the prototype and the peak of population—the second part emphasizes the same period as the beginning of the 1–7...4–3 structure's decline. In particular, a gradual return of subsidiary schemata and overlapping processes served to greatly complicate the 1–7...4–3 style structures of the late 1770s. These changes are especially evident in the discussion of a large group of 1–7...4–3 style structures by Haydn and Mozart. As we shall see, one very complex phrase from Mozart's "Posthorn" Serenade melds a 1–7...4–3 style structure into a larger form that constituted a standard vehicle for extending and concluding a phrase. Finally, in a return to a topic touched on at the end of chapter 4, I address the active role of schematic perception as an interpreter of incoming experiences. Two musical examples present further instances of schematic interpretations slightly at odds with what one views in the composers' scores.

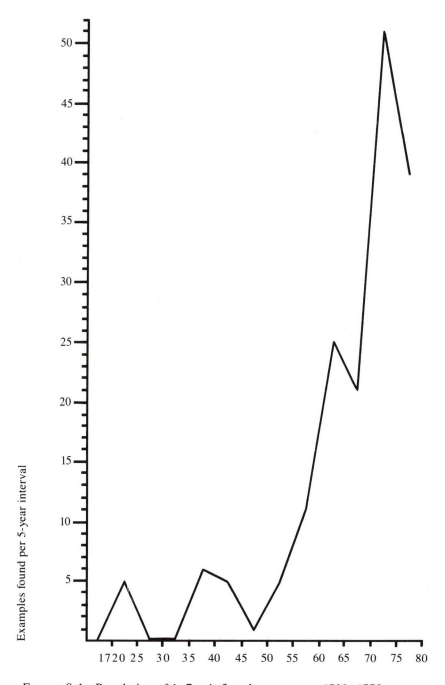

FIGURE 9-1. Population of 1–7…4–3 style structures, 1720–1779

PROTOTYPES AND NEAR PROTOTYPES

Earlier I predicted that if the range of variation among 1–7...4–3 style structures from any single year decreases as the structure's population increases, then the examples from the years of highest population should most closely resemble each other. In the 1770s this is largely the case. Of the phrases to be discussed in this section, almost half have near twins in other compositions. The upper limit of similarity would, of course, be two phrases that are identical in every respect. Although I found no such examples, the previously mentioned phrase from Mozart's Symphony KV 114 and the opening theme of Vanhal's Symphony C9 do approach this limit (see example 9-1).

EXAMPLE 9-1. (*a*) Mozart, Symphony in A Major, KV 114 (1771), iii, Trio, meas. 9–12; (*b*) Vanhal, Symphony in C Major, Bryan C9 (1772), i, Allegro, meas. 1–4

According to the model of chapter 6, these two phrases should be the 1−7...4−3 prototypes par excellence: they occur at the peak of population, are maximally similar, and present the central features of the schema to the exclusion of almost any other pattern. One is tempted to cite the Vanhal phrase as *the* prototype, because the Mozart phrase contains an active inner voice that steals attention from the 1−7...4−3 schema. Yet low-level rhythmic activity is the norm in the 1770s. Vanhal's phrase is thus slightly unusual in having only a single attack per measure. Indeed, the second statement of Vanhal's theme incorporates the low-level rhythmic activity that characterizes the movement as a whole (example 9-2). These considerations point up the two slightly different meanings of *prototype* discussed in chapter 5: one, "a hypothetical most typical instance of a category";[1] the other, "a perfect example of a particular type."[2]

Vanhal's opening phrase (example 9-1b) coincides with the hypothetical central tendency suggested for the 1−7...4−3 schema, but perhaps its lack of low-level rhythmic activity makes it unsuited as a "perfect example." Example 9-3 is more animated. The requisite low-level activity is created by repeated notes in both the melody and accompaniment. The inventive arrangement of example 9-3 creates a type of echo or call-and-response relationship between the eighth-notes in the melody and those in the accompaniment. This is also idiosyncratic, and cannot be considered prototypical. A more common melodic arrangement of repeated notes is given by the incipit of an undated Ordonez symphony (example 9-4).

EXAMPLE 9-2. Vanhal, Symphony in C Major, Bryan C9 (1772), i, Allegro, meas. 14−17

EXAMPLE 9-3. Mozart, Overture to *La finta giardiniera*, KV 121 (207a) (1774), iii, Allegro, meas. 21–24

EXAMPLE 9-4. Ordonez, Symphony in E Major, Brown I:E2 (n.d.), i, Allegro, meas. 1–4

Perhaps the implicit stipulation that a 1–7…4–3 prototype can have only the two basic dyads in its melody is unrealistic, reflecting a confusion of analytical reduction with the psychological question of prototypicality. If an upbeat note is allowed before each dyad, then several more phrases can be considered "perfect examples." For instance, the phrase by Mozart in example 9-5 employs upbeat ⑤s prior to each dyad. A four-measure version of the same structure was composed by Joseph Fiala, a composer at the small court of Öttingen-Wallerstein (example 9-6).

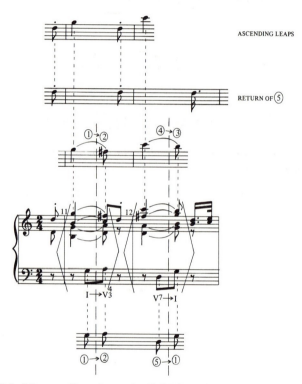

EXAMPLE 9-5. Mozart, Symphony in G Major, KV 124 (1772), ii, Andante, meas. 11–12

EXAMPLE 9-6. Fiala, Symphony in C Major, Murray C1 (1775), iv, Allegro assai, meas. 31–34

The two phrases in examples 9-5 and 9-6 demand consideration as "perfect examples," because they not only clearly present the 1−7...4−3 style structure without suggesting any other schema but also are generic, ordinary segments of eighteenth-century music. This is not the case with the superficially similar phrase by Haydn in example 9-7. Here the last two grace notes continue the linear descent implied by the 1−7 dyad (see example 9-7). This small variation from the preceding examples is idiosyncratic in two ways. First, together with the sequence 1−7−4−3, the linear descent creates an unusual network of style structures. Second, the intimation of parallel sixths in the final two measures contradicts the standard use of parallel thirds in the same situation (example 9-8).

EXAMPLE 9-7. Haydn, Symphony No. 45 in F♯ Minor, "Farewell" (1772), ii, Adagio, meas. 21−24

EXAMPLE 9-8. Different versions of the 4−3 dyad

A second example from the same symphony further illustrates Haydn's idio-syncratic treatment of detail (example 9-9). The small neighbor-note figures are only loosely connected to the 1–7...4–3 dyads. Normally, these figures would be fixed to ⑤ and ①, matching the harmonic roots of the overall form and setting up two conformant descending thirds (example 9-10). This arrangement better serves the large-scale design of the phrase but involves a small-scale contrapuntal problem—an implied dissonant fourth (example 9-11). Haydn's phrase avoids this small-scale problem but creates another idiosyncratic melody.

EXAMPLE 9-9. Haydn, Symphony No. 45 in F♯ Minor, "Farewell" (1772), iii, Trio, meas. 65–68

EXAMPLE 9-10. An alternate melody for example 9-9

EXAMPLE 9-11. The problem of a disso-nant fourth in the melody of ex-ample 9-10

The examples shown thus far all feature melodies whose four main pitches are evenly spaced and clearly grouped into two dyads. Each of the next two phrases lacks one of these characteristics. In the first phrase, by Mozart, the tendency toward the stratification of rhythmic activity seen in example 9-1a is taken a step further; the inner voices have not only most of the rhythmic activity but much of the melodic activity as well (example 9-12).

Quite different in effect is the incipit given for Fiala's Symphony F1 (example 9-13). Rather than being overtly paired in some way as two dyads, the melody is presented as four individual notes. In fact, the whole phrase is "schematized," in the sense of excluding everything except the structural skeleton.

This incipit is probably the simplest in structure and the shortest in duration of all the phrases yet presented in this chapter. Not surprisingly, the phrase with the longest duration, the Haydn Adagio excerpt of example 9-7, is structurally the most complex. The other phrases could all be aligned somewhere between these two extremes; if complexity were quantifiable, a graph similar to that shown in figure 9-2 might result.

EXAMPLE 9-12. Mozart, Symphony in E♭ Major, KV 132 (1772), ii, Andante, meas. 8–9

EXAMPLE 9-13. Fiala, Symphony in F Major, Murray F1 (1776), i, Allegro assai, meas. 1–2

This hypothetical graph can be used to make two general predictions. The first is that the very simplest 1–7...4–3 style structures of the 1770s are probably two seconds or less in duration (perhaps in two seconds or less we can do little more than to process the unadorned schema). The second prediction is that a 1–7...4–3 schema longer than six seconds but still restricted to the type of prototypical melodies discussed in this chapter would have to accommodate the required low-level rhythmic and melodic activity with repeated notes, an active inner voice, or some other means.

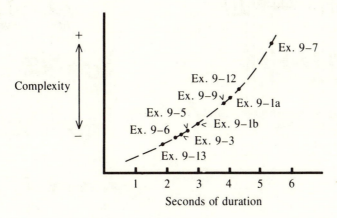

FIGURE 9-2. Hypothetical relationship between complexity and duration

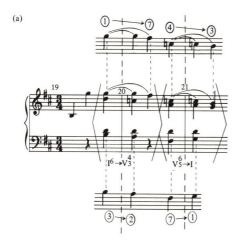

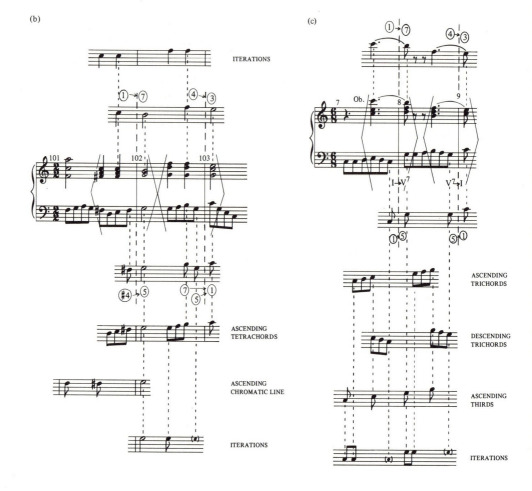

EXAMPLE 9-14. (*a*) Mozart, Serenade in D Major, "Haffner," KV 250 (248b) (1776), ii, Menuetto galante, meas. 19–21; (*b*) Ordonez, Symphony in C Major, Brown I:C9 (1773), iii (Finale), meas. 101–3; (*c*) Mozart, Symphony in C Major, KV 162 (1773), iii, Presto assai, meas. 7–9

The three phrases in example 9-14, all about two seconds or less in duration, do indeed have simple melodies. Only the first of these can be considered prototypical, however. The others introduce atypical basses significantly more complex than the melody. Thus the prediction made above about the simplicity of brief examples is applicable only to the melody.

The second prediction, that long 1−7...4−3 structures restricted to the prototypical melody will have many repeated notes or some similar enlivenment of the texture, cannot be confirmed by a symphonic example from this period because I could find no such phrase. The Haydn string quartet in example 9-15 does, however, contain a phrase that appears to confirm the above prediction. Not only does Haydn employ a host of repeated notes to maintain low-level rhythmic activity, but he also uses varied dynamics to further animate the phrase [3]

EXAMPLE 9-15. Haydn, String Quartet in E♭ Major, Op. 33, No. 2 (1781), iii,
    Largo e sostenuto, meas. 21–24

The foregoing comments about low-level rhythmic and melodic activity apply only to the period of the 1770s. The norms of these low-level features have an important bearing on what prototypical phrases were possible during the population peak of the 1–7...4–3 style structure. When these low-level norms changed, new possibilities emerged. In the early 1790s Louis Massonneau could produce the ponderous relative of the Haydn string quartet excerpt shown in example 9-15 (example 9-16). And in the late teens of the next century Schubert could write the whirring drone behind the otherwise prototypical phrase in example 9-17. But these options were not employed in the 1770s

EXAMPLE 9-16. Massonneau, Symphony in E♭ Major, Op. 3, Book 1 (1792), i, Grave e sostenuto, meas. 1–4

EXAMPLE 9-17. Schubert, Piano Quintet in A Major, "The Trout," D667 (1819), v, Allegro giusto, meas. 195–98

Looking back over the many examples presented thus far, it is interesting to note that a practically unknown composer like Fiala produced phrases that are more prototypical than those of a famous composer like Haydn. If the ability to write typical examples of most eighteenth-century musical schemata was one prerequisite for employment as a court composer during this period, then Fiala may represent someone who attained mastery over that aspect of his craft. Haydn, on the other hand, would seem to represent someone for whom eighteenth-century musical schemata were conventions against which his idiosyncratic techniques could project emotion and personality. Haydn's approach represents much of the future course of late eighteenth- and early nineteenth-century compositional method.

THE DESCENDING-TRIADS MELODIC COMPLEX

The major types of 1–7...4–3 melodic complexes have their own histories, population curves, and prototypes. For example, the high-② melodic complex discussed in the previous chapter has a population curve that peaks around 1755 or 1760. The graph in figure 9-3 shows the approximate relationship of the high-② population to the overall population of the 1–7...4–3 structure. There are still several examples of the high-② melodic complex written in the 1770s—for example, the rather emphatic phrase by Vanhal in example 9-18. Their number, however, is not as great as in the previous decade, and the complex becomes rare after 1780.

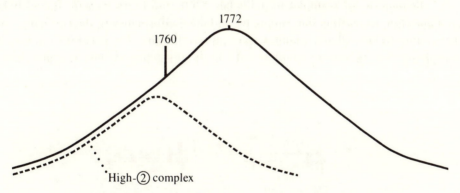

FIGURE 9-3. Population of high-② melodic complex compared with that of 1–7...4–3 style structure

EXAMPLE 9-18. Vanhal, Symphony in C Major, Bryan C11 (1775), iv, "l'Alle-grezza," Allegro, meas. 1–4 after a minor mode introduction

A different melodic complex involves prefixing the 1–7 and 4–3 dyads with descending triads. The population curve of this complex peaks a decade later than that of the high-② complex (i.e., in the late 1760s and the 1770s instead of the late 1750s and the 1760s). Indeed the descending-triads melodic complex is probably the successor to the high-② complex, inasmuch as the later pattern can be viewed as a variation of the earlier one. Two clear instances of the descending-triads melodic complex were discussed in the preceding chapter (examples 8-14 and 8-15). Several more examples, found in the period covered by the present chapter, are discussed below.

The obvious descending triads to use in this melodic complex are the tonic and the dominant. Two types of basic units result from combining these triads with the 1–7 and 4–3 dyads—a linked unit and a juxtaposed unit (example 9-19). If a composer wished to make the two halves of a descending-triads complex more conformant, he could either take the linked unit as a model and alter the juxtaposed unit, or vice versa (example 9-20). There are four different permutations of these basic units, all of which have been represented by examples previously discussed: linked-juxtaposed (example 7-10); juxtaposed-juxtaposed (example 7-16); juxtaposed-linked (example 8-14); and linked-linked (example 8-15).

The majority of examples from the late 1760s and 1770s have the linked-linked configuration, suggesting that simplicity and the conformance of the two halves of a descending-triads melodic complex were preferred traits. The excerpt from Haydn's Symphony No. 35 seen as example 8-15 in the preceding chapter is quite close to

EXAMPLE 9-19. Combining descending triads with schema dyads

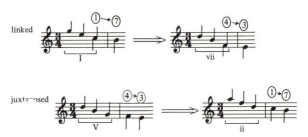

EXAMPLE 9-20. Conjunct and disjunct complexes

EXAMPLE 9-21. Mozart, Symphony in G Major, KV 129 (1772), iii, Allegro, meas. 46–49

EXAMPLE 9-22. Mozart, Keyboard Sonata in G Major, KV 283 (189h) (early 1775), i, Allegro, meas. 1–4

being a prototype for this configuration. The examples I found in the 1770s all have slightly more complicated structures. For instance, even though the phrase by Mozart in example 9-21 has a melody restricted to just the two basic conjunct units, the effect of the four tied notes is quite sophisticated. The first two notes of each descending triad are subtly disassociated from the third note—a technique that Mozart further developed in his Keyboard Sonata in G Major (example 9-22).

In contrast to the economy of the two preceding phrases by Mozart, the following examples by Jean-Guillain Cardon and Vanhal are somewhat prolix. Cardon uses a large number of low-level iterations in the incipit to his Symphony in B♭ Major, Op. 10 (example 9-23). Vanhal also uses repeated notes, but a more interesting feature of his phrase is the interaction of the descending triads with the half notes ① and ④ in the melody (example 9-24). He chooses not to create the more conformant versions in example 9-25. Vanhal's original version has a more balanced tessitura,

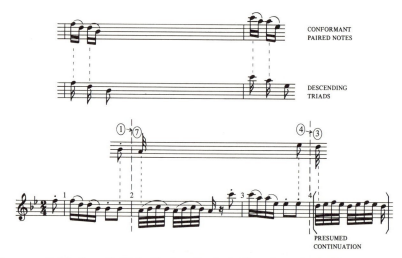

EXAMPLE 9-23. Jean-Guillain Cardon (le père), Symphony in B♭ Major, Op. 10, No. 2, Brook II, p. 177 (1772), i, Allegro ma non troppo, meas. 1–4

EXAMPLE 9-24. Vanhal, Symphony in F Major, Bryan F5 (1771), i, Allegro, meas. 1–4

and the complete rhythmic conformance of its two halves is tempered with a slight structural variation.

The majority of descending-triads melodic complexes are, as mentioned, of the linked-linked configuration. Occasionally it is possible to suggest why a particular example departs from this pattern. Consider the phrase from the *presto* finale of Haydn's "Laudon" Symphony in example 9-26. This phrase alternates stable and unstable measures: measures 27 and 29 have each a single, consonant triad; measures 28 and 30 have dissonances, descending melodic tetrachords, and moving basses. This alternation or, if you will, higher-level conformance of odd and even measures would have been upset by the normal linked-linked configuration and the attendant substitution of a C for the final D in the third measure.

EXAMPLE 9-25 (above). More
    conformant versions of
    example 9-24

EXAMPLE 9-26 (right). Haydn,
    Symphony No. 69 in C Major, "Laudon" (?c1775–76),
    iv, Presto, meas. 27–30

MOZART AND HAYDN IN THE 1770S

Many examples by Haydn and Mozart have already been presented in this and the preceding chapter in connection with various special topics. In this section I want to show a broader sample of the more than four dozen 1–7...4–3 style structures that these composers included in their symphonies from this period. Lest this section become inordinately long, I have generally provided only brief commentary on each phrase, and since most of the compositional techniques displayed by these phrases have already been analyzed, I indicate only a few central features in each case.

The initial outlining of an octave, seen earlier in example 9-24 by Vanhal, is a feature shared by the two phrases by Mozart in example 9-27. The first of these (example 9-27a) has a complementary, up-then-down contour. The second one has matching, conformant halves. This tendency toward conformance is even more evident in the two phrases in example 9-28.

(a)
(b)

EXAMPLE 9-27. Mozart: (*a*) Symphony in A Major, KV 134 (1772), i, Allegro, meas. 1–4; (*b*) Symphony in A Major, KV 201 (186a) (1774), iv, Allegro con spirito, meas. 1–4

(a)
(b)

EXAMPLE 9-28. Mozart: (*a*) Symphony in D Major, KV 202 (186b) (1774), i, Molto allegro, meas. 19–20; (*b*) Serenade in D Major, KV 204 (213a) (1775), iv, Allegro, meas. 54–57

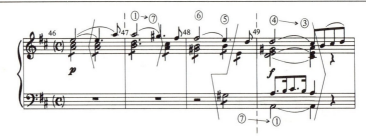

EXAMPLE 9-29. Mozart, Serenade in D Major, "Posthorn," KV 320 (1779), i,
Allegro con spirito, meas. 46–49

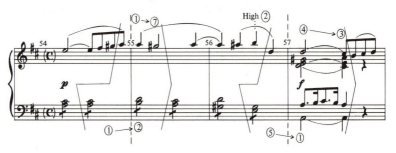

EXAMPLE 9-30. Mozart, Serenade in D Major, "Posthorn," KV 320 (1779), i,
Allegro con spirito, meas. 54–57

EXAMPLE 9-31. Mozart, Serenade in D Major, "Posthorn," KV 320 (1779), i,
Allegro con spirito, meas. 197–200

EXAMPLE 9-32. Mozart, Serenade in D Major, "Posthorn," KV 320 (1779), i,
Allegro con spirito, meas. 205–8

In the first part of this study I presented examples from Haydn and Massonneau (see examples 2-23 and 2-24) of slight variations on 1−7...4−3 themes. As might be expected, the best example that I found of this technique comes from the 1770s. The second theme in the first movement of Mozart's "Posthorn" Serenade appears four times in four different guises (examples 9-29 to 9-32). Only the basic complex of a 1−7...4−3 style structure and a subsidiary 5...4−3 descending third is retained in every instance. The first appearance of the theme features the descending linear progression 1−7−6−5−4−3 (example 9-29). The second appearance features a chromatic variant of the high-② melodic complex (example 9-30). The third appearance (example 9-31), now in the tonic key, begins with what is often a cadential gesture, the closure of which is here forestalled by the melodic D♯. Notice that in the second and third measures the bass line now ascends where in the previous two examples it descended. The last appearance of this theme (example 9-32) has the same general structure as the first appearance, but here the descending bass line is allowed to continue downward past the third measure, pulling the harmonic center of the phrase down toward its relative minor. The only constants that allow all the four disparate phrases to be viewed as the same theme are orchestration, texture, and the 1−7...4−3 complex mentioned above.

There are only a handful of 1−7...4−3 style structures by Mozart prior to 1770; he thus had relatively little experience with the structure to bring into the period discussed in this chapter. Haydn, on the other hand, had extensive experience with this structure, and he continued using many of the techniques discussed in the previous chapter well into the 1770s. For instance, in example 9-33 the four-measure version of a two-measure 1−7...4−3 model uses both the unison writing and the inflection of ⑤ in the bass with ♭⑥ seen in previous examples from the 1760s (see examples 8-24 to 8-28). Once again the unison texture distinguishes the extension from the harmonized schema events.

EXAMPLE 9-33. Haydn, Symphony No. 42 in D Major (1771), i, Moderato e
    maestoso, meas. 9−12

Of course there were also marked changes in Haydn's use of the 1−7...4−3 structure. Some of the processes of simplification that led toward 1−7...4−3 prototypes in the early 1760s contributed to new types of complications in the later 1770s.

To illustrate various aspects of these new complications I have assembled six Haydn examples extending from 1765 to 1779 that show movement toward and then, almost at the same time, away from the prototypes of the early 1770s.

A sense of the changes I am referring to can be gained from comparing the two eight-measure 1−7...4−3 structures in example 9-34. In terms of harmony, example 9-34b is a far simpler structure. Furthermore, the small note values and the active bass line of example 9-34a are both absent from the later example. But example 9-34b has other features that, in the course of the 1770s and beyond, emerge to create problems for the schema's perceptibility. For example, the *forte* chords in measures 1 and 5 stand apart from the other sections of the phrase, creating a type of foreground (*forte*) and background (*piano*) effect. This does not significantly complicate the perception of the 1−7...4−3 structure in example 9-34b, but failing to emphasize the 1−7 and 4−3 dyads may, in other examples, make them seem like subsidiary or ornamental patterns. Another feature of example 9-34b is the pitch relationship of the two *piano* sections prior to the 1−7 and 4−3 dyads: the second section is transposed down one step. This transposition is not normally part of a 1−7...4−3 style structure and, in the absence of any indication of a high-②, descending-triads, or any other stock pattern to signal the 1−7...4−3 schema, a listener has little reason to expect a 4−3 termination. The stepwise descent more likely implies a termination on the tonic C, and in fact a 7−1 ending concludes the next statement of the theme (example 9-35). I do not mean to say that the 1−7...4−3 structure of example 9-34b is analytically suspect. The point is that further development of latent features from the period of the 1−7...4−3 structure's greatest currency can (and will) destroy much of the structure's coherence.

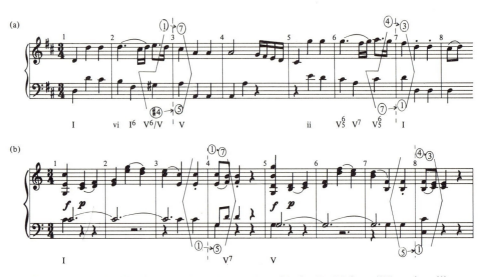

EXAMPLE 9-34. Haydn: (*a*) Symphony No. 31 in D Major, "Hornsignal" (1765), iii, Menuet, meas. 1−8; (*b*) Symphony No. 41 in C Major (−1770), i, Allegro con spirito, meas. 1−8

EXAMPLE 9-35. Haydn, Symphony No. 41 in C Major (–1770), i, Allegro con spirito, meas. 23–26

Another feature that is of little consequence in the early 1770s but later becomes a basis for elaboration that obscures the schema is the filling in of a triad to create a scalar pattern. The technique is obvious in the context of an indicated descending-triads melodic complex (example 9-36). But in example 9-37, by Haydn, the same sort of procedure leaves the nominal ① as a rather insignificant sixteenth-note, and the 4–3 dyad is blurred by sixteenth-notes as well.

EXAMPLE 9-36. Mozart, Symphony in A Major, KV 114 (1771), iv, Allegro molto, meas. 82–88

EXAMPLE 9-37. Haydn, Symphony No. 43 in E♭ Major, "Mercury" (−1772), i, Allegro, meas. 1–4

Notice in examples 9-36 and 9-37 how prominent the initial notes of both halves of the structure are. These phrases have a close affinity with the high-② melodic complex and its near relative, the descending-triads melodic complex. In example 9-38 this standard pattern breaks down, and ② moves to the bottom and middle of the two versions of the phrase, a "second theme" written toward the latter part of the decade.

[accompaniment as above (in D major)]

EXAMPLE 9-38. Haydn, Symphony No. 53 in D Major, "Imperial" (1778), iv, version B, Allegro: (*a*) meas. 42–45; (*b*) meas. 137–40

Another feature of example 9-38 is the placement of the 1–7 and 4–3 dyads in the middle of strings of eighth-notes. Haydn was apparently aware that this reduces the closure of each dyad; in their larger contexts, the two versions of example 9-38 are both immediately repeated, and to give more closure to their repetitions Haydn allows the final 4–3 dyads to end without any ensuing eighth-notes (example 9-39). This placement of the 1–7 and 4–3 dyads *in medias res* is quite typical of Haydn, as in example 9-40.

In the phrase in example 9-41, from the very end of the 1770s, most of the potentially deforming features mentioned in this discussion of Haydn come together: the prominent initial notes of each half of the phrase, the filling in of a melodic triad, the string of eighth-notes following the 1–7 and 4–3 dyads, and the transposition by one step of corresponding sections of the phrase (see the oboe lines). Haydn assimilates all these features and still maintains a very clear schema by staying close to the basic descending-triads melodic complex with the string section, and by giving the remaining melodic material to the oboes—in other words, by using orchestration to organize the listener's perception of the phrase's structure. Notice also how Haydn capitalizes on the prominence of the first notes of each phrase half, creating a large 1–2–3 pattern. He probably did not invent this complex; the incipit in example 9-42 by Antonio Rosetti (né Rössler) antedates example 9-41 by four years. But Haydn's phrase gives a better indication of both the scope and the complexity that were being reintroduced into the 1–7…4–3 style structure during the later 1770s.

instead of

EXAMPLE 9-39. Haydn, Symphony No. 53 in D Major, "Imperial" (1778), iv, version B, meas. 143–44 compared with meas. 139–40

EXAMPLE 9-40. Haydn, Symphony No. 54 in G Major (1774), i, Presto, meas. 21–24

EXAMPLE 9-41. Haydn, Symphony No. 71 in B♭ Major (?1778–79), iv, Vivace, meas. 11–14

EXAMPLE 9-42. Rosetti, Symphony in E♭ Major, Murray E♭1 (1776), i, Allegro moderato, meas. 1–5

EXAMPLE 9-43. Mozart, Serenade in D Major, "Posthorn," KV 320 (1779), v, Andantino, meas. 1–6

Example 9-43 by Mozart, also from the end of the 1770s, shows that he too was now creating large, complicated 1–7...4–3 structures. In this case, the phrase is so intricately designed that I must revert to using a detailed network representation. There is a rich fund of relationships in example 9-43 reflecting a wide array of

EXAMPLE 9-44. Mozart, Overture to *La finta giardiniera,* KV 121 (207a) (1774), iii, Allegro: (*a*) meas. 21–25; (*b*) meas. 29–33

EXAMPLE 9-45. Hypothetical components of example 9-43

compositional techniques. At a low level we see the intricate melodic network, rhythmic uniformity, and inner-voice suspension characteristic of some of the earliest examples of the 1–7…4–3 structure. At the mid-level there is the basic 1–7…4–3 schema with a prototypical bass line. At a higher level there is a very sophisticated version of an overlapping process. To better illustrate this overlapping process, let me first return to the earlier part of the decade and one of the 1–7…4–3 prototypes (example 9-44). Superimposed on the two-part 1–7…4–3 structure is a three-part process of ascending dyads. The two types of this process shown in example 9-44 might be called, borrowing terms from the study of fugue, "tonal" and "real" variants: the tonal variant maintains the principal key but alters the interval of ascent; the real variant maintains the interval of ascent but alters the key.

In example 9-43 this three-part "tonal" process is combined with two interlocking four-measure units, the hypothetical normal forms of which are shown in example 9-45. The original, of course, does not end this way. Line *C* of example 9-45 would require another two measures for a full cadence, as shown in example 9-46. Mozart compresses the last four measures of example 9-46 into two measures by using a smaller 1–7...4–3 structure with a linear-descent melodic complex (example 9-47). The acceleration of the linear descent and its continuation past the 4–3 dyad give this structure quite low typicality. Only one note is lacking in order to make example 9-47 the same as Mozart's original phrase—the low D in the melody in measure 4 (example 9-48). This low D (example 9-48) completes some of the other schemata indicated in the network representation of example 9-43. The low D also expands the ascent to the high D, providing an early example of the stretching of intervals that characterizes later Romantic music (example 9-49).[4]

EXAMPLE 9-46. Hypothetical conclusion of example 9-45

EXAMPLE 9-47. Small 1–7...4–3 style structure embedded in example 9-43

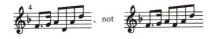

EXAMPLE 9-48. The low D in measure 4
of example 9-43

EXAMPLE 9-49. The stretching of intervals

As a synopsis of the various forms and processes mentioned over the last several pages, the diagram in example 9-50 may be helpful.

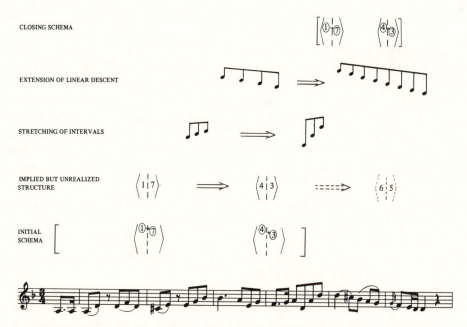

EXAMPLE 9-50. A summation of structures present or suggested in example 9-43

An even more abstract representation of example 9-50 symbolizes what was one of the standard higher-level forms of the late eighteenth and early nineteenth centuries (figure 9-4). One or more processes lead up from an initial schema to a closing schema, the whole form having an arclike melodic contour.[5]

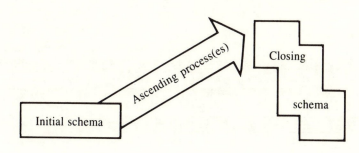

FIGURE 9-4. A further abstraction of example 9-50

SCHEMATIC PERCEPTION

Imagine a foreign language interpreter hired by a king to simultaneously translate an ambassador's speech. The interpreter is told beforehand that perfect grammar must be used at all times, regardless of how the ambassador speaks, and that he is forbidden to admit that he did not understand what the ambassador said. Imagine also that the ambassador has a speech impediment and speaks an obscure dialect little known to the interpreter. Obviously, what the king thinks the ambassador said and what he actually said may be quite different—everything depends on the interpreter.

Our cognitive schemata function somewhat like the interpreter in the story, processing the confusing messages of sensory stimuli and providing us with coherent perceptions. This schematic perception is a great time-saver—the king does not have to look up every word of the ambassador's speech in a dictionary—but the time saved is at the cost of occasionally being misled, of having to accept the interpreter's version of a message.

In this short section, I present two examples of phrases that sound like or, perhaps more accurately, are remembered to have sounded like 1–7...4–3 style structures when in fact they lack central features of this schema. In both cases it appears that the composers took advantage of schematic perception to conceal or smooth over the effect of a harmonic modulation.

The first example is from the Andante of Mozart's Symphony KV 200 (example 9-51). The 1–7 dyad is placed in parentheses to indicate that only in retrospect can it be considered as such. In the main key of F major the repeated note C is not ① but ⑤, and at the beginning of the second measure the movement of the bass does not make this C dissonant (example 9-52). The descending tetrachord in the bass is also unsuited to form part of a 1–7...4–3 style structure. A simpler version of such a combination makes this incompatibility obvious (example 9-53). In terms of voice-leading norms, this bass would have been more likely to have had the melody in example 9-54.

EXAMPLE 9-51. Mozart, Symphony in C Major, KV 200 (189k) (?1773), ii, Andante, meas. 11–14

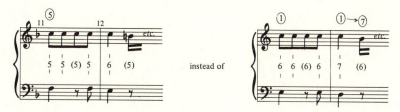

EXAMPLE 9-52. Counterpoint in meas. 11–12 of example 9-51

EXAMPLE 9-53. Potential for parallel fifths when 1–7…4̂–3 melody is combined with descending tetrachord

EXAMPLE 9-54. Likely melody for bass of example 9-53

EXAMPLE 9-55. Mozart, Symphony in C Major, KV 200 (189k) (?1773), ii, Andante, meas. 1–4

The actual opening theme of this Andante combines a slightly less processive version of the bass and harmony of example 9-54 with a latent 1–7…4–3 melody (example 9-55). In the phrase first cited in example 9-51, the first two measures of example 9-55 are repeated, but then a change in the harmony (V$^4_3$ in C major) helps to bring about a reinterpretation of the latent 1–7…4–3 melody. Such a reinterpretation must begin after the phrase's second measure and is probably not confirmed until after the phrase's cadence.

An interesting technical matter is the placement of the metric boundary of the 4–3 dyad. Mozart had two options, shown in example 9-56. Because Mozart chose the delayed placement (example 9-56a), and because the two metric boundaries of a 1–7...4–3 schema are usually placed in the same metric position, it is likely that the first metric boundary of Mozart's own mental reinterpretation of this phrase had the position shown in example 9-57. This placement makes sense not only because the melodic C in the second measure is not a dissonance (as would be required if it followed the metric boundary), but also because the process of reinterpretation will extend the area of dominant harmony in C major back to the appearance of the B♮–F tritone.

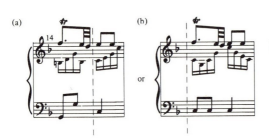

EXAMPLE 9-56. Optional metric boundaries for the 4–3 dyad of example 9-51

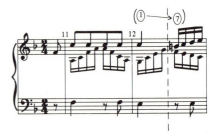

EXAMPLE 9-57. Retrospective metric boundary for the 1–7 dyad of example 9-51

The second example of schematic perception comes from the Andante of Cambini's Symphony in D Major of 1776 (example 9-58). In contrast to the Mozart example, the opening two measures of this phrase form the perfectly regular first half of a 1–7...4–3 style structure. The position of the high A in the second measure suggests some expanded form of a high-② melodic complex, perhaps like the hypothetical realization in example 9-59. Cambini's own phrase uses the likelihood of such a realization to smooth over a modulation to the dominant key area (example 9-60). The strong conformance of measures 18 and 20 serves to weld this phrase together and to give the impression of a four-measure 1–7...4–3 style structure, even though paradoxically the same pitches (G and F♯) that were ① and ⑦ at the beginning of the schema are ④ and ③ at its end. The regularizing effect of the 1–7...4–3 schema is quite strong; if after playing through this phrase one thinks back to the 1–7 dyad in measure 18, it is difficult not to remember it as D–C♯ rather than the actual G–F♯. The large, illusory 1–7...4–3 style structure seems more vivid than the small 1–7...4–3 structure embedded in the last two measures (example 9-61).

EXAMPLE 9-58. Cambini, Symphony in D Major, Op. 5, No. 1 (1776), ii, Andante, meas. 17–18

EXAMPLE 9-59. Hypothetical continuation of example 9-58

EXAMPLE 9-60. Cambini, Symphony in D Major, Op. 5, No. 1 (1776), ii, Andante, meas. 17–20

EXAMPLE 9-61. Small 1–7…4–3 style structure embedded in example 9-60

Summary

A distinction was made between a prototype as a hypothetical abstraction and as "a perfect example of a particular type." It was found that some examples, though close to the hypothetical abstraction of a 1–7...4–3 prototype, were actually too idiosyncratic to be considered perfect examples of this structural category. The most representative, most generic examples of the 1–7...4–3 style structure conformed not only with the mid-level, structural requirements but also with the low-level norms of rhythmic and melodic activity of the 1770s.

In previous chapters, two common 1–7...4–3 melodic complexes were discussed: the linear-descent complex (chapter 7) and the high-② complex (chapters 7 and 8). In this chapter, a third type was introduced, the descending-triads melodic complex. This complex, a close relative and possible descendant of the high-② complex, can exist in four different configurations. The fact that the configuration predominantly chosen is the simplest and has two conformant halves suggests that simplicity and conformance were two preferred traits.

Conformance remained a preferred trait throughout the 1770s, but the same cannot be said of simplicity. The wide selection of examples by Mozart and Haydn presented in this chapter shows that 1–7...4–3 style structures became increasingly complicated as the decade progressed. There was a reemergence of subsidiary patterns and overlapping processes. Haydn, in particular, frequently places the 1–7 and 4–3 dyads in the midst of a stream of eighth-notes. This technique reintegrates the dyads into a more continuous melodic flow but also makes them less prominent. Some of the possible confusions that these complications might have brought about were allayed by the growing use of orchestration to highlight and differentiate the multiple structures of complex phrases. Tone color proved to be a readily perceived feature that was ideal for establishing an immediate sense of similarity between short passages (or even single chords) separated by other material.

CHAPTER 10

1780–1794: New Complications

A precipitous decline in the population of the 1–7...4–3 schema occurs between the late 1770s and the early 1780s. As figure 10-1 shows, during 1780–84 the number of examples is only half that of the preceding five-year interval. The population then rises a little in the later 1780s, but it remains far below the peak of the early 1770s.

The model of chapter 6 predicted this overall decline in population. The additional dip in population in the early 1780s, however, was not predicted. There are at least two possible explanations, not mutually exclusive, for this phenomenon. First, the dip and subsequent slight rebound in population could have been created by the rise of a new 1–7...4–3 melodic complex, as shown in figure 10-2. Or, second, the dip might reflect a lowering of the total number of musical examples for that five-year interval (figure 10-3).

Regarding the first explanation, there does not appear to be any single new 1–7...4–3 complex that has the subsidiary population curve called for in figure 10-2 (although a new formal type does become more prominent later in this period). Regarding the second explanation, it is possible that the low number of 1–7...4–3 style structures in the interval 1780–84 is a result of a sharp decrease in the number of symphonies Mozart composed at that time. Mozart and Haydn symphonies figure prominently in the statistics used in this study, and it is only to be expected that significant changes in their rates of composing symphonies should have some impact on the reported population curve. Of course this anomaly in the population curve might also be attributable to flaws in my sampling method. The whole matter of statistics of this kind will be discussed again in chapter 12.

This chapter begins with a description of the retention in the 1780s of 1–7...4–3 structural types characteristic of the 1770s. Although several basic structural types did persist into the 1780s, the typicality of individual examples is generally lower than in the 1770s. Part of the decline in typicality is due to a general complication of the melodic pattern networks; more subsidiary patterns are incorporated, and the schema boundaries are blurred by overlapping processes. This is especially evident

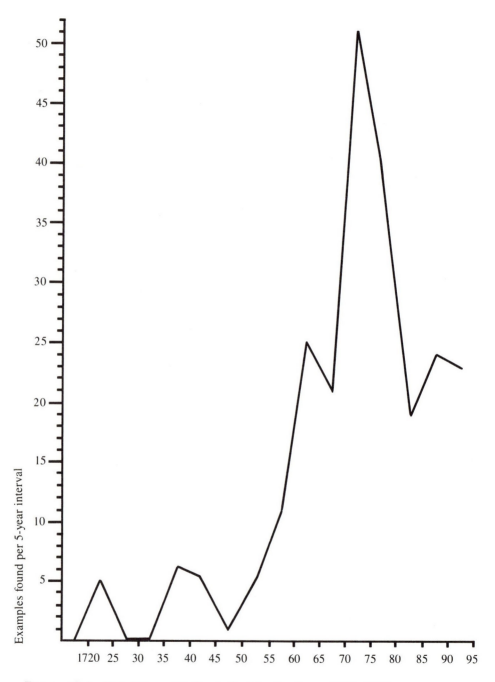

FIGURE 10-1. Population of 1–7...4–3 style structures, 1720–1794

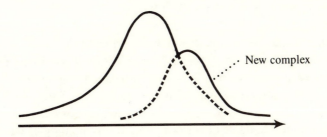

FIGURE 10-2. A change in a schema's population due to a temporary rise of a new melodic complex

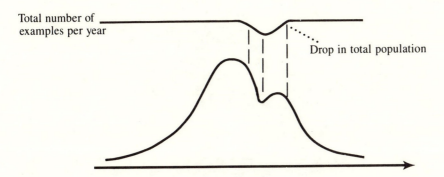

FIGURE 10-3. A change in a schema's population due to a temporary drop in the sampled population

in Mozart's last symphonies. One manifestation of this trend is the melodic ornamentation of the terminal schema dyad 4–3, discussed in relation both to the aria "Batti, batti" from Mozart's *Don Giovanni* and to several examples from late Haydn symphonies. There are also changes in musical form that adversely affected typicality. One alteration, frequent in Haydn, is simply to stretch the form by delaying the terminal schema event. Another more fundamental change is to adopt a less closed formal type—the $\overline{x}$ 1–$\overline{7}$...$\overline{4}$–3 style structure (see the discussion of example 5-33 in chapter 5). The appearance of this phrase type, with its dynamic linkage of subphrases, may be viewed on the one hand as a type of schema mutation in response to new trends, or on the other hand as a return to an old pattern seldom seen since the late Baroque.

THE RETENTION OF STRUCTURAL TYPES

In conjunction with the lowered population and typicality of 1–7…4–3 style structures in this period, there is an increasing range of variation among examples. Nowhere is this more apparent than in the most constrained structural type—prototypes and near prototypes. Even examples with the prototypical 1–7…4–3 melody demonstrate new departures from the norms of the previous period. For instance, in the small episode from the Andante of Mozart's "Linz" Symphony in example 10-1, the diminished seventh chords, the larger F-major context, the chromatic line C–B♮–B♭, and the weak metric positions of the resolutions of the several dissonances combine to give this phrase very low typicality in spite of its prototypical melody and simple bass.

EXAMPLE 10-1. Mozart, Symphony in C Major, "Linz," KV 425 (1783), ii, Andante, meas. 96

Another example, from the Sanctus of Haydn's *Missa Cellensis,* introduces fermatas (example 10-2). The fermatas on ⑦ and ③ help to close off the two dyads and do not interfere with the larger 1–7…4–3…6–5 pattern (example 10-3). When Haydn restates the theme, however, he chooses to use a lower-level, linear continuation of the structure and, perhaps because a fermata on ③ would interrupt this linear continuation, he removes both fermatas (example 10-4).

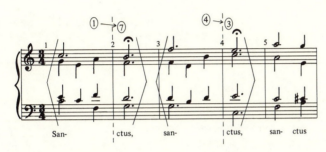

EXAMPLE 10-2. Haydn, Mass No. 6, *Missa Cellensis* (*Mariazellermesse*) (1782), Sanctus, meas. 1–5

EXAMPLE 10-3. The 1–7…4–3…6–5 pattern of example 10-2

EXAMPLE 10-4. The melody of example 10-2 as repeated at meas. 11

Some of the more prototypical 1–7…4–3 structures from this period are not found in symphonies. For example, I could find no symphonic equivalents of the two phrases in example 10-5, from a Vanhal string quartet. There are, to be sure, fea-

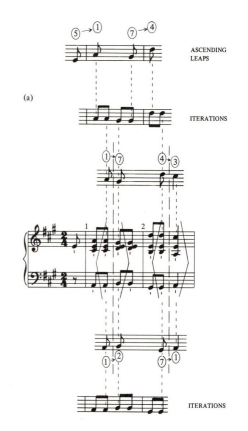

EXAMPLE 10-5. Vanhal, String Quartet
No. 5 in A Major, Bryan A4 (1784),
iv, Allegro molto: (*a*) meas. 1–2;
(*b*) meas. 80–83

tures that distinguish these examples from prototypes of the early 1770s. For instance, the retrospective conformance of the ascending melodic intervals 5–1 and 7–4 in example 10-5a is an early indication of a pattern favored in the early decades of the next century, and the relationship of stepwise transposition between the two descending triads in the bass of example 10-5b is atypical of the early 1770s. But in spite of these technical details, both phrases are far closer to the prototypes of the early 1770s than is a typical symphonic example like the phrase from Haydn's Symphony No. 74 in example 10-6.

EXAMPLE 10-6. Haydn, Symphony No. 74 in E♭ Major (?1780), iii, Allegretto, meas. 2–3

(a)

(b)

EXAMPLE 10-7. (*a*) The melody of example 10-6 rewritten without the super-ordinate 3–4–5 pattern; (*b*) the melody of example 10-6 rewritten with less motivic conformance

EXAMPLE 10-8. Haydn, Symphony No. 93 in D Major (1791), i, Allegro assai, meas. 120–22

Haydn's decision to incorporate the superordinate pattern 3–4–5 while maintaining all the subordinate rhythmic and conformant melodic patterns forced the mid-level 1–7…4–3 structure of example 10-6 out of balance; for the first time in this study an example's 4–3 dyad is placed ahead of its second metric boundary. Had either the superordinate pattern or one of the subordinate patterns been sacrificed, the mid-level structure could have been regularized (example 10-7). Thus, just as was seen much earlier in the phrase by Pollarolo from the 1720s (example 7-5), compositional attention directed toward a lower or a higher level of structure can leave a mid-level pattern like the 1–7…4–3 schema slightly out of focus.

The standard 1–7…4–3 melodic complexes were also retained into the 1780s and early 1790s. For instance, the high-② complex, though rare, can be found in both the original form (example 10-8) and the simplified form (example 10-9). Notice how in example 10-9 the tendency toward larger patterns involving a 6–5 continuation is evident (line C).

EXAMPLE 10-9. Haydn, Symphony No. 85 in B♭ Major, "La reine" (?1785), iv, Presto, meas. 9–12

EXAMPLE 10-10. Haydn, Symphony No. 85 in B♭ Major, "La reine" (?1785), iv, Presto, meas. 25–28

EXAMPLE 10-11. Haydn, Symphony No. 89 in F Major (1787), i, Vivace: (*a*) meas. 15–16; (*b*) meas. 25–26

From the same movement as example 10-9 comes an example of the descending-triads melodic complex (example 10-10). The shift of the B♭ in the first measure of the melody to the higher octave keeps the phrase in a narrower range, creates a complementary melodic contour, and also permits the forming of an overlapping 1–2–3 pattern. Haydn weakens the closure of the 1–7 and 4–3 dyads by appending to each a string of sixteenth-notes (line *B*).

Two versions of another descending-triads complex show the now common transformation of descending triads into descending scales (example 10-11).

A linear-descent melodic complex is found in the incipit to Boccherini's Symphony G520 (example 10-12, lines *D* and *E*). This incipit shares most of the idiostructural arrangement of the 1–7...4–3, 5...4–3, and linear-descent patterns found in Mozart's "Posthorn" Serenade (see examples 9-29 to 9-32) of ten years earlier. The main difference between the Boccherini and Mozart examples is that Boccherini makes the 5...4–3 pattern more prominent by placing it above the rest of the phrase. Of course, in doing this he has to weaken the lower-level continuation of the linear descent by placing the final G and F♯ up an octave.

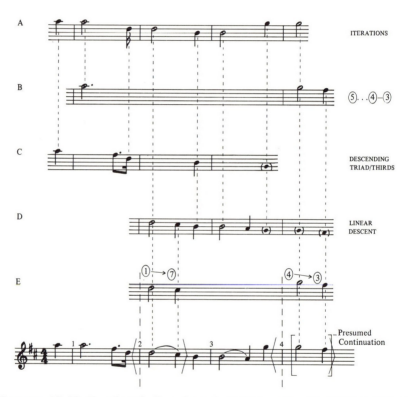

EXAMPLE 10-12. Boccherini, Symphony in D Major, Op. 42, G520 (1789), i,
        Allegro, meas. 1–4

Besides retaining most of the structural types of the 1770s, this later period also retained and developed the structural complications that reemerged in the later 1770s. One of these complications was the reintroduction of overlapping processes. In example 10-13, two four-measure processes—a linear descent in the bass (line *G*) and an ascending 6–5...1–7...4–3 process in the melody (line *B*)—subsume a two-measure 1–7...4–3 structure.

EXAMPLE 10-13. Haydn, Symphony No. 73 in D Major, "La chasse" (?1781), i, Allegro, meas. 27–30

There also occur conformant, as well as processive, overlaps with larger contexts. The 1–7…4–3 style structure in example 10-14 is a G-minor episode in an F-major context (the same situation encountered in example 10-1), connected to the previous two measures by a recurring A–B♭–C motive (line *C*). The effect of this integration on the schema itself is lowered typicality, because it is very rare for a 1–7…4–3 style structure to begin with ② in the melody.

As a final example of techniques from the later 1770s retained in this period, I present the opening phrase of the Minuet from Haydn's Symphony No. 99 (example 10-15). Notice Haydn's trademark of following each dyad with a descending string of equal note values leading down first to ⑤ and then to ① (line *F*). Notice also the distinction made between background (*piano,* high, unison) and foreground (*forte,* low, chordal).

EXAMPLE 10-14. Haydn, Symphony No. 98 in B♭ Major (1792), iv, Presto, meas. 43–48

EXAMPLE 10-15. Haydn, Symphony No. 99 in E♭ Major (1793), iii, Allegretto, meas. 1–8

These last few examples have shown the trend toward the integration of 1–7…4–3 style structures into larger contexts. The result of this integration is increasingly lower typicality, because to be clearly perceptible the style structure must in some way be set apart from a larger context. Thus the late Classic style (like the Baroque) often achieves the effect of continuity by attenuating, eliding, or overlapping the boundaries of mid-level forms.

ALTERATION OF THE 4–3 DYAD

One of the destabilizing developments in the 1–7…4–3 style structures written during this period is a tendency to avoid the simple 4–3 dyad implied by the form of the 1–7 dyad and to substitute an ornamented or protracted version. To illustrate this tendency, example 10-16 gives the well-known theme from Mozart's aria "Batti, batti." In this aria the nominal 4–3 dyad has only a faint overt presence, ④ being placed in the metrically weak middle of the descending third 5–4–3. Yet this ④ has a strong psychological presence that can be explained in several ways. In terms of schema theory, the concept of default values can account for much of the strength of the 4–3 dyad of the "Batti, batti" theme. That is, the ornamented 4–3 dyad of "Batti, batti" is an acceptable confirmation of a 1–7…4–3 style structure, because even though the dyad is altered, it coincides with and is corroborated by the expected default values of the schema. And at a lower level, basic voice-leading patterns require that the descent from ⑤ to ④ over the dominant in the bass continue on to ③ over the tonic in the bass.

As was mentioned in chapter 5 (see the section "Melodic Dyads"), the 4–3 dyad was far more frequently altered than the 1–7 dyad. A repetition of a phrase was also more likely to be highly ornamented than the original. Not surprisingly, it was in the 4–3 dyad of a phrase repetition that composers tended to utilize their most intricate melodic ornaments, in effect countering with melodic innovation the high predictability of the last 4–3 dyad. Example 10-17 shows the original and repeated statements of a subsidiary theme from a Mozart rondo. The 4–3 dyad from the repeat of the phrase is one of the most highly ornamented presented in this study.

EXAMPLE 10-16 (top, facing page). Mozart, *Don Giovanni* (1787), Act I, No. 12, Aria di Zerlina, "Batti, batti," meas. 1–4

EXAMPLE 10-17 (bottom, facing page). Mozart, Piano Concerto in E♭ Major, "Jeunehomme," KV 271 (1777), iii, Menuetto, Cantabile: (*a*) meas. 237–40; (*b*) meas. 249–52

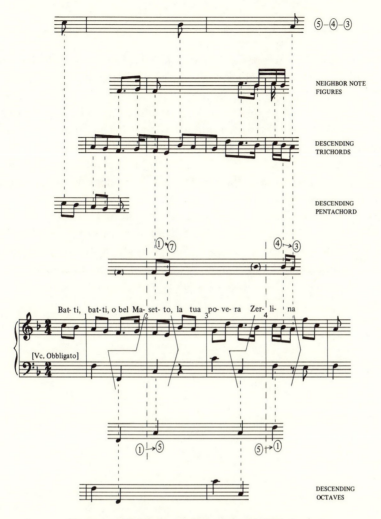

NEIGHBOR NOTE
FIGURES

DESCENDING
TRICHORDS

DESCENDING
PENTACHORD

Bat- ti, bat- ti, o bel Ma- set- to, la tua po- ve- ra Zer- li- na

[Vc. Obbligato]

DESCENDING
OCTAVES

EXAMPLE 10-16 above, EXAMPLE 10-17 below

(a)

(b)

Melodic variation in repeated phrases does not, of course, always have to be in the direction of shorter note values, trills, turns, and other devices. Later in Mozart's "Batti, batti," for example, the theme itself is presented by the orchestra while Zerlina adds what might be described as a simplified melodic commentary that emphasizes the underlying schema (example 10-18). These "added" melodies are neither distinct countermelodies nor straightforward simplifications of the "Batti, batti" theme. Instead, they are simpler 1–7...4–3 melodic complexes presented simultaneously with the "Batti, batti" theme. The first is a linear-descent complex and the second a high-② complex.[1]

Mozart was not alone in altering the 4–3 dyad of 1–7...4–3 style structures. Haydn also produced several comparable examples. In his Symphony No. 81 one can see a phrase where the 1–7 dyad, though brief, at least has a direct melodic connection, while the 4–3 dyad is both ornamented and indirect (example 10-19). In Haydn's Symphony No. 96 a rest is actually introduced to separate the 4–3 dyad (example 10-20).

EXAMPLE 10-18. Mozart, *Don Giovanni* (1787), Act I, No. 12, Aria di Zerlina, "Batti, batti": (*a*) meas. 9–12; (*b*) meas. 45–48

EXAMPLE 10-19. Haydn, Symphony No. 81 in G Major (1784), i, Vivace, meas. 28–31

EXAMPLE 10-20. Haydn, Symphony No. 96 in D Major, "The Miracle" (1791), ii, Andante, meas. 2–3

EXAMPLE 10-21. Rigel, Symphony in D Minor, Op. 21, No. 2, Brook III, p. 86 (1785), i, Allegro maestoso, meas. 1–4

EXAMPLE 10-22. Ragué, Symphony in D Minor, Op. 10, No. 1, Brook III, p. 109 (1786), i, Allegro maestoso, meas. 1–10

French symphonists of the period also begin avoiding the obvious 4–3 dyad, somewhat more in line with Haydn's procedures than with Mozart's. For instance, Henri-Joseph Rigel uses an ornate 4–3 dyad, as shown in the violins of example 10-21, although he clarifies the dyad with the simpler 3–2...4–3 pattern in the oboes. In the last three examples, ③ has been preceded by a fleeting ②. Louis-Charles Ragué makes this ② a little longer to capitalize on the opposition of descending 5–4–3–2–1 and ascending 2–3–♯4–5 (in the violins). This opposition is worked out in four measures of extended "struggle" (example 10-22). Note that in the later section, where 4–3 becomes the antithesis of ♯4–5, the 4–3 dyad has a direct, unobscured presence. The final 4–3 dyad (measure 10) even appears as an appoggiatura, though perhaps too late to recall the earlier 1–7 dyad.

The final example of an obscured 4–3 dyad can also serve as the first example of delaying the arrival of ③ (example 10-23). The foreground (*fortissimo*)/background (*piano*) effect and the stepwise transposition of the second half of the phrase are additional characteristics of the style of the 1780s.

In example 10-23, Haydn obscures the 4–3 dyad by moving it into the second violin part and delays the arrival of ③ and the attendant tonic harmony by an extra two beats. The held ⑤ in the first violins then resumes its descent to ①, making the smoothest possible juncture between the 1–7...4–3 and the cadential 5–4–3–2–1 style structures.

EXAMPLE 10-23. Haydn, Symphony No. 75 in D Major (−1781), i, Grave, meas. 1–7

Haydn's oeuvre contains numerous instances of delaying the arrival of ③. Like melodic ornamentation, a delaying technique can be used to vary and extend a repetition of a 1–7...4–3 structure. For instance, when the Minuet theme (example 10-24a) returns in Haydn's "Surprise" Symphony (example 10-24b), ④ is first put off for an additional measure and then held by a fermata. The ③ finally arrives, but it is a mere upbeat, the full tonic cadence forestalled for another six measures. The same combined use of variation and extension characterizes the repeat of a small 1–7...4–3 structure from Haydn's Symphony No. 97 (example 10-25). Example 10-25a is distinguished from the near prototypes of the 1770s only by the technical detail of having the bass note C under the dominant chord in the second measure. In example 10-25b, on the other hand, ④ is greatly prolonged and ③ is harmonized with a deceptive cadence.

EXAMPLE 10-24. Haydn, Symphony No. 94 in G Major, "The Surprise" (1791), iii, Allegro molto: (*a*) meas. 1–8; (*b*) meas. 41–50

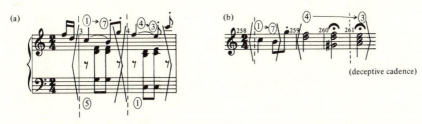

EXAMPLE 10-25. Haydn, Symphony No. 97 in C Major (1792), iv, Presto assai:
(*a*) meas. 3–4; (*b*) meas. 258–61

While examples 10-24 and 10-25 represent playful alterations of previously established phrases, example 10-26 shows the potential abrogation of the 4–3 dyad used to portray a dramatic character's indecision.[2] Haydn stretched the normal four-measure compass of this type of 1–7…4–3 structure to eight measures by literally bringing the phrase to a complete halt, tentatively beginning again with ④ still in the melody and ② in the bass, and then finally placing ⑦ in the bass and moving the melody convincingly toward the 4–3 dyad. One could hardly ask for a better matching of musical syntax and poetic text.

EXAMPLE 10-26. Haydn, *Orlando Paladino* (1782), Aria No. 13, Un poco adagio, meas. 1–8

EXAMPLE 10-27. Mozart, Symphony in E♭ Major, KV 543 (1788), i, Allegro, meas. 26–33

1–7…4–3 Style Structures in
Mozart's Symphonies No. 39 and 40

The Allegro of Mozart's Symphony in E♭, No. 39, begins with an eight-measure 1–7…4–3 style structure (example 10-27). To say this phrase is a 1–7…4–3 style structure with ascending triads in each conformant subphrase belies the complexities of its network of patterns. Comparable phrases by Haydn are much simpler, with perhaps overly conformant subphrases (examples 10-28 and 10-29). Mozart, on the other hand, tempers the rhythmic conformance of his two phrase halves with small melodic variations that maintain the surface simplicity seen in the two Haydn phrases (examples 10-28 and 10-29) but result in a host of supplementary conformant and complementary relationships.

EXAMPLE 10-28. Haydn, Symphony No. 88 in G Major (1787), ii, Andante, meas. 1–4

EXAMPLE 10-29. Haydn, Symphony No. 100 in G Major, "Military" (1793–94), iv, Presto, meas. 125–28

Economy of means would not describe example 10-30—the last full statement of the theme in the opening movement of Mozart's G-Minor Symphony. It is interesting to contrast the four statements of the secondary theme from Mozart's "Posthorn" Serenade analyzed in chapter 9 (see examples 9-29 to 9-32) with the four main state-

EXAMPLE 10-30. Mozart, Symphony in G Minor, KV 550 (1788), i, Allegro molto, meas. 184–91

ments of the G-Minor Symphony's theme. In the earlier work, the $1-7\ldots4-3$ schema remains constant while much of the melody, rhythm, and harmony is varied for each appearance of the theme. In the G-Minor Symphony, rhythm and melodic figuration are held constant while three different schemata are introduced. The first and third statements of the theme, beginning the exposition and recapitulation, use the basic schema given in example 10-31. The second and fourth statements of the theme have modulatory functions. The second statement uses a $3-2\ldots4-3$ schema (viewed retrospectively) to move to the relative major (example 10-32). The fourth statement, analyzed in example 10-30, uses a $1-7\ldots4-3$ schema to move from G minor to E♭ major (example 10-33).

EXAMPLE 10-31. The basic schema of the opening theme of the G-Minor Symphony (meas. 2–9)

EXAMPLE 10-32. The theme of the G-Minor Symphony transformed into a $3-2\ldots4-3$ schema (meas. 21–28)

EXAMPLE 10-33. The theme of the G-Minor Symphony transformed into a $1-7\ldots4-3$ schema (meas. 184–91)

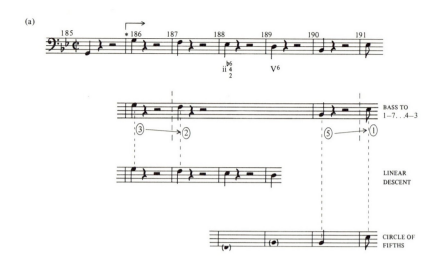

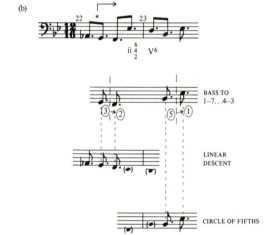

EXAMPLE 10-34. (*a*) The bass line of example 10-30; (*b*) the bass line of example 7-27 (*The Well-Tempered Clavier,* Book I, Prelude No. 13 in F♯ Major, after Kirnberger, transposed to E♭ major)

In general, the technique of holding melodic and rhythmic figures constant while varying structural schemata is more characteristic of the first half of the eighteenth century than of the second half. Another indication of early eighteenth-century technique is found in the bass line of example 10-30. Compare, in example 10-34, the patterns of the basses of example 10-30 and a 1−7...4−3 style structure from the Bach/Kirnberger F♯-Major Prelude in *The Well-Tempered Clavier,* Book I (see example 7-28). Though slightly distinguished by their larger contexts and by Mozart's use of the more poignant ii$^{♭6}_{4}$ to Bach's plain ii$^{6}_{4}$, in almost all other respects these are the same basses. Mozart may indeed have studied this prelude; he may also have arrived at his bass independently, because after the early 1770s the reintroduction of subsidiary patterns, overlapping processes, and other complications brought to 1−7...4−3 style structures of the late 1780s and early 1790s some

EXAMPLE 10-35. Mozart, Symphony in G Minor, KV 550 (1788), ii, Andante, meas. 20–23. The basic schema of the second theme

of the same compositional techniques used in the earlier part of the century. Seen in this light, Mozart's interest in Bach and Handel had a practical and applied aspect. That is, he could study their scores for ideas about how to attenuate the boundaries and formal divisions of mid-level schemata and thus create more continuous, integrated structures.

The only other large 1–7…4–3 style structure in Mozart's last symphonies appears in the second movement of the G-Minor Symphony. Like the 1–7…4–3 structure in the first movement, this one is a restatement of what was originally a different schema. That is, the 1–7…2–1 schema at measure 20 (example 10-35) is transformed into a 1–7…4–3 schema at measure 86 (example 10-36; only the most important patterns are presented in the analytic diagram).

EXAMPLE 10-36. Mozart, Symphony in G Minor, KV 550 (1788), ii, Andante, meas. 86–89

In the 1–7...2–1 structure at measure 20 (see example 10-35) the initial, *forte* high B♭ is answered two measures later by a *forte* high C. In the 1–7...4–3 structure at measure 86 (see example 10-36) the initial, *forte* high C is answered *four* measures later by a *forte* high B♭. This high B♭ begins a second 1–7...4–3 style structure a step lower than that of example 10-36.

Perhaps no better demonstration can be made of the remarkable developments in the 1–7...4–3 schema since its population and typicality peaks in the early 1770s than to compare example 10-36 and its one-step-lower restatement with an analogous passage by Mozart from 1771 (example 10-37). Example 10-37b can be performed in about five seconds. Its simple, juxtaposed combination of two 1–7...4–3 structures needs little comment. The passage from the G-Minor Symphony's Andante, on the other hand, can take over half a minute to perform, and several pages would be required to describe just its internal network of melodic relationships, not to mention its melodic and motivic relationships with other parts of the movement.

EXAMPLE 10-37. (*a*) Example 10-36 and its one-step-lower restatement; (*b*) Mozart, Symphony in F Major, KV 112 (1771), iv, Molto allegro, meas. 17–24

The single most telling feature of this complex passage may be its sheer length. Each of the two 1–7...4–3 structures is so drawn out that fully six or seven seconds elapse between the respective 1–7 and 4–3 dyads. Given the great complexity of this passage, such a span of time may approach the upper limit of short-term memory. In fact, one has to look to Mahler for a comparable 1–7...4–3 example (see example 11-41).

NEW FORMAL TYPES

The two hypothetical melodies in example 10-38 have the form of possible 1–7...4–3 style structures. In their original forms these melodies are divided between two voices, with the sections of dominant harmony overlapping (example 10-39).

EXAMPLE 10-38. A hypothetical 1–7...4–3 melody modeled after: (*a*) KV 183
(cf. example 10-39a); (*b*) KV 385 (cf. example 10-39b)

EXAMPLE 10-39. Mozart: (*a*) Symphony in G Minor, "Little G-Minor," KV 183
(173dB) (1773), i, Allegro con brio, meas. 29–34; (*b*) Symphony in D
Major, "Haffner," KV 385 (1782), i, Allegro con spirito, meas. 117–21

The two phrases of example 10-39 might be considered contrapuntal versions of the hypothetical phrases in example 10-38. But these phrases are of interest here not because they give indications of Mozart's interest in counterpoint; rather, these phrases represent a trend toward a new, hybrid formal type. The more established formal types, 1−7...4−3 and 1...7−4...3 structures, are distinguished by their melodic and harmonic forms. For example, the theme from Mozart's Symphony KV 201 in example 10-40 is clearly a 1−7...4−3 style structure with the melodic form $\overbrace{\underset{X\ \ Y}{A}}\ \overbrace{\underset{X'\ \ Y'}{A'}}$, and harmonic form ABB′A. The 1...7−4...3 style structure in example 10-41 tends, on the other hand, toward a small AB form in which the melodic ③ begins a repetition (A′B′). Compared to a 1−7...4−3 style structure, the closure at the end of a 1...7−4...3 style structure is weak. As is shown by example 10-41, such 1...7−4...3 style structures often establish an oscillation of contrasting tonic and dominant subsections that continues in subsequent measures.

The phrase from the "Little" G-Minor Symphony (shown above in example 10-39a) has both the paired dyads of a 1−7...4−3 structure and the tonic dominant alternation of a 1...7−4...3 structure (example 10-42). This is a hybrid form, which I label the $\overline{x\ \ }$ 1−7...4−3 style structure, using dashes to mark the dyads and brackets to indicate the overall form (this form is also discussed in chapter 5; see figure 5-4 and example 5-33).

The $\overline{x\ \ }$ 1−7...4−3 style structure existed long before this period and did not always involve overlapping voices. For instance, example 10-43 gives a large phrase by Veracini from the 1740s. In the 1780s and 1790s, composers other than Mozart also produced examples of this type of style structure, some with and some without overlapping voices. Louis-Charles Ragué wrote the phrase in example 10-44 in 1786 or 1787. The 1−7...2−1 style structure seems likewise to have been susceptible to the same formal changes, as can be seen in the phrase by Jean-Baptiste Bréval in example 10-45.

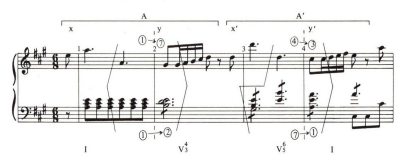

EXAMPLE 10-40. Mozart, Symphony in A Major, KV 201 (1774), iv, Allegro con spirito, meas. 1−4

EXAMPLE 10-41. Mozart, Piano Concerto in A Major, KV 488 (1786), i, Allegro, meas. 71–72

EXAMPLE 10-42. The melody of example 10-39a

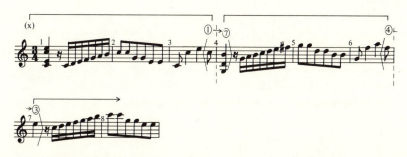

EXAMPLE 10-43. Veracini, Sonate Accademiche, Op. 2 (1744), No. 3, i, Allegro, meas. 1–8

EXAMPLE 10-44. Ragué, Symphony in D Minor, Op. 10, No. 1, Brook III, pp. 128–29 (1786–87), iii, Vivace non tanto, meas. 20–24

EXAMPLE 10-45. Bréval, Symphonie concertante in F Major, Op. 38, Brook III,
    p. 208 (?1795), ii, Adagio, meas. 54–57

The reemergence of the $\overline{x\quad 1-7}...\overline{4}-3$ style structure is but another sign of
late eighteenth-century composers either rediscovering or reinventing ways of writing more open-ended, processive phrases. The specified differences between a
1–7... 4–3 and an $\overline{x\quad 1-7}...\overline{4}-3$ style structure may seem slight, but the effect of
these differences on a phrase's closure is surprisingly great. A 1–7...4–3 structure
from the early 1770s can be such a closed entity that practically all its implications
are realized or neutralized within the phrase itself. The incipit in example 10-46,
from an Ordonez symphony, presents such a phrase. To change this incipit into a
more processive, implicative phrase—in other words, to bring it into line with
phrases of the late 1780s and early 1790s—all that is necessary is to make the two
phrase halves overlap, thereby creating an $\overline{x\quad 1-7}...\overline{4}-3$ style structure. I have provided such an altered version in example 10-47, along with a possible continuation.

We shall see in the next chapter that the more open-ended $\overline{x\quad 1-7}...\overline{4}-3$ style
structure was preferred by many nineteenth-century composers.

EXAMPLE 10-46. Ordonez, Symphony in F Minor, Brown I:F12(min) (1773), i,
    Allegro moderato, meas. 1–6

EXAMPLE 10-47. A hypothetical transformation of example 10-46 into an
    $\overline{x\quad 1-7}...\overline{4}-3$ style structure

CHAPTER 11

1795–1900: A Legacy

With this final chapter of historical exposition we return to a situation not unlike that of the period 1720–1754 (chapter 7). As the graph in figure 11-1 indicates, the 1–7...4–3 schema in the nineteenth century has the very low population that it had in the early eighteenth century. We will see that this period also resembles the early eighteenth century in having 1–7...4–3 structures of very low typicality. Whereas many of the examples presented in relation to the 1760s, 1770s, and 1780s are representative of entire categories of 1–7...4–3 structures, most of the examples presented in this chapter are one-of-a-kind phrases—true idiostructural creations.

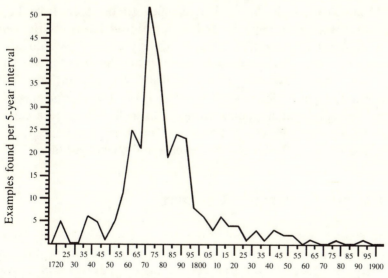

FIGURE 11-1. Population of 1–7...4–3 style structures, 1720–1900

I have chosen five topics through which to approach these idiosyncratic phrases. In the first I examine the end of the eighteenth century and include examples by Haydn, Bréval, Beecke, and Vandenbroeck. In the second I discuss the retention in the nineteenth century of the type of large 1–7...4–3 style structure seen, for example, in the opening theme of Mozart's Symphony No. 39 in E♭ Major. The Franco-Italian focus of this phrase type is evident from some of the composers involved: Rossini, Mercadante, Berlioz, and Méhul. The third topic is organized more by stylistic affinity, and includes examples by Weber, Schubert, Eberl, Beethoven, and Cherubini. The fourth topic is directed toward a younger, somewhat more northern group of composers—Berwald, Henselt, Schumann, and Wagner. Finally, in the fifth topic I address the anomalous appearance of 1–7...4–3 style structures with high typicality in a period of very low population. Some phrases can be explained as evocations of the past. For example, a composer might use an eighteenth-century musical schema as a sign for the eighteenth century itself. Other phrases seem to be outside the realm of art music. In a few cases the denigratory term *Trivialmusik* may be applicable; in others, the more objective term *Schema-Musik* better explains the structures under consideration.

In many instances, the early nineteenth-century phrases to be discussed are examples of juvenilia. Whether by exposure to provincial repertories or to the stylistic preferences of elderly teachers, several composers with mature styles antithetical to the 1–7...4–3 schema produced 1–7...4–3 structures in their teens or twenties. Wagner is the obvious example, though this phenomenon can also be observed in Mendelssohn and Schubert. As the composers of the Classic style died and the eighteenth-century legacy came to be regarded as Bach, some late Mozart, late Haydn, and Beethoven, it is possible that by the 1840s and 1850s student composers were no longer exposed to music from the peak period of the 1–7...4–3 style structure. This may explain why the 1–7...4–3 structure appears to be absent from the early works of Brahms. My single example by Brahms comes from late in his life, perhaps in his role as conservator of tradition. Even then, the phrase in question is an instance of the gap-fill, linear-descent melodic complex (like that found in Schumann's "Wehmut"), rather than a reworking of a specifically Classic phrase type. Those composers of Brahms's generation who did write 1–7...4–3 style structures of high typicality—for example, Anton Rubinstein and Ponchielli—have been censured, even in their own day, for their "conventionality." The basis for this censure will be shown to be critical distaste for scriptlike schemata in Romantic art music.

THE CLOSE OF THE EIGHTEENTH CENTURY

Relatively few symphonies are available from the last five years of the eighteenth century, making it difficult to discern any unifying characteristics among the handful of 1–7...4–3 style structures from the period. For instance, example 11-1 by Ignaz

(Franz) von Beecke—a tiny structure deformed by a much larger descending linear pattern—is quite different from the more conventional phrase of example 11-2 by Othon-Joseph Vandenbroeck.

EXAMPLE 11-1. Ignaz (Franz) von Beecke, Symphony in C Minor, Murray Cm1 (1795), ii, Siciliana, Larghetto, meas. 1–2

EXAMPLE 11-2. Othon-Joseph Vandenbroeck, Symphony in E♭ Major, Brook II, p. 717 (1795), i, Allegro moderato, meas. 1–4

If Beecke's phrase represents a fairly large departure from tradition and Vandenbroeck's hardly any, then the 1–7...4–3 style structures in Haydn's last two symphonies would appear to fall somewhere in between. Several of Haydn's techniques have already been discussed in the previous chapter. For example, in the second movement of his Symphony No. 103 we see the now familiar transformation of the two dyads (in the oboe parts) into scalar descending ninths (example 11-3), and in the last movement he uses the x̄ 1–7̄...4̄–3 style structure with overlapping voices (example 11-4).

EXAMPLE 11-3. Haydn, Symphony No. 103 in E♭ Major, "Drumroll" (1795), ii, Andante più tosto allegretto, meas. 117–18

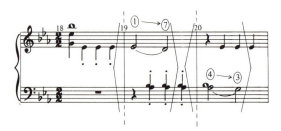

EXAMPLE 11-4. Haydn, Symphony No. 103 in E♭ Major, "Drumroll" (1795), iv, Allegro con spirito, meas. 18–20

Many of the phrases presented in this chapter are poorly described by such labels as *Classic* or *Romantic*. Consider, for example, the phrase from Haydn's "London" Symphony in example 11-5. On the one hand, the melodic structure of this phrase recalls an earlier stage in the 1–7...4–3 style structure's history. Compare this melody, for instance, with one by Georg (Anton) Benda, written perhaps in the late 1750s or early 1760s (example 11-6). On the other hand, the plenitude of countermelodies and orchestral forces employed by Haydn is quite characteristic of the early nineteenth century.

EXAMPLE 11-5. Haydn, Symphony No. 104 in D Major, "London" (1795), ii, Andante, meas. 42–45

EXAMPLE 11-6. Georg (Anton) Benda, Symphony No. 4 in F Major (?1760), i, Allegro, meas. 9–10

EXAMPLE 11-7. Jean-Baptiste Bréval, Symphonie concertante in F Major, Op. 38, Brook III, p. 188 (?1795), i, Allegro maestoso, meas. 142–45

A bassoon solo from a symphonie concertante of Jean-Baptiste Bréval may serve as a final example of a 1–7...4–3 style structure from the close of the eighteenth century (example 11-7). Notice in particular how all the complexities of this phrase are concentrated in the melody. Bréval's combination of both the linear-descent and descending-triads melodic complexes creates a rich network that is intricate yet easily intelligible; neither melodic complex alone produces the same effect.

THE HYPERTROPHY OF THE 1–7...4–3 STYLE STRUCTURE

Consider the phrase by Joseph Fiala in example 11-8. This phrase is an early example of a type of inflated, highly rhetorical, and occasionally bombastic 1–7...4–3 structure that became common in the early nineteenth century. In both this phrase and example 11-9 by Rossini, the basic technique of the triadic or scalar extention of the tonic and dominant chords with the 1–7...4–3 dyads serving as punctuation is easily seen. Even larger versions came later. Méhul produced the eight-measure phrase in example 11-10 in 1809. Examples from concertos by Spohr and Mercadante show the more florid style of the 1810s (examples 11-11 and 11-12). Mercadante's phrase takes about fifteen seconds to perform, and the time between the dyads (about 7.5 seconds) is at the upper bounds of short-term memory as defined in chapter 3. This may explain why the temporal expansion of the phrase type halted at about this length. Examples of this phrase type did, however, continue to be written.

EXAMPLE 11-8. Fiala, Symphony in C Major, Murray C1 (1775), ii, Romance:
andante poco allegretto, meas. 60–65

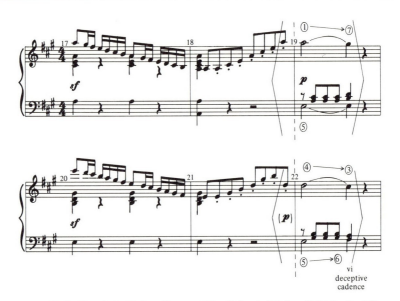

EXAMPLE 11-9. Rossini, String Sonata No. 2 in A Major (1804), i, Allegro, meas. 17–22

EXAMPLE 11-10 (above). Méhul, Symphony No. 1 in G Minor (1809), i, Allegro, meas. 1–8

EXAMPLE 11-11 (top, facing page). Spohr, Violin Concerto No. 8 in A Minor, "In the Form of a Vocal Scene" (1816), i, Allegro, meas. 1–10

EXAMPLE 11-12 (bottom, facing page). Mercadante, Clarinet Concerto in B♭ Major (1819), i, Allegro maestoso, meas. 1–8

EXAMPLE 11-11 above, EXAMPLE 11-12 below

The fourteen-year-old Mendelssohn must have been aware of this phrase type when he penned example 11-13. Note in particular how he overlaps the end of the phrase's first half with the beginning of its second half, resulting in the x̄ 1̄– 7̄...4̄–3 style structure.

EXAMPLE 11-13. Mendelssohn, String Symphony No. 11 in F Minor (1823), i, Allegro molto, meas. 68–76

What is probably the longest example of a 1–7...4–3 style structure on paper, but in performance only half as long as, for instance, Mercadante's phrase, is the well-known theme from the *Symphonie fantastique* of Berlioz (example 11-14). This phrase has been discussed at length by Leonard Meyer.[1]

It might be thought that these large phrases represent an inevitable "dinosaur" phase of giantism at the end of the schema's heyday. That is, just as the dinosaurs reached the structural limits of bone and muscle, these phrases perhaps reached the perceptual limits of short-term memory. However tempting such a view may be, it founders on a simple fact—musical phrases are artifacts, not organisms. Only composers can reproduce musical schemata. A simpler and more plausible explanation for the appearance of these large phrases may be the general trend toward monumentality and, under Napoleon, imperial grandeur that dominated this period. This trend found musical support in the fashion for eight-, sixteen-, and even thirty-two-measure phrases composed of nested binary subdivisions. Thus the 1–7...4–3 schema did not provide a metaphysical seed for growth, but rather a simple pattern that could be enlarged in conformance with general artistic trends.

EXAMPLE 11-14. Berlioz, *Symphonie fantastique,* Op. 14 (1830), i, Allegro agitato e appassionato assai, meas. 72–86 [adapted from his *Herminie* of 1828]

CHALLENGES TO THE 1–7…4–3 SCHEMA

For the composers mentioned in this section—Beethoven, Weber, Schubert,[2] Eberl, and Cherubini—the 1–7…4–3 schema was not a prominent mid-level form. These composers have a melodic style often based more on low-level motives than on mid-level melodic schemata. In addition, the processive higher-level structures of these composers often deform their subsumed mid-level structures. As a result, a stable, highly closed, mid-level form like the 1–7…4–3 style structure was forced out of the structural center by pressures from both above and below.

In the previous chapter the small and very brief phrase by Vanhal in example 11-15 was cited as a remnant of the more prototypical examples of the 1770s. I have circled the implicit conformance of the two ascending leaps 5–1 and 7–4. This pattern of two ascending leaps was not always present in similarly miniaturized 1–7… 4–3 melodies from the 1780s. For example, the opening of the Haydn string quartet in example 11-16 lacks the initial leap 5–1.

EXAMPLE 11-16. Haydn, String Quartet in B♭ Major, Op. 55, No. 3 (1789), i, Vivace assai, meas. 1–4

EXAMPLE 11-15. Vanhal, String Quartet No. 5 in A Major, Bryan A4 (1784), iv, Allegro molto, meas. 1–2

By the beginning of the nineteenth century, however, the explicit pattern of two ascending leaps was firmly established. Notice how in example 11-17, by Anton Eberl, the motivic conformance of four consecutive ascending leaps suppresses almost all the closure of the first 4–3 dyad. Other examples are found in Beethoven's Sixth Symphony (example 11-18) and Cherubini's String Quartet in E♭ (example 11-19). Examples of this melodic pattern were also composed by Schubert (example 11-20).

The low-level deformation caused by what might be called the "Wanderer" pattern of ascending leaps is formally related to the mid-level x͞ 1̄–7̄...4̄–3 style structure. This style structure was quite common in the early nineteenth century, appearing almost as frequently as the 1–7...4–3 structure. In the phrase by Weber in example 11-21, notice how the x͞ 1̄–7̄...4̄–3 structure is combined with a 1–2–3 bass line that continues its ascent to ④ and then ⑤. Apparently it is for the sake of this linear bass that in measure 58 Weber tolerates the quite atypical doubling in the outer voices of the third of the tonic triad (③ over ③). The actual melodic dyads in example 11-21 have receded from the perceptual foreground, ① and ④ being represented only by eighth-notes. This perfunctory role for the 1–7 and 4–3 dyads is even more evident in the slow movement of Beethoven's "Emperor" Concerto (example 11-22).

EXAMPLE 11-17. Eberl, Piano Sextet (Cl. and Hn.), Op. 47 (1800), iii, Allegro, meas. 1 [3]

EXAMPLE 11-18. Beethoven, Symphony No. 6 in F Major, "Pastorale" (1808), iii, Allegro, meas. 181–84

EXAMPLE 11-19. Cherubini, String Quartet in E♭ Major (1814), i, Allegro, meas. 1–4

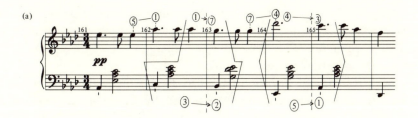

EXAMPLE 11-20. Schubert: (*a*) Wanderer Fantasy, D760 (1822), Presto, meas.
161–65; (*b*) "Das Wandern," *Die schöne Müllerin* No. 1 (1823), Mässig
geschwind, meas. 5–6

EXAMPLE 11-21. Weber, Clarinet Concerto in E♭ Major, Op. 74 (1811), i, Allegro, meas. 54–58

EXAMPLE 11-22. Beethoven, Piano Concerto No. 5 in E♭ Major, "Emperor,"
Op. 73 (1809), ii, Adagio un poco mosso, meas. 16–20

Mendelssohn is a little younger than the other composers discussed in this section, but the theme from the Scherzo of his Octet is such a good example of the nominal presence of the 1–7 and 4–3 dyads in a large x ⌐1–7...4–3 structure that I have included it nevertheless (see example 11-23).

Before concluding this section I want to discuss higher-level deformations of 1–7...4–3 structures. For example, the phrase by Cherubini in example 11-24 opens as the kind of very large 1–7...4–3 (or possibly 1–7...2–1) structure discussed in the previous section. But the second half of this phrase turns out not to close in C major but to veer toward D minor. The mid-level closure of Cherubini's

EXAMPLE 11-23. Mendelssohn, Octet (1825), iii, Scherzo, meas. 1–9

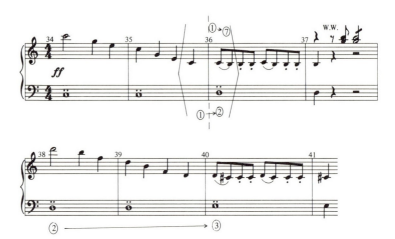

EXAMPLE 11-24. Cherubini, Symphony in D Major (1815), iv, Allegro assai, meas. 34–41

phrase is traded for the higher-level processes of the ascending bass line and tonal modulation. An even more processive deformation of a potential $1-7...4-3$ structure is given in the storm scene of Beethoven's Sixth Symphony, where the melodic motion $1-7$ continues downward to $\flat 7$ and the bass motion $1-2$ continues upward to ③ (example 11-25). A less drastic deformation of a very large $1-7...4-3$ style structure is found in Beethoven's Seventh Symphony, where the tonality is deflected at the last second from the lowered mediant (C major) toward the overall tonic (A major) (example 11-26).

EXAMPLE 11-25. Beethoven, Symphony No. 6 in F Major, "Pastorale" (1808), iv, Allegro, meas. 21–29

EXAMPLE 11-26. Beethoven, Symphony No. 7 in A Major (1812), i, Vivace, meas. 201–12

The various deformations of the 1−7...4−3 style structure at all structural levels—the "Wanderer" motivic pattern, x̄ 1−7̄...4̄−3 patterns with just perceptible 1−7...4−3 dyads, and the tonal deflection of implied structures—are symptomatic of the demise of the 1−7...4−3 style structure. Whether or not these deformations actually *caused* this structure to diminish in importance, the virtual disappearance of 1−7...4−3 examples was a fact by the end of the 1820s. Most of the remaining examples to be discussed in this chapter are therefore not representative instances of general types, as has been the case in much of this study, but rather single cases of a schema no longer in favor.

SCHUMANN, WAGNER, HENSELT, AND BERWALD

Of the four composers mentioned in this section, Schumann is the only one for whom the 1−7...4−3 style structure has some significance. Wagner's mature style is quite alien to symmetrical, closed phrases. One could hardly imagine the following phrase from the overture to *Die Feen* (example 11-27) in the prelude to *Tristan und Isolde*. Wagner's sole symphony is in a rather different style from *Die Feen;* if *Die Feen* recalls the Franco-Italian opera of Spontini and Meyerbeer, the Symphony in C is closer to middle-period Beethoven. Not surprisingly, it contains an x̄ 1−7̄...4̄−3 style structure (example 11-28). Each time this phrase returns it acquires a larger orchestration. For its third appearance an active inner voice is also added (see example 11-29).

EXAMPLE 11-27. Wagner, *Die Feen* (1833), Overture, meas. 9−16 after Più allegro

EXAMPLE 11-28. Wagner, Symphony in C Major (1832), ii, Andante ma non troppo, un poco maestoso, meas. 15–17

EXAMPLE 11-29. Wagner, Symphony in C Major (1832), ii, Andante ma non troppo, un poco maestoso, meas. 42–44

Much the same technique is used in Henselt's Piano Concerto in F Minor. As is shown in example 11-30, the three successive statements of the x $\overline{1-7}...\overline{4}-3$ structure become louder and increasingly ornate. The nominal $1-7$ and $4-3$ dyads in the Henselt phrases have the perfunctory, perceptually weak presence already discussed in connection with examples from the 1810s and 1820s.

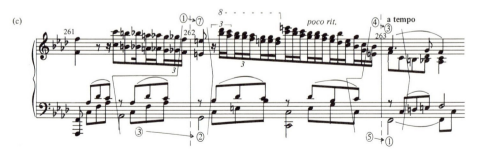

EXAMPLE 11-30. Henselt, Piano Concerto in F Minor, Op. 16 (1838), i, Allegro patetico: (*a*) meas. 12–14; (*b*) meas. 73–75; (*c*) meas. 261–63

Franz Berwald's singular contribution to the history of the 1–7...4–3 schema appears in the polonaise from his opera *Estrella de Soria* (example 11-31b). This phrase is a stretched version of the rather conventional high-② phrase type shown below in example 11-31a.

EXAMPLE 11-31. (*a*) A hypothetical normal form of example 11-31b; (*b*) Berwald, *Estrella de Soria* (1841), Polonaise, 2d theme[4]

Schumann, on the other hand, made repeated use of the 1–7...4–3 schema. Example 11-32 is from mid-century. Within his symphonies, Schumann used for the most part the altered forms of the 1–7...4–3 structure. For instance, in the same movement containing the previous phrase there is a good example of the "Wanderer" motive of ascending leaps (example 11-33). Both his First and Second Symphonies contain examples of the x‾‾ 1–7̄...4̄–3 pattern formed by overlapping halves of the melody (example 11-34).

None of the phrases presented in this section is *highly* typical of the 1–7...4–3 schema. This would be expected from the model of chapter 6. What is unexpected is that composers of the same generation and general locality—Schumann and Wagner—would be so clearly distinguished by their use of this schema. Wagner used the 1–7...4–3 schema only in his youth; Schumann used it throughout his life. Wagner's few examples have relatively large and complex melodies; Schumann's phrases are terse, with often only one note preceding each schema dyad. These observations, in conjunction with comparisons of the ways in which these composers used other common schemata, may suggest avenues toward a fuller discussion of how Schumann and Wagner each develop different methods of transforming the Classic phrase, of how Schumann implodes and Wagner explodes their common inheritance.

EXAMPLE 11-32. Schumann, Symphony No. 3 in E♭ Major, "Rhenish" (1850), v, Vivace, meas. 47–48

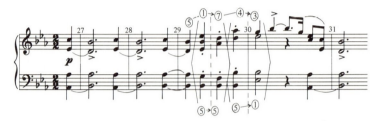

EXAMPLE 11-33. Schumann, Symphony No. 3 in E♭ Major, "Rhenish" (1850), v, Vivace, meas. 27–31

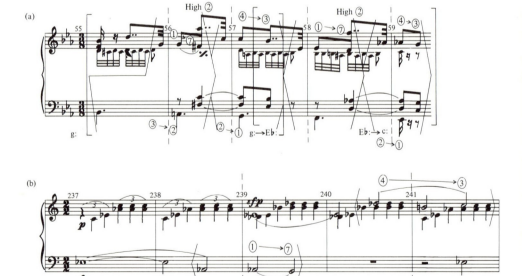

EXAMPLE 11-34. Schumann: (a) Symphony No. 1 in B♭ Major, "Spring" (1841), ii, Larghetto, meas. 55–59; (b) Symphony No. 2 in C Major (1845), iv, Allegro molto vivace, meas. 237–41

THE LATER NINETEENTH CENTURY

Characteristic examples of the 1–7...4–3 schema are rare after the 1820s, and even the mutations of the schema—the x̄ 1–7̄...4̄–3 and "Wanderer" patterns—are seldom found after the 1840s. The model of chapter 6 suggests that any 1–7...4–3 style structures found later in the century would have the lowest possible typicality. In a few instances, this does appear to be true. For example, let us compare the phrase from Schumann's "Wehmut" analyzed in chapter 2 with a phrase from a late Brahms intermezzo (example 11-35).

(a)

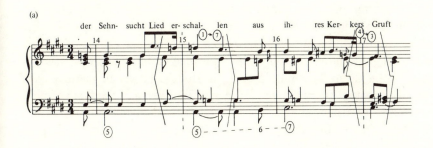

(b)

EXAMPLE 11-35. (*a*) Schumann, *Liederkreis,* Op. 39 (1840), No. 9, "Wehmut," Sehr langsam, meas. 14–17; (*b*) Brahms, Intermezzo in B Minor, Op. 119, No. 1 (1893), Adagio, meas. 24–31

These phrases have strikingly similar initial schema events and share the same gap-fill/linear-descent melodic complex. But what distinguishes the Brahms phrase and makes it so much less typical than the Schumann phrase is its extraordinary delay of the melodic ③. The two schema events in Schumann's phrase occur, in a typical performance, about six seconds apart—for short-term memory a long but not unmanageable period. The melodic ③ in the Brahms phrase, however, is separated from the initial schema event by easily fifteen seconds of complicated chromatic music.

This length of time would ordinarily exceed the capacity of short-term memory. Brahms's use of a memory aid called "rehearsal," however, segments the phrase into more manageable five-second units.[5] The first segment extends from the initial schema event to the ④ of the terminal schema event. There the second segment begins with the creation of a small descending gap in the melody (G–E) that avoids the expected ③ (F♯). By then repeating this second segment Brahms rehearses the ④ of the schema, maintaining it in short-term memory. The small chromatic ascent (E–E♯...F♯) at the end of this third segment simultaneously fills in the small gap of the second and third segments, provides a "reversal before closure" for the large melodic descent of the first segment, and provides the terminal ③ implied by the first segment. In its possession of a clear initial implication (1–7...4–3 schema with an ascending melodic gap), an ambivalent middle section, and a terminal event that seems to follow from a different schema (*descending* gap, *ascending* fill), this phrase might be thought to present some of the aspects of cognition better known in the type of visual conundrum shown in figure 11-2. But such a visual example cannot represent the fact that in Brahms's phrase the gap-fill schema of the first segment and the opposite gap-fill schema of the second and third segments both share the same terminal event. That is, the whole phrase resolves, and we are not forced, as in figure 11-2, to exclude one pattern in order to perceive the other.

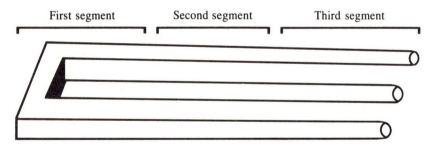

FIGURE 11-2. A visual conundrum

In contrast to this example from Brahms, there are several phrases from the later nineteenth century that do not fit the model of chapter 6. These phrases constitute examples of high typicality found anomalously in a period of low population. Musicologists concerned with the nineteenth century have always been aware that some phrases and even entire compositions stand apart from general stylistic trends. The terms already developed to describe these stylistic anomalies can serve to organize the following discussion.

One cluster of terms implies a reverence for, or a yearning after, the past—
homage, neoclassicism, nostalgia, and historicism. Among the earliest pieces to
which this cluster has been attached is Beethoven's Eighth Symphony. The opening
theme is a large 1−7...4−3 style structure with a Haydnesque stream of eighth-notes
following the initial schema event (example 11-36). Even though this phrase is much
less closed than its antecedents in Haydn, it nevertheless evokes the stability and
regularity of the Classic phrase. Rey M. Longyear is persuaded to declare the entire
work "genuinely neo-Classic."[6]

EXAMPLE 11-36. Beethoven, Symphony No. 8 in F Major (1812), i, Allegro vivace e con brio, meas. 1−8

Beethoven's later uses of 1–7...4–3 style structures become, contrary to expectation, more and more typical of the schema. In his Piano Sonata Op. 111, for instance, he creates a linear-descent melodic complex that, although supported by a pedal ⑤ in the bass and contracted in length, is quite similar to a Boccherini phrase written over thirty years earlier (example 11-37). Beethoven had probably become acquainted with a near prototype of this schema complex in his youth through exposure to Clementi's Piano Sonatas Op. 10 (example 11-38), and the thought presents itself that its appearance in Op. 111 is a "remembrance of things past." Yet this notion is just one of many possible interpretations of the meaning of conventional Classic schemata in Beethoven's later works. Thomas Mann, for example, writing of Op. 111 in the persona of Kretschmar in *Doctor Faustus,* claims that late in Beethoven's life the composer's relation to convention changed. Instead of reshaping conventions as before, he presented them "untouched, untransformed by the subjective, . . . in a baldness, one might say an exhaustiveness, an abandonment of self, [that gives] an effect more majestic and awful than any reckless plunge into the personal."[7]

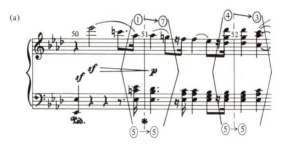

EXAMPLE 11-37. (*a*) Beethoven, Piano Sonata in C Minor, Op. 111 (1821), i, Allegro con brio ed appassionato, meas. 50–52; (*b*) Boccherini, Symphony in D Major, Op. 42, G520 (1789), i, Allegro, meas. 1–4

EXAMPLE 11-38. Clementi, Piano Sonata, Op. 10, No. 1 (1783), ii, Trio, meas. 1–4

For his String Quartet Op. 132 Beethoven chose an even more typical 1–7…
4–3 style structure. A survey of the sketches for this theme (example 11-39) shows
that Beethoven's final choice avoids the rhythmic asymmetry of sketches I and II, the
stepwise transposition of phrase halves in sketch III, or the complication of the
strong ② to ③ termination of sketch IV.[8] In other words, he rejected late-Classic
complications and chose rhythmic regularity along with the tried-and-true linear-
descent melodic complex.

EXAMPLE 11-39. Sketches for the melody of Beethoven's String Quartet in A
    Minor, Op. 132 (1825), i, Allegro, meas. 13–20

Finally, at the end of his life, Beethoven reverted to a pristine type of 1–7...4–3 style structure not far removed from the schema prototype (example 11-40), a theme that Wagner characterized as "the incarnation of innocence."[9]

EXAMPLE 11-40. Beethoven, String Quartet in C♯ Minor, Op. 131, No. 4 (1826), iv, Andante ma non troppo e molto cantabile, meas. 1–4

My use of the word "pristine" and Wagner's use of "innocence" suggest that nineteenth-century reverence for the classical past may include associations of purity, youth, or even "eternal peace." A fine example that evokes all these associations comes from the slow movement of Mahler's Fourth Symphony (example 11-41). In harmony, form, and bass line this is a highly typical 1–7...4–3 style structure. The melody, however, is not so much typical as idealized. Compare its studied calm with the livelier character of its Classic antecedents in example 11-42. Still more unusual is the steadily ascending inner voice of example 11-41 (the opening melody of this movement), which attenuates the closure provided by the 1–7...4–3 schema when, in the fourth measure, an E is placed against the tones of the G-major triad—a decidedly un-Classic procedure.

Two very different reactions are possible to such a phrase. The first views its retrospection in light of the associations discussed above: innocence, purity, repose, and so on. As an example, here is Deryck Cooke's description of the first part of this movement:

> The slow movement opens with some of the most heart-easing music ever written by Mahler or anyone else—a *transfigured cradle song* [italics mine]. . . . The present writer, hearing this movement for the first time, found it bringing a line of Hardy irresistibly into his head—"I seem where I was before my birth, and after death may be"—and was amazed to discover later that Mahler had actually written the movement under the inspiration of "a vision of a tombstone on which was carved an image of the departed, with folded arms, in eternal sleep."[10]

On the other hand, some might see in Mahler's use of the classical tradition the mark of an imitator, a debaser, and an epigone. His enemies frequently labeled him as such, and even his friends at times questioned his retrospection. When Mahler first demonstrated parts of his Fourth Symphony at the piano for his then fiancée Alma, she had the frankness to say, "I think Haydn has done that better." [11]

EXAMPLE 11-41. Mahler, Symphony No 4 (?1899), iii, Ruhevoll, meas. 17–21

EXAMPLE 11-42. (a) Mozart, Serenade in D Major, "Posthorn," KV 320 (1779), i, Allegro con spirito, meas. 197–200; (b) Haydn, Symphony No. 81 in G Major (1784), i, Vivace, meas. 28–31

Of course Haydn never did anything quite like Mahler's Fourth Symphony. But Alma's remark does suggest the general antipathy that many nineteenth- and twentieth-century listeners have felt toward post-Beethovenian music composed with pre-Beethovenian musical schemata. In Mahler's case, musicologists deflect such disparagement by pointing out the appropriateness of the terms already mentioned: homage, nostalgia, neoclassicism, historicism, and so on. But for other, presumably inferior composers, musicologists are likely to legitimize such disparagement by invoking the concept of *Trivialmusik* (trivial music).

The traditional approaches to *Trivialmusik* involve entangled issues of aesthetic evaluation, intended audience, genre, music commerce, artistic pretension, class, performance medium, subject, and the deprecation of one music subculture by another.[12] Musical analysis has played only a minor role in discussions of *Trivialmusik*, because it has been found difficult to cite features or procedures that set trivial apart from so-called art music. Both Sousa and Brahms, for instance, wrote antecedent-consequent phrases. Of course, as pointed out elsewhere in this study, distinctions made on the basis of a single musical feature may not be very discriminating. Subtler discriminations require a knowledge of feature complexes which, if common enough, can be termed musical schemata. Let us examine ways in which nineteenth-century art music and *Trivialmusik* may differ in their use of musical schemata.

NOTES ON *TRIVIALMUSIK*

Three nineteenth-century phrases have already been discussed that are unquestionably examples of Romantic art music—from Schumann's "Wehmut," Brahms's B-Minor Intermezzo, and Mahler's Fourth Symphony. In each case the scriptlike schema of the 1–7...4–3 style structure was either merged with or overlaid on a planlike schema: a gap-fill pattern for Schumann and Brahms, and a rising linear pattern for Mahler. Partly as a result of this integration, the composers were able to deflect, delay, or attenuate the strong closure of the terminal schema event (4–3).

How different is the case with the bald script presented by Anton Rubinstein in example 11-43. The melody is prototypical and highly closed; the presence of a tonic pedal (F) in the bass can hardly be said to conceal the obvious conventionality of this structure. At the same time the pretension of profundity exhibited by this phrase—it is preceded by a grandiloquent introduction—is completely at odds with its meager content. Rubinstein's whole concerto is not *Trivialmusik,* but this one phrase probably is (example 11-43).

Edward Garden, writing of a comparable work (Rubinstein's "Ocean" Symphony), said "Good ideas . . . are developed in a trivial manner and . . . reveal his fatal facility as a note spinner."[13] Mozart and Haydn were, to be sure, also note spinners of schematized music. The difference is that by Rubinstein's day the types of schemata favored in art music had changed from stereotyped scripts to generalized plans. Later nineteenth-century composers who continued to write scriptlike musi-

cal schemata risked censure for "conventionality," "banality," "triteness," "triv-
iality," "lack of inspiration," and so on, when in fact the real issue of criticism was
their preferred type of schematization. Thus the wonderful—but scriptlike—*idée
fixe* of Berlioz's *Symphonie fantastique* (see example 11-14) could be criticized by
Fétis as "flat, insipid" and by Schumann as "[not] significant in itself, . . . un-
distinguished." [14] To his credit, however, Schumann discerned that Berlioz's intention
"was not to present a great thought, but rather a persistent, tormenting idea of the
kind that one often cannot get out of one's head for days at a time; and he could not
have succeeded better in depicting something monotonous and maddening." [15]

EXAMPLE 11-43. Rubinstein, Piano Concerto No. 4 in D Minor, Op. 70 (1864),
    ii, Andante, meas. 65–72

Schumann (like Fétis) also recognized the asymmetry and frequent deformations of the *idée fixe*. He made a point of distinguishing Berlioz's deformed schematic melodies from those "of the Italian type, which one knows by heart even
before they have begun." [16] The huge 1–7…4–3 style structures discussed earlier in
this chapter (examples 11-8 through 11-14) may be the sort of predictable scripts

that Schumann had in mind when he referred to the "Italian type." The slur was directed not against Italian composers, but against the type of schematism toward which Italian composers may have been kindly disposed. Certainly the blatant manner in which Donizetti presents the 1–7...4–3 schema in an aria from *Torquato Tasso* (example 11-44) would have been unthinkable for a composer "of the German type" like Schumann.

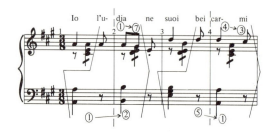

EXAMPLE 11-44. Donizetti, *Torquato Tasso* (1833), meas. 1–4 of the aria "Io l'udia ne suoi bei carmi"

Is Donizetti's phrase then an example of *Trivialmusik?* True, the high typicality of the phrase is, according to the model of chapter 6, anachronistic in 1833; true, there is little to be claimed for the melody other than a knowledge of convention; and true, the accompaniment provides only the default values of harmony, bass, and rhythm. But *Trivialmusik* seems too heavy a charge to lay against such a lighthearted phrase. The deprecation implied by the term *Trivialmusik* would here seem unwarranted and even snobbish.

Hans Dieter Zimmermann has made an interesting critique of the adjective *trivial* as it is applied to literature (*Trivialliteratur*).[17] He argues that the term is ultimately of little use and that the supposed dichotomy between the good and the bad, the high art and the trivial must be abandoned. In its place he establishes a dichotomy based on two traditions of what we expect of a literary creation. In the one tradition, that of "modern literature," we expect each new work to extensively vary or even to transform the schemata it employs. In the other tradition, that of gothic novels, romances, detective stories, westerns, and so on, we expect only a slight variation of schemata. Stated another way, we fully expect the authors to present and respect all the schemata demanded by the particular genre. Because clearly presented schemata are the essence of this second tradition, Zimmermann labels it *Schema-Literatur.*

Could there not also be *Schema-Musik?* Donizetti's phrase, for instance, clearly presents the 1–7...4–3 schema without the pretension characteristic of *Trivialmusik,* without the irony or caricature to be found in some Romantic art music (e.g., Berlioz), and without the air of nostalgia in the neo-Romantic art music of Mahler or

Brahms. The whole tradition of *primo ottocento* opera, in fact, seems a candidate for the appellation *Schema-Musik*. Likewise, the many genres of "light music"— waltzes, operettas, marches, quadrilles, and so on—are characterized by the faithful reproduction of scriptlike musical schemata. The phrase by Jean-Baptiste Arban in example 11-45, for instance, unashamedly and unpretentiously presents a clever 1–7...4–3 style structure no more deserving of the label *trivial* than would be a passage from the detective fiction of Agatha Christie or Dorothy Sayers.

EXAMPLE 11-45. Jean-Baptiste Arban, Fantasie and Variations on "The Carnival of Venice" (1864), piano ritornello [18]

For the first generation of Romantics—Schumann and Berlioz in particular— *Schema-Musik* was a competing, and hence pernicious, product, a "prosaic" rather than "poetic" medium (borrowing Schumann's terms). Later in the century, the art music tradition was so far removed from the tradition of *Schema-Musik* that neither posed any threat to the other. Brahms was not sullied in his friendship with Johann Strauss, Jr., nor was Strauss in any way ennobled by association with Brahms. Only when composers of *Schema-Musik* attempted to produce art music was there serious criticism.

George Bernard Shaw, for example, had a positive loathing for grand opera produced by composers of *Schema-Musik:*

> Nobody except the directors of the Philharmonic Society will claim any higher than fourth place for those who have borrowed both their ideas and their music, and vulgarized both in the process—your Bruchs, Rubin-steins, Moszkowskis, Benoits, [and] Ponchiellis.[19]

His criticism of Ponchielli's *La Gioconda,* though intended to prove how "inorganic" it was, can in fact be reinterpreted as a perceptive evaluation of some salient features of *Schema-Musik:*

If the score were to be lost, and someone . . . had to reconstruct it from the voice parts alone, with the first violin copy thrown in, there is not the slightest reason to suppose that the result would be any worse than the original.[20]

Shaw's antipathy is not toward *Schema-Musik* itself but rather toward its intrusion in a genre reserved for art music. Were this not the case, Shaw wouldn't have expressed admiration for the ballet music in *La Gioconda*. Balletic interludes in grand opera were a traditional preserve of *Schema-Musik,* as can be seen in the well-known phrase in example 11-46.

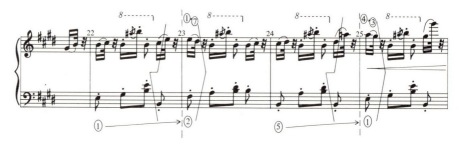

EXAMPLE 11-46. Ponchielli, *La Gioconda* (1876), Theme of the Daylight Hours (meas. 22–25 of Entrance of the Evening Hours), moderato

The fact that such a perceptive critic as Shaw could have praise for a trifle like the *Dance of the Hours* and at the same time excoriate the more substantial *La Gioconda* seems to lend support to the notion of a separate and distinct critical response to *Schema-Musik*. The distinction between the purely scriptlike presentation of 1–7...4–3 style structures in nineteenth-century *Schema-Musik* and the dual script-and-planlike presentation of 1–7...4–3 style structures in nineteenth-century art music also suggests that there may be objectively analyzable characteristics of *Schema-Musik*. In any event, the concept of *Schema-Musik* appears to afford a new and provocative avenue for the analysis and discussion of large segments of nineteenth-century music.

SUMMARY

There is little doubt that the use of the 1–7...4–3 schema was already in sharp decline when the nineteenth century began. Were this study interested solely in tracing a population curve, the nineteenth century could have been accommodated by a mere footnote appended to the discussion of the eighteenth century. But this is not the case. The scattered examples of 1–7...4–3 style structures in the nineteenth century are, in fact, quite revealing of important aspects of Romantic musical style.

In the earlier part of the century one can detect two very different trends. On the one hand, German and Austrian composers attacked the strong closure of the 1–7...4–3 schema by employing various deformations or mutations of the form: the x̄ 1–7̄...4̄–3 pattern, the "Wanderer" pattern, and harmonic deflections of the cadence. On the other hand, composers more allied with the Franco-Italian school left the form of the 1–7...4–3 style structure intact and concentrated on aggrandizing and lengthening its conformant phrase halves. By the 1840s both trends had resulted in the general extinction of the 1–7...4–3 schema.

The appearance of typical 1–7...4–3 style structures later in the nineteenth century seems to call for special explanation. For Brahms an explanation might be framed in terms of veneration or nostalgia, as it might also be for Mahler (though in Mahler's case there is an admixture of irony). For a less talented composer like Rubinstein, the pretentious use of a scriptlike 1–7...4–3 style structure might suggest the derogatory category of *Trivialmusik*. Within the tradition of art music, historians and critics scarcely recognize a middle ground between "good" (i.e., Brahms) and "bad" (i.e., Rubinstein) uses of traditional eighteenth-century schemata. It may well be that such a middle ground exists outside the art music tradition—in the parallel tradition of *Schema-Musik*. There, in so-called light music, the expectation is not for the transformation of schemata but instead for their faithful reproduction.

CHAPTER 12

Conclusions

In figure 12-1 I have overlaid a normal statistical distribution on the population curve used in this study. As was predicted in chapter 6, the historical outline of the 1–7…4–3 schema approximates a normal distribution. Moreover, the predicted asymmetry due to the effects of memory—more examples to the right of the peak of population than to the left—is also evident.

Before commenting on the significance of figure 12-1, I want to consider the traditional skepticism that accompanies the use of statistics in a humanistic arena. This skepticism toward statistics per se is unwarranted; almost any discussion of style is based on implicit informal statistics. What I have done is to make the counting explicit and open to empirical verification. The broad outline of the population curve of the 1–7…4–3 schema is patent and unequivocal. The number of examples from the 1770s is nearly double that of the 1760s or 1780s, and the number of examples from those two decades is nearly half again as large as that of the 1750s or 1790s. Furthermore, the bald population statistics can be interpreted in relation to a specific theoretical prediction—a modified normal distribution.

This last point bears on the question of what constitutes an adequate sample. There is, of course, no hope of canvassing every composition or even every tenth composition. A survey of ten thousand pieces would still be but a minute sample of a century or more of music. Thus the ability to interpret a limited sample is crucial. In figure 12-1 two samples are graphed. The solid line represents all the musical examples counted for this study, while the dotted line represents an earlier stage of this same sample—only symphonies by Mozart and Haydn. At points A and B on the smaller sample there are sharp dips in population not predicted by my theory. These anomalies place the reliability of both the theory and the sample in question. If the theory is nonetheless correct, enlarging the sample ought to make it more representative and hence more like the normal distribution. As is shown by the solid line in figure 12-1, the larger sample does in fact temper these two dips in population. Thus it appears that the larger sample is adequate in the sense that further sampling should

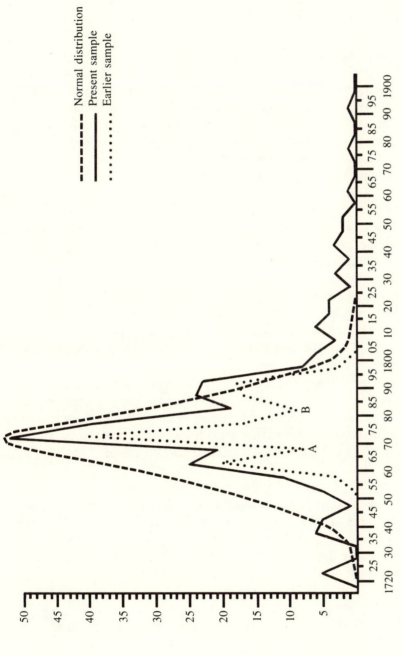

FIGURE 12-1. Population of 1–7...4–3 style structures, 1720–1900

only bring the population curve closer to its predicted shape. Clearly such an interpretation is possible only with a theory to guide it.

The real significance of figure 12-1 lies in its coordination of theories of musical structure with theories of musical history. This coordination is possible because the several attendant concepts of schemata—features, events, typicality, fuzzy categories, pattern networks, prototypes, central tendencies, default values, scripts, and plans—address with equal applicability the stability and instability of musical structure. In other words, the theoretical definitions of musical structure are not, as is sometimes the case, formulated in such a way as to preclude the possibility of fundamental structural changes. So figure 12-1 represents both a static figure (a stable musical category) and a trajectory of changing realizations.

The predictions of chapter 6 concerned not only the quantitative profile confirmed in figure 12-1 but also the qualitative changes confirmed in the preceding five chapters. The schema prototype was, generally speaking, found at the peak of population in the early 1770s, while progressively more atypical examples were found before or after that peak. In fact, the typicality of the examples in this study follows the population curve more closely than I had assumed possible when I first thought about such a relationship. There is little change, for instance, in the typicality of the few idiosyncratic examples from the 1720s through the 1740s. Then, as the population skyrockets, very characteristic examples suddenly emerge, which by the 1760s begin to approach the schema prototype. Following the population peak, there occurs a precipitous increase in the complexity of 1–7...4–3 style structures that neatly conforms to their sharp drop in population. By the early nineteenth century, many examples are already characterized by deformations or transformations that make this closed form more open-ended and processive. The few nineteenth-century examples that are, unexpectedly, highly typical of the 1–7...4–3 schema appear to be used either as a sign of the musical past, for nostalgic or ironic effect, or more naively as part of a fixed tradition of *Schema-Musik*—the music of ballets, waltzes, marches, and salons.

As perhaps the first comprehensive investigation of a mid-level musical schema, this study can be taken as a realization of the intimations, suggestions, and hypotheses of several scholars. The derivation of my work from concepts of Narmour and Meyer has, of course, already been discussed in chapter 3. Other scholars also warrant mention because they demonstrate a growing recognition of the concepts and problems considered here.

A pioneer of musical schema research was the late Charles Cudworth, whose 1949 article "Cadence galante: The Story of a Cliché"[1] prefigures my own work in several respects. His willingness to view a complex musical pattern as an element of history rather than as simply, for instance, a harmonic progression is perceptive, and his recognition that certain late instances of a schema may become "symbol[s] of something ludicrously old-fashioned" shows his sensitivity to the role of schema history in critical analysis. To be sure, he expressed his history of a schema through an organic metaphor rather than in the psychological terms of the present study:

From its obscure birth, probably in some Italian opera-house, it had grown into universal favor, only to die of old age an out-of-date mannerism fit only for derision, passing away with the *galant* period from which it can take its name.[2]

But for Cudworth, this was no more than metaphor; his actual arguments present change as a result of whim, fashion, style, and "human invention."

In more recent times, there are indications that elements of schema theory are becoming accepted as central to many of the questions of musical structure. Leonard Ratner, in his summa *Classic Music*, proposes that eighteenth-century melodies be interpreted as elaborations of "basic structural melodies":

Basic structural melodies are relatively few, simple, and neutral in expressive quality. Elaborations are uncountable and embody topic, affect, and expressive nuance; they also contribute to periodicity as they create tensions against structural tones.[3]

The sample melodic analyses given by Ratner reveal that he has a firm conception of complex harmonic/rhythmic/melodic schemata, even though the "basic structural melodies" he cites might more accurately be referred to as melodic style forms in the restricted contexts of certain style structures. Elements of schema theory are also evident in various updated formulations of Schenkerian analysis. Schenker's universal *Ursatz* is now frequently rationalized as a high-level schema whose plan-like specifications make it well adapted to represent several nineteenth-century musical structures.

Among less conservative analysts, the sense that musical schemata are of signal importance and pose a serious challenge to past analytical systems is more clearly articulated. As Wayne Slawson puts it in a critical review of Meyer's archetypes, "These concepts seem to be intended as alternative formulations to the hierarchical structures postulated by Schenker."[4] Similarly, even in rejecting traditional schemata as elements in their analytical system, Lerdahl and Jackendoff affirm that "the study of archetypal patterns is a matter of serious interest. All experienced listeners intuitively apprehend a phrase, for example, as relatively normal or unusual."[5] Schema theory, as was of course mentioned in chapter 1, already has an established and growing presence in the psychology of music. Both of the most recent books on music cognition treat the subject of musical schemata from several perspectives.[6]

The scholar who has most clearly adumbrated my own research is James R. Meehan. As early as 1979 he concluded (as I did independently in 1982) that an analysis of music restricted to tree-structures of pitches might constitute a methodological dead end, and that an alliance of Narmour's structural categories with the concepts of "natural language processing" in computer science, especially Schank and Abelson's various types of schemata (i.e., scripts and plans), offers a more fruitful avenue for further research. In his "An Artificial Intelligence Approach to Tonal Music Theory,"[7] no analyses are presented, nor are the details of his proposals made explicit. I suspect also that he may not realize the various distinctions among Narmour's categories—there is no mention of style structures or idiostructures, only of style forms. Nevertheless, his trenchant outline of why music theory should move away from outdated models derived from linguistics and toward the more sophisticated and flexible models of current cognitive psychology and artificial intelligence is persuasive. His concluding remark that "what music theory lacks is not the concept of expectations or semantic primitives, but rather the organization and detailed specification of such concepts, which would lead to higher-level information structures and reasonable process models for analysis and composition," calls for the very type of in-depth research provided in the present study.

As a contribution to music theory, the present work offers an alternative to the tree-structures that dominate contemporary analysis. Flexible network representations of diverse musical patterns allow the richness and subtlety of musical phrases to be better apprehended, while indications of schema boundaries and events provide simple mid-level parsings. Since I assume that the comprehension of music requires a mix of bottom-up feature recognition and top-down pattern matching, I have made my analytical apparatus, with its dichotomy between higher-level schemata and lower-level features, reflect such a strategy. This approach leads to a more fluid, less systematized view of structural hierarchy in music, a clearer recognition of how analysis can balance its determination of what is normal and what is abnormal, and a realization that since schemata are the products of experience (hence subject to great change over the centuries), theorists must take a new look at music history.

As a contribution to music history, this study opens up two new areas. The first and most obvious is the history of specific phrase types. Just as much can be learned of a composer's style through the way he handles a high-level schema, such as sonata form, so can much be learned from the way he treats a mid-level schema like the 1–7...4–3 style structure. I do not claim to have discovered the phrase as an object of study—eighteenth-century writers themselves discussed musical phrases. But my research establishes an agenda for the study of the phrase that looks beyond the single considerations of size, harmony, form, or melodic contour toward an integrated definition of what constitutes a phrase type.

The second new area of study might be called the history of musical schematization—that is, the study of what types of schemata composers used in a particular musical period, where their schemata came from, and which schemata survived into the next period. I am not proposing merely a catalogue of clichés and mannerisms, but rather a consideration of the psychological differentiations among various types of schemata. For example, purely in terms of schemata the claim can be made that while eighteenth-century composers preferred conventional scripts, nineteenth-century composers favored more open-ended plans. No doubt this dichotomy is an oversimplification, yet it could nonetheless provide a point of departure for specific comparisons with the histories of schemata in the other arts (e.g., narrative arche-types in literature, or visual schemata in painting).

As a final point I want to suggest that the careful study of Classic schemata can result in an analytical description of eighteenth-century music that may qualify as a "music-producing model," [8] to use Jeff Titon's term. Titon argues that while any analysis is concerned with enumerating and classifying the individual elements of a music, a production model must go further and provide "a set of instructions for their use." In this study a large set of instructions has been advanced for how to combine the 1–7...4–3 schema with other patterns. Following these instructions, one can in fact produce representative passages of eighteenth-century music. The results are by definition conventional, but then most eighteenth-century music was written not by geniuses but by musical tailors—men who stitched and sewed to-gether swatches woven by others.

Perhaps an example is in order. Imagine a young eighteenth-century composer who needs to produce eight stable measures of music to place within a minuet trio. His first task would be to decide which eight-measure schema to use. Let us assume he selects the initial-schema → ascending-process(es) → closing-schema pattern discussed in chapter 9, assigns the 1–7...4–3 schema to the first four measures, and then assigns a long version of Cudworth's "cadence galante" to the last four mea-sures. If he were satisfied with the default values of these schemata, then his produc-tion would closely resemble what the fifteen-year-old Mozart produced for the trio of his Symphony KV 114 (example 12-1). If, on the other hand, he wished to incor-porate a richer network of patterns, then a process of matching and adjustment must ensue. Let us say he wanted to include the high-② leap, a melodic 5–4–3 descent, the sequential 1–7...4–3...♭7–6 melodic/harmonic process, and a small gap-fill plan. Given his rather specific knowledge of how these patterns combine—his "set of instructions for their use"—he would probably decide on a network like that shown in example 12-2.

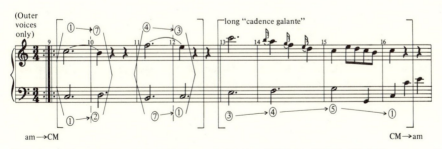

EXAMPLE 12-1. Mozart, Symphony in A Major, KV 114 (1771), iii, Trio, meas. 9–16

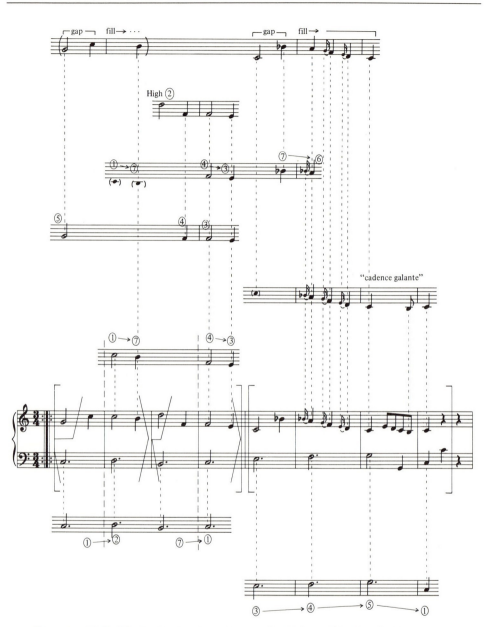

EXAMPLE 12-2. The basic structure of example 12-1 modified by the incorporation of a network of additional patterns

Like an apprentice tailor, our composer has now stitched together a serviceable frock. It lacks rhythmic decoration, of course, and shows no flair for fashion, but the basic design is solid, and the craftsmanship well in hand. How an eighteenth-century master tailor like Franz Schneider might finish it off is shown in example 12-3.

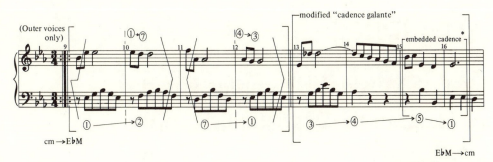

* The embedded two-measure cadence cannily delays the melody's downbeat tonic until the final measure.

EXAMPLE 12-3. Franz Schneider, Symphony in C Major, Freeman d514 (also attributed to Haydn, Hob. I:C11) (before 1777), iii, Trio, meas. 9–16

The conventions of eighteenth-century music ultimately reside in the minds of listeners. While those conventions we fail to recognize cease to exist in any meaningful way, those we can recognize unlock for us experiences shared by generations of musicians and their audiences. If this recognition and sharing of experience can be deepened through the study of musical schemata, then we should be willing to accept all the uncertainties inherent in the study of cognition. We should concern ourselves less with systematizing the elements of music and take a closer look at what the elements of music might be.

APPENDIX

List of Musical Examples Cited or Used in the Statistical Sample

All of the musical phrases listed in this appendix fall into one or more of the following three categories:

1. 1–7...4–3 style structures counted for the statistics of this study. These are indicated by asterisks (*) preceding the entries.
2. 1–7...4–3 style structures presented as examples in the text. These are indicated by small circles (°).
3. Other types of musical phrases used as examples in the text.

The number of a musical example in the text is given in brackets following entries in the second and third categories.

Entries in the first category are here given specific, single-year dates, even when the exact year of a composition's origin is unknown. For example, a composition believed to come from the period 1765–1769 is dated simply as 1767—the mid-point of its presumed time frame. This is done merely to simplify computing the population statistics and in no way represents a "dating" of works in the full sense of the word. Properly circumscribed dates are given in the text for those 1–7...4–3 style structures presented only as musical examples.

The following abbreviations are used in this appendix:

Brook   Brook, Barry S. *La symphonie française dans la seconde moitié du XVIIIe siècle*. 3 vols. Paris: Publications de l'institut de musicologie de l'université de Paris, 1962.

Brown	Brown, A. Peter. *Carlo d'Ordonez (1734–1786): A Thematic Catalogue*. Detroit: Detroit Studies in Music Bibliography, 1978.
Bryan	Bryan, Paul R. *The Symphonies of Johann Vanhal*. Ph.D. dissertation, University of Michigan, 1955.
DDT	Mayer-Reinach, Albert, ed. *Montezuma*. Denkmäler Deutscher Tonkunst. Herausgegeben von der Musikgeschichtlichen Kommission. Leipzig: Breitkopf & Härtel, 1892–1931.
DTÖ	Horwitz, Karl, and Karl Riedel, eds. *Wiener Instrumentalmusik vor und um 1750, I*. Denkmäler der Tonkunst in Österreich, edited by Guido Adler, vol. 31 (Jahrgang 15,2). Vienna: Artaria, 1894–.
Freeman	Freeman, Robert N. *Franz Schneider (1737–1812): A Thematic Catalogue of His Works*. New York: Pendragon, 1979.
G	Gérard, Yves. *Thematic, Bibliographical, and Critical Catalogue of the Works of Luigi Boccherini*. London: Oxford University Press, 1969.
Hill	Hill, George R. *A Thematic Catalog of the Instrumental Music of Florian Leopold Gassmann*. Hackensack, N.J.: Joseph Boonin, 1976.
Hort. mus.	*Hortus musicus*. Kassel: Barenreiter, 1936–.
It. Op.	Lampugnani, Giovanni Battista, *L'amor contadino*. Italian Opera 1640–1770, selected and arranged by Howard Mayer Brown. New York: Garland Publishing, 1978.
Jenkins/Churgin	Jenkins, Newell, and Bathia Churgin. *Thematic Catalogue of the Works of Giovanni Battista Sammartini*. Cambridge: Harvard University Press, 1976.
Krebs	Krebs, Carl. *Dittersdorfiana*. Berlin: Gebrüder Paetel, 1900.
MAB	*Musica antiqua bohemica*. Prague.
Murray	Murray, Sterling E., ed. *Seven Symphonies from the Court of Oettingen-Wallerstein, 1773–1795*. The Symphony, 1720–1840, series C, vol. 6. New York: Garland Publishing, 1981.
Strohm	Strohm, Reinhard, *Italienische Opernarien des frühen Settecento (1720–1730)*. Cologne: Arno Volk Verlag, 1976.
Wq	Wotquenne, Alfred. *Thematisches Verzeichnis der Werke von Carl Philipp Emanuel Bach*. Leipzig: Brcitkopf & Härtel, 1905.
WV	Scholz-Michelitsch, H. *Das Orchester- und Kammermusikwerk von G. C. Wagenseil: thematischer Katalog*. Vienna, 1972.

* Albrechtsberger, Johann Georg, Symphony in D Major (1770), i, meas. 13–15
———, Symphony in D Major (1770), iii, meas. 1–3 [fig. 3-9]
° Arban, Jean-Baptiste, Fantasie and Variations on "The Carnival of Venice" (1864), piano ritornello [11-45]
* Bach, Carl Philipp Emanuel, 3d Orchestral Symphony in F Major, Wq 183 (1776), i, meas. 28–29
* ———, 3d Orchestral Symphony in F Major, Wq 183 (1776), i, meas. 38–39
* ———, 3d Orchestral Symphony in F Major, Wq 183 (1776), i, meas. 74–75
* ———, 3d Orchestral Symphony in F Major, Wq 183 (1776), iii, meas. 60–63
* Bach, Johann Christian, Symphony in G Minor, Op. 6, No. 6 (1770), i, meas. 33–34
Bach, Johann Sebastian, *The Well-Tempered Clavier,* Book I, Prelude No. 8 in E♭ Minor (1722), meas. 1–4 [7-23]
———, *The Well-Tempered Clavier,* Book I, Prelude No. 13 in F♯ Major (1722), meas. 21–24 [7-27]
° ———, *The Well-Tempered Clavier,* Book II, Prelude No. 7 in E♭ Major (?1744), meas. 1–4 [7-31]
———, *The Well-Tempered Clavier,* Book II, Prelude No. 7 in E♭ Major (?1744), meas. 57–65 [7-32]
° ———, *The Well-Tempered Clavier,* Book II, Fugue No. 12 in F Minor (?1744), meas. 1–4 [7-29]
* Barthélemon, François-Hippolyte, Symphony in D Major, Op. 3, No. 2, Brook II, p. 58 (1774), i, meas. 2–4
* ———, Symphony in F Minor, Op. 3, No. 5, Brook II, p. 58 (1775), i, meas. 1–3
* Beecke, Ignaz (Franz) von, Symphony in C Minor, Murray Cm1 (1795), i, meas. 34–36
°* ———, Symphony in C Minor, Murray Cm1 (1795), ii, Siciliana, meas. 1–2 [11-1]
* Beethoven, Ludwig van, Symphony No. 1 in C Major, Op. 21 (1800), ii, meas. 8–11
* ———, Symphony No. 2 in D Major, Op. 36 (1801), i, meas. 12–14
°* ———, Symphony No. 6 in F Major, Op. 68, "Pastorale" (1808), iii, meas. 181–84 [11-18]
———, Symphony No. 6 in F Major, Op. 68, "Pastorale" (1808), iv, meas. 21–29 [11-25]
°* ———, Symphony No. 7 in A Major, Op. 92 (1812), i, meas. 201–12 [11-26]
°* ———, Symphony No. 8 in F Major, Op. 93 (1812), i, meas. 1–8 [11-36]
°* ———, Piano Concerto No. 5 in E♭ Major, "Emperor," Op. 73 (1809), ii, meas. 16–20 [11-22]
°* ———, String Quartet in C♯ Minor, Op. 131, No. 4 (1826), iv, meas. 1–4 [11-40]
° ———, String Quartet in A Minor, Op. 132 (1825), i, meas. 13–20 [11-39]

Beethoven, Ludwig van (*continued*), Piano Sonata in F Major, Op. 10, No. 2 (1796–97), i, meas. 19–26 [5-9]

° ———, Piano Sonata in D Major, Op. 10, No. 3 (1797–98), iii, Trio, meas. 1–8 [5-23]

———, Piano Sonata in D Major, Op. 10, No. 3 (1797–98), iv, meas. 35–37 [1-1, 5-37]

° ———, Piano Sonata in E♭ Major, Op. 27, No. 1 (1800–1801), i, meas. 37–40 [5-30]

° ———, Piano Sonata in E♭ Major, Op. 27, No. 1 (1800–1801), ii, meas. 9–12 [5-40]

———, Piano Sonata in C♯ Minor, "Moonlight," Op. 27, No. 2 (1801), ii, meas. 1–8 [5-19]

° ———, Piano Sonata in D Major, "Pastoral," Op. 28 (1801), i, meas. 138–40 [5-5a]

° ———, Piano Sonata in D Minor, "Tempest," Op. 31, No. 2 (1802), ii, meas. 1–5 [5-33a]

° ———, Piano Sonata in E♭ Major, Op. 31, No. 3 (1802), iii, meas. 1–4 [5-13]

° ———, Piano Sonata in C Major, "Waldstein," Op. 53 (1803–04), iii, meas. 14 [5-26]

———, Piano Sonata in E♭ Major, "Lebewohl," Op. 81a (1809–10), iii, meas. 53–54 [5-35]

———, Piano Sonata in E Minor, Op. 90 (1814), ii, meas. 9–10 [5-38]

° ———, Piano Sonata in C Minor, Op. 111 (1821–22), i, meas. 50–54 [5-12, 11-37a]

°* Benda, Georg (Anton), Symphony in F Major, MAB No. 4 (1760), i, meas. 9–10 [11-6]

°* Berlioz, Hector, *Symphonie fantastique*, Op. 14 (1830), i, meas. 72–86 [11-14]

°* Berwald, Franz, *Estrella de Soria* (1841), Polonaise, 2d theme (transcribed from Nonesuch H71218) [11-31b]

°* Boccherini, Luigi, Symphony in D Major, Op. 42, G520 (1789), i, meas. 1–4 [10-12, 11-37b]

* Boyce, William, Symphony No. 2 in A Major (1760), i, meas. 45–47

Brahms, Johannes, Symphony No. 1 in C Minor, Op. 68 (1876), iii, meas. 1–9 [fig. 3-7]

°* ———, Intermezzo in B Minor, Op. 119, No. 1 (1892), meas. 24–31 [11-35b]

°* Bréval, Jean-Baptiste Sébastien, Symphonie concertante in F Major, Op. 38, Brook III, p. 188 (1795), i, meas. 142–45 [11-7]

———, Symphonie concertante in F Major, Op. 38, Brook III, p. 208 (?1795), ii, meas. 54–57 [10-45]

———, Symphonie concertante in F Major, Op. 38 (?1795), iii, Rondeau, meas. 73–77 [2-n.18]

* ———, Symphonie concertante in F Major, Brook III, p. 215 (1795), iii, Rondeau, meas. 328–49

°* Cambini, Giuseppe Maria, Symphonie concertante No. 6 in F Major, Brook II, p. 144 (1776), i, meas. 1–4 [8-20b]

* ———, Symphonie concertante in C Major, Brook II, p. 161 (1780), i, meas. 1–4

°* ———, Symphony in D Major, Op. 5, No. 1 (1776), ii, meas. 17–20 [9-58, 9-60]

°* Cardon, Jean-Guillain (le père), Symphony in B♭ Major, Op. 10, No. 2, Brook II, p. 177 (1772), i, meas. 1–4 [9-23]

* Cherubini, Luigi, Symphony in D Major (1815), i, meas. 153–54

    ———, Symphony in D Major (1815), iv, meas. 34–40 [11-24]

°* ———, String Quartet in E♭ Major (1814), i, meas. 1–4 [11-19]

° Clementi, Muzio, Piano Sonata, Op. 10, No. 1 (1783), ii, Trio, meas. 1–4 [11-38]

    Corelli, Arcangelo, Trio Sonata, Op. 3, No. 2 (1689), Allegro, meas. 95–96 [7-3]

°* Dittersdorf, Carl Ditters von, Symphony in C Major, Krebs 1 (1766), i, meas. 1–4 [8-16]

°* Donizetti, Gaetano, *Torquato Tasso* (1833), meas. 1–4 of the aria "Io l'udia ne suoi bei carmi" [11-44]

    Dvořák, Antonin, Symphony No. 9 in E Minor, "From the New World," Op. 95 (1893), iv, meas. 10–12 [fig. 3-8]

* Eberl, Anton, Symphony in E♭ Major, Op. 33 (1804), i, meas. 158–59

°* ———, Piano Sextet (Cl. and Hn.), Op. 47 (1800), iii, meas. 1 [11-17]

°* Fiala, Joseph, Symphony in C Major, Murray C1 (1775), ii, meas. 60–65 [11-8]

°* ———, Symphony in C Major, Murray C1 (1775), iv, meas. 31–34 [9-6]

°* ———, Symphony in F Major, Murray F1 (1776), i, meas. 1–2 [9-13]

    Froberger, Johann Jakob, Suite No. 3 for Harpsichord (?1649), Allemande, meas. 6–7 [6-1a, 7-2]

* Gassmann, Florian Leopold, Symphony in C Minor, Hill No. 23 (1765), ii, meas. 14–16

°* ———, Symphony in C Minor, Hill No. 23 (1765), iv, meas. 37–40 [8-20a]

°* ———, Symphony in E♭ Major, Hill No. 26 (1765), i, meas. 19–20 [8-23]

* ———, Symphony in E♭ Major, Hill No. 26 (1765), iv, meas. 33–35

°* ———, Symphony in E♭ Major, Hill No. 85 (1769), iv, meas. 1–2 [8-22]

°* Gossec, François Joseph, Symphony in G Major, Op. 12, No. 2 (1766), ii, meas. 40–44 [8-25]

* ———, Symphony in G Major, Op. 12, No. 2 (1766), ii, meas. 51–54

° Graun, Carl Heinrich, *Montezuma* (1755), Sinfonia, i, meas. 7–9 [8-n.2]

°* ———, *Montezuma* (1755), Sinfonia, i, meas. 44–46 [8-1]

* ———, *Montezuma* (1755), Sinfonia, i, meas. 65–67

* ———, *Montezuma* (1755), Sinfonia, iii, meas. 17–19

    ———, *Montezuma* (1755), Aria di Narvès, DDT, p. 54, meas. 1–3 [8-n.3]

°* ———, *Montezuma* (1755), Aria di Narvès, DDT, p. 54, meas. 8–10 [8-4]

°* ———, *Montezuma* (1755), Aria di Eupaforice, DDT, p. 156, meas. 21–24 [8-6]

°* Graun, Carl Heinrich (*continued*), Trio Sonata in E♭ Major, Hort. mus. 211 (1750), ii, meas. 1–2 [7-17]

°* Haydn, Franz Josef, Mass No. 6, *Missa Cellensis (Mariazellermesse)* (1782), Sanctus, meas. 1–4 [10-2]

°* ———, *Orlando Palladino* (1782), Aria No. 13, Un poco adagio, meas. 1–8 [10-26]

* ———, *Orlando Palladino* (1782), Aria No. 26, Presto, meas. 1–4

°* ———, Symphony B in B♭ Major, Hob. I:108 (1759), ii, meas. 7–8 [8-8]

* ———, Symphony No. 1 in D Major (1759), ii, meas. 1–3

* ———, Symphony No. 3 in G Major (1762), iv, meas. 39–42

* ———, Symphony No. 6 in D Major, "Le matin" (1761), ii, meas. 17–20

* ———, Symphony No. 7 in C Major, "Le midi" (1761), i, meas. 55

°* ———, Symphony No. 7 in C Major, "Le midi" (1761), i, meas. 121–24 [8-11]

* ———, Symphony No. 7 in C Major, "Le midi" (1761), ii, meas. 3

°* ———, Symphony No. 12 in E Major (1763), ii, meas. 1–5 [8-28]

* ———, Symphony No. 12 in E Major (1763), ii, meas. 34–36

* ———, Symphony No. 12 in E Major (1763), iii, meas. 38–39

°* ———, Symphony No. 14 in A Major (1764), iii, Trio, meas. 29–32 [2-23]

°* ———, Symphony No. 15 in D Major (1761), i, meas. 37–38 [8-7a]

* ———, Symphony No. 17 in F Major (1761), iii, meas. 9–12

°* ———, Symphony No. 19 in D Major (1759), i, meas. 42 [8-7b]

* ———, Symphony No. 20 in C Major (1760), ii, meas. 19–22

°* ———, Symphony No. 20 in C Major (1760), iv, meas. 45–48 [8-12]

* ———, Symphony No. 22 in E♭ Major, "The Philosopher" (1764), Alternate ii, meas. 12–14

* ———, Symphony No. 24 in D Major (1764), iv, meas. 21–22

* ———, Symphony No. 25 in C Major (1761), i, meas. 156–57

* ———, Symphony No. 26 in D Minor, "Lamentatione" (1770); ii, meas. 9–11

* ———, Symphony No. 30 in C Major, "Alleluja" (1765), iii, meas. 12–14

°* ———, Symphony No. 31 in D Major, "Hornsignal" (1765), i, meas. 27–28 [8-14]

* ———, Symphony No. 31 in D Major, "Hornsignal" (1765), i, meas. 93–94

°* ———, Symphony No. 31 in D Major, "Hornsignal" (1765), iii, meas. 1–8 [9-34a]

°* ———, Symphony No. 32 in C Major (1760), i, meas. 161–64 [8-13]

°* ———, Symphony No. 32 in C Major (1760), ii, Trio, meas. 1–4 [8-19]

°* ———, Symphony No. 35 in B♭ Major (1767), i, meas. 17–20 [8-15]

* ———, Symphony No. 36 in E♭ Major (1763), iv, meas. 17–18

* ———, Symphony No. 38 in C Major (1769), iv, meas. 43–45

°* ———, Symphony No. 41 in C Major (1770), i, meas. 1–8 [9-34b]

°* ———, Symphony No. 42 in D Major (1771), i, meas. 9–12 [9-33]

* ———, Symphony No. 42 in D Major (1771), iii, meas. 41–42

* ———, Symphony No. 42 in D Major (1771), iv, meas. 65–75

°* ———, Symphony No. 43 in E♭ Major, "Mercury" (1772), i, meas. 1–4 [9-37]

* Haydn, Franz Josef (*continued*), Symphony No. 43 in E♭ Major, "Mercury" (1772), iv, meas. 1–5

* ———, Symphony No. 44 in E Minor, "Trauersinfonie" (1772), i, meas. 5–8

°* ———, Symphony No. 45 in F♯ Minor, "Farewell" (1772), ii, meas. 21–24 [9-7]

°* ———, Symphony No. 45 in F♯ Minor, "Farewell" (1772), iii, Trio, meas. 65–68 [9-9]

* ———, Symphony No. 45 in F♯ Minor, "Farewell" (1772), iv, meas. 2–3

* ———, Symphony No. 51 in B♭ Major (1774), ii, meas. 5–7

* ———, Symphony No. 51 in B♭ Major (1774), iv, meas. 13–15

* ———, Symphony No. 51 in B♭ Major (1774), iv, meas. 17–20

* ———, Symphony No. 51 in B♭ Major (1774), iv, meas. 33–37

°* ———, Symphony No. 53 in D Major, "Imperial" (1778), iv (version B), meas. 42–45 [9-38]

°* ———, Symphony No. 54 in G Major (1774), i, meas. 21–24 [9-40]

* ———, Symphony No. 54 in G Major (1774), ii, meas. 27–28

* ———, Symphony No. 56 in C Major (1774), i, meas. 53–56

* ———, Symphony No. 60 in C Major, "Il distratto" (1774), v, meas. 1–4

* ———, Symphony No. 61 in D Major (1776), ii, meas. 1–2

* ———, Symphony No. 61 in D Major (1776), ii, meas. 100–104

* ———, Symphony No. 61 in D Major (1776), iii, meas. 1–5

* ———, Symphony No. 61 in D Major (1776), iv, meas. 1–3

* ———, Symphony No. 63 in C Major, "La Roxelane" (1779), iv (version 1), meas. 94–97

°* ———, Symphony No. 69 in C Major, "Laudon" (1776), iv, meas. 27–30 [2-16, 9-26]

°* ———, Symphony No. 71 in B♭ Major (1779), iv, meas. 11–14 [9-41]

* ———, Symphony No. 72 in D Major (1764), ii, meas. 1

°* ———, Symphony No. 73 in D Major, "La chasse" (1781), i, meas. 29–30 [10-13]

°* ———, Symphony No. 74 in E♭ Major (1780), iii, meas. 2–3 [10-6]

°* ———, Symphony No. 75 in D Major (1779), i, meas. 1–6 [10-23]

* ———, Symphony No. 76 in E♭ Major (1782), ii, meas. 81–84

* ———, Symphony No. 80 in D Minor (1784), iv, meas. 111–17

°* ———, Symphony No. 81 in G Major (1784), i, meas. 28–31 [10-19, 11-42b]

* ———, Symphony No. 84 in E♭ Major (1786), iv, meas. 120–23

°* ———, Symphony No. 85 in B♭ Major, "La reine" (1785), iv, meas. 9–10 [10-9]

°* ———, Symphony No. 85 in B♭ Major, "La reine" (1785), iv, meas. 25–28 [10-10]

* ———, Symphony No. 87 in A Major (1785), iv, meas. 28–31

°* ———, Symphony No. 88 in G Major (1787), ii, meas. 1–4 [10-28]

* ———, Symphony No. 88 in G Major (1787), iv, meas. 37–38

°* ———, Symphony No. 89 in F Major (1787), i, meas. 15–16 [10-11a]

———, Symphony No. 90 in C Major (1788), iv, meas. 54–56

°* Haydn, Franz Josef (*continued*), Symphony No. 93 in D Major (1791), i, meas. 120–22 [10-8]

°* ———, Symphony No. 94 in G Major, "The Surprise" (1791), iii, meas. 1–8 [10-24a]

* ———, Symphony No. 94 in G Major, "The Surprise" (1791), iv, meas. 45–46

* ———, Symphony No. 95 in C Minor (1791), i, meas. 6–9

* ———, Symphony No. 95 in C Minor (1791), ii, meas. 8–9

* ———, Symphony No. 96 in D Major, "The Miracle" (1791), i, meas. 14–18

°* ———, Symphony No. 96 in D Major, "The Miracle" (1791), ii, meas. 2–3 [10-20]

°* ———, Symphony No. 97 in C Major (1792), iv, meas. 3–4 [10-25a]

* ———, Symphony No. 98 in B♭ Major (1792), i, meas. 109–12

°* ———, Symphony No. 98 in B♭ Major (1792), iv, meas. 45–48 [10-14]

* ———, Symphony No. 99 in E♭ Major (1793), i, meas. 3

°* ———, Symphony No. 99 in E♭ Major (1793), iii, meas. 1–8 [10-15]

* ———, Symphony No. 99 in E♭ Major (1793), iv, meas. 173–76

°* ———, Symphony No. 100 in G Major, "Military" (1794), iv, meas. 125–28 [10-29]

* ———, Symphony No. 101 in D Major, "The Clock" (1794), i, meas. 27–28

°* ———, Symphony No. 101 in D Major, "The Clock" (1794), i, meas. 81–84 [10-n.1]

* ———, Symphony No. 102 in B♭ Major (1794), i, meas. 43–44

* ———, Symphony No. 102 in B♭ Major (1794), iv, meas. 71–72

°* ———, Symphony No. 103 in E♭ Major, "Drumroll" (1795), ii, meas. 117–18 [11-3]

°* ———, Symphony No. 103 in E♭ Major, "Drumroll" (1795), iv, meas. 18–20 [11-4]

°* ———, Symphony No. 104 in D Major, "London" (1795), ii, meas. 42–45 [11-5]

°* ———, Overture in D Major, Hob. Ia:4 (1783), i, meas. 1–4 [5-21]

* ———, Violin Concerto in C Major, Hob. VIIa:1 (1765), i, meas. 3–4

* ———, Violin Concerto in C Major, Hob. VIIa:1 (1765), iii, meas. 29–31

* ———, Violin Concerto in C Major, Hob. VIIa:1 (1765), iii, meas. 204–7

* ———, Violoncello Concerto No. 1 in C Major, Hob. VIIb:1 (1763), i, meas. 1

* ———, Violoncello Concerto No. 1 in C Major, Hob. VIIb:1 (1763), i, meas. 27–28

°* ———, String Quartet in E♭ Major, Op. 33, No. 2 (1781), iii, meas. 21–24 [9-15]

° ———, String Quartet in B♭ Major, Op. 55, No. 3 (1789), i, meas. 1–4 [11-16]

* ———, String Quartet in G Major, Op. 64, No. 4, Hob. III:66 (1790), i, meas. 1–3

* ———, Keyboard Trio in F Major, Hob. XV:17 (1790), i, meas. 54–56

° ———, Keyboard Sonata in B♭ Major, Hob. XVI/2 (−?1760), ii, meas. 1–4 [5-15a]

° Haydn, Franz Josef (*continued*), Keyboard Sonata in D Major, Hob. XVI/4 (?c1765), ii, meas. 1–4 [5-11]

° ———(?), Keyboard Sonata in A Major, Hob. XVI/5 (−1763), i, meas. 38–41 [5-4a]

° ———, Keyboard Sonata in C Major, Hob. XVI/21 (−?1765), i, meas. 1–4 [5-31]

° ———, Keyboard Sonata in F Major, Hob. XVI/23 (1773), i, meas. 12–15 [5-6b]

———, Keyboard Sonata in F Major, Hob. XVI/23 (1773), i, meas. 61–64 [5-7]

° ———, Keyboard Sonata in F Major, Hob. XVI/23 (1773), iii, meas. 1–4 [5-3]

° ———, Keyboard Sonata in D Major, Hob. XVI/24 (?1773), ii, meas. 9–12 [5-15b]

° ———, Keyboard Sonata in G Major, Hob. XVI/27 (?1776), ii, meas. 1–2 [5-27]

° ———, Keyboard Sonata in G Major, Hob. XVI/27 (?1776), iii, meas. 1–4, 25–28, 49–52, 81–84, 105–8, 113–16 [5-1]

° ———, Keyboard Sonata in C Major, Hob. XVI/35 (−1780), ii, meas. 1–2 [5-16]

° ———, Keyboard Sonata in C♯ Minor, Hob. XVI/36 (?c1770–75), ii, meas. 17–18 [5-22]

° ———, Keyboard Sonata in D Major, Hob. XVI/37 (−1780), iii, meas. 1–4 [5-2]

———, Keyboard Sonata in E♭ Major, Hob. XVI/38 (−1780), ii, meas. 1–2 [5-8a]

° ———, Keyboard Sonata in E♭ Major, Hob. XVI/38 (−1780), ii, meas. 5–6 [5-8b]

° ———, Keyboard Sonata in G Major, Hob. XVI/39 (−1780), ii, meas. 8–11 [5-15c]

° ———, Keyboard Sonata in B♭ Major, Hob. XVI/41 (−1784), i, meas. 8–11 [5-4b]

° ———, Keyboard Sonata in A♭ Major, Hob. XVI/46 (c1767–70), i, meas. 9–10 [5-6a]

° ———, Keyboard Sonata in E♭ Major, Hob. XVI/49 (1789–90), i, meas. 13–14 [5-25]

° ———, Keyboard Sonata in E♭ Major, Hob. XVI/49 (1789–90), i, meas. 81–84 [5-4c]

———, Keyboard Sonata in E♭ Major, Hob. XVI/49 (1789–90), i, meas. 84–85 [5-36]

———, Keyboard Sonata in E♭ Major, Hob. XVI/52 (1794), ii, meas. 3 [5-34]

° ———, Keyboard Sonata No. 18 in E♭ Major in Wiener Urtext Ed. (?c1764), i, meas. 23–24 [5-5b]

°* Henselt, Adolf, Concerto for Piano in F Minor, Op. 16 (1838), i, meas. 12–14 [11-30a]

* Lampugnani, Giovanni Battista, *L'amor contadino,* It. Op., p. 30, meas. 4–5 (1760), Aria di Clorideo

* Leo, Leonardo, *Lucio Papirio* (1737), Overture, i, meas. 5–6
°* Mahler, Gustav, Symphony No. 4 (1899), iii, meas. 17–21 [11-41]
°* Massonneau, Louis, Symphony in E♭ Major, Op. 3, Book 1 (1792), i, meas. 1–4 [9-16]
°* ———, Symphony in E♭ Major, Op. 3, Book 1 (1792), i, meas. 19–22 [2-24]
°* Méhul, Etienne-Nicolas, Symphony No. 1 in G Minor (1809), i, meas. 1–8 [11-10]
* Mendelssohn, Felix, String Symphony No. 8 in D Major (1822), iv, meas. 25–29
°* ———, String Symphony No. 11 in F Minor (1823), i, meas. 68–76 [11-13]
* ———, String Symphony No. 11 in F Minor (1823), iv, meas. 1–2
°* ———, Octet (1825), iii, meas. 1–9 [11-23]
°* Mercadante, Saverio, Clarinet Concerto in B♭ Major (1819), i, meas. 1–8 [11-12]
* Monn, Matthias Georg, Symphony in D Major, DTÖ (1740), ii, meas. 51–54
°* ———, Symphony in B Major, DTÖ (?1742), ii, meas. 9 [7-19]
* Mozart, Leopold, Symphony in G Major, No. 2, "Sinfonia burlesca" (1753), i, meas. 62–64
°* Mozart, Wolfgang Amadeus, *Don Giovanni* (1787), Act I, No. 12, Aria di Zerlina, "Batti, batti," meas. 1–4 [10-16]
° ———, *Don Giovanni* (1787), Act I, No. 12, Aria di Zerlina, "Batti, batti," meas. 9–12, 45–48 [10-18]
 ———, *Don Giovanni* (1787), Act I, Finale, meas. 218–19 [2-25]
°* ———, *La finta giardiniera*, KV 121 (207a) (1774), Overture, iii, meas. 21–24 [9-3, 9-44]
* ———, Symphony in B♭ Major, KV 22 (1765), ii, meas. 32–35
°* ———, Symphony in F Major, KV 43 (1767), ii, meas. 1–4 [8-18]
* ———, Symphony in C Major, KV 73 (1772), iv, meas. 107–10
* ———, Symphony in D Major, KV 84 (73q) (1770), iii, meas. 159–61
°* ———, Symphony in F Major, KV 112 (1771), iv, meas. 17–20 [10-37]
* ———, Symphony in A Major, KV 114 (1771), i, meas. 48–50
°* ———, Symphony in A Major, KV 114 (1771), iii, Trio, meas. 9–12 [4-11, 5-28, 8-17, 9-1a, 12-1]
* ———, Symphony in A Major, KV 114 (1771), iv, meas. 16–20
°* ———, Symphony in A Major, KV 114 (1771), iv, meas. 82–88 [7-22, 9-36]
°* ———, Symphony in G Major, KV 124 (1772), ii, meas. 11–12 [4-9, 9-5]
 ———, Symphony in G Major, KV 124 (1772), ii, meas. 43–44 [4-10]
 ———, Symphony in C Major, KV 128 (1772), iii, Finale, meas. 12–13 [7-n.3]
°* ———, Symphony in G Major, KV 129 (1772), iii, meas. 46–49 [9-21]
* ———, Symphony in F Major, KV 130 (1772), ii, meas. 5–6
°* ———, Symphony in E♭ Major, KV 132 (1772), ii, meas. 8–9 [9-12]
°* ———, Symphony in A Major, KV 134 (1772), i, meas. 1–4 [9-27a]
°* ———, Symphony in C Major, KV 162 (1773), iii, meas. 7–9 [9-14c]
* ———, Symphony in B♭ Major, KV 182 (173dA) (1773), ii, meas. 28–29
°* ———, Symphony in G Minor, KV 183 (173dB) (1773), i, meas. 29–32 [10-39a]
* ———, Symphony in G Minor, KV 183 (173dB) (1773), ii, meas. 17–18

* Mozart, Wolfgang Amadeus (*continued*), Symphony in E♭ Major, KV 184 (161a) (1773), iii, meas. 3–4

———, Symphony in C Major, KV 200 (189k) (1773), ii, meas. 1–4 [9-55]

°* ———, Symphony in C Major, KV 200 (189k) (1773), ii, meas. 11–14 [9-51]

°* ———, Symphony in A Major, KV 201 (186a) (1774), iv, meas. 1–4 [9-27b, 10-40]

°* ———, Symphony in D Major, KV 202 (186b) (1774), i, meas. 19–20 [9-28a]

* ———, Serenade in D Major, KV 204 (213a) (1775), ii, meas. 23–24

°* ———, Serenade in D Major, KV 204 (213a) (1775), iv, meas. 54–57 [9-28b]

°* ———, Serenade in D Major, "Haffner," KV 250 (248b) (1776), ii, meas. 19–21 [9-14a]

* ———, Symphony in D Major, "Paris," KV 297 (300a) (1778), i, meas. 33–34

* ———, Symphony in B♭ Major, KV 319 (1779), iv, meas. 208–9

°* ———, Serenade in D Major, "Posthorn," KV 320 (1779), i, meas. 46–49 [2-17, 9-29]

° ———, Serenade in D Major, "Posthorn," KV 320 (1779), i, meas. 54–57, 197–200, 205–8 [8-20c, 9-30, 9-31, 9-32, 11-42a]

* ———, Serenade in D Major, "Posthorn," KV 320 (1779), v, meas. 1–4

° ———, Serenade in D Major, "Posthorn," KV 320 (1779), v, meas. 1–6 [9-43]

* ———, Serenade in D Major, "Posthorn," KV 320 (1779), v, meas. 38–39

* ———, Symphony in C Major, KV 338 (1780), ii, meas. 154–56

°* ———, Symphony in D Major, "Haffner," KV 385 (1782), i, meas. 117–21 [10-39b]

°* ———, Symphony in C Major, "Linz," KV 425 (1783), ii, meas. 96 [10-1]

* ———, Symphony in D Major, "Prague," KV 504 (1786), ii, meas. 97–99

* ———, Symphony in D Major, "Prague," KV 504 (1786), iii, meas. 59–60

°* ———, Symphony in E♭ Major, KV 543 (1788), i, meas. 26–33 [10-27]

* ———, Symphony in E♭ Major, KV 543 (1788), i, meas. 84–85

°* ———, Symphony in G Minor, KV 550 (1788), i, meas. 184–91 [10-30]

———, Symphony in G Minor, KV 550 (1788), ii, meas. 20–23 [10-35]

* ———, Symphony in G Minor, KV 550 (1788), ii, meas. 71–72

°* ———, Symphony in G Minor, KV 550 (1788), ii, meas. 86–89 [10-36]

* ———, Symphony in G Minor, KV 550 (1788), iii, meas. 28–31

* ———, Symphony in C Major, "Jupiter," KV 551 (1788), iv, meas. 190–91

°* ———, Piano Concerto in E♭ Major, "Jeunehomme," KV 271 (1777), iii, meas. 237–40 [10-17a]

———, Piano Concerto in A Major, KV 488 (1786), i, meas. 71–72 [10-41]

° ———, String Quartet in G Major, KV 387 (1782), i, meas. 68–72 [5-32]

* ———, Fugue in G Minor, KV 401 (375e) (1782), meas. 1–3

° ———, Keyboard Sonata in F Major, KV A135 (547a) (?1788), i, meas. 17–24 [5-17]

° ———, Keyboard Sonata in G Major, KV 283 (189h) (1775), i, meas. 1–4 [2-9, 2-10, 2-11, 2-14, 4-12, 5-29, 9-22]

° Mozart, Wolfgang Amadeus (*continued*), Keyboard Sonata in C Major, KV 309 (284b) (1777), ii, meas. 33–36, 53–56 [5-14]

° ———, Keyboard Sonata in B♭ Major, KV 333 (315c) (1778), i, meas. 11–14 [4-15]

° ———, Keyboard Sonata in C Minor, KV 457 (1784), iii, meas. 1–4 [4-13]

Müller, A. E. (?), once attributed to Mozart as KV³ 498a (1786), Keyboard Sonata in B♭ Major, iv, meas. 110–13 [5-18]

°* Ordonez, Carlo d', Symphony in C Major, Brown I:C1 (?1753), iii, meas. 8 [7-21]

* ———, Symphony in C Major, Brown I:C1 (?1753), iii, meas. 14–15

* ———, Symphony in C Major, Brown I:C9 (1773), i, meas. 55–58

°* ———, Symphony in C Major, Brown I:C9 (1773), iii, Finale, meas. 101–3 [9-14b]

* ———, Symphony in C Major, Brown I:C14 (1775), i, meas. 21–22

° ———, Symphony in E Major, Brown I:E2 (n.d.), i, meas. 1–4 [9-4]

* ———, Symphony in F Major, Brown I:F11 (1767), ii, meas. 17–18

°* ———, Symphony in F Minor, Brown I:F12(min) (1773), i, meas. 1–6 [10-46]

* ———, Symphony in G Minor, Brown I:G8(min) (1773), i, meas. 1–4

* ———, Symphony in A Major, Brown I:A8 (1765), ii, meas. 1–4

* ———, Symphony in B♭ Major, Brown I:B♭4 (1778), i, meas. 39–40

* ———, Symphony in B♭ Major, Brown I:B♭4 (1778), ii, meas. 9–12

Orlandini, Giuseppe Maria, *Ormisda,* Strohm, ex. 101 (1722), meas. 21–22 [7-4]

° Pleyel, Ignaz, piano arrangement by Hummel (1789) of Benson No. 432, iii, meas. 97–100 [3-4]

°* Pollarolo, Antonio, *Lucio Papirio dittatore,* Strohm, ex. 102 (1721), meas. 50–53 [7-5]

°* Ponchielli, Amilcare, *La Gioconda* (1876), Theme of the Daylight Hours (meas. 22–25 of Entrance of the Evening Hours) [11-46]

Poulenc, Francis, Flute Sonata (1956), i, meas. 5–7 [6-1b]

°* Ragué, Louis-Charles, Symphony in D Minor, Op. 10, No. 1, Brook III, p. 109 (1786), i, meas. 1–6 [10-22]

* ———, Symphony in D Minor, Op. 10, No. 1, Brook III, p. 119 (1786), i, meas. 111–14

°* ———, Symphony in D Minor, Op. 10, No. 1, Brook III, pp. 128–29 (1786), iii, meas. 20–24 [10-44]

°* Rigel, Henri-Joseph, Symphony in D Minor, Op. 21, No. 2, Brook III, p. 86 (1785), i, meas. 1–4 [10-21]

* Rosetti, Antonio, Symphony in D Major, Murray D3 (1788), iv, meas. 44–47

°* ———, Symphony in E♭ Major, Murray E♭1 (1776), i, meas. 1–5 [9-42]

* ———, Symphony in F Major, Murray F1 (1776), i, meas. 44–47

* ———, Symphony in F Major, Murray F1 (1776), i, meas. 73–75

°* Rossini, Gioachino, String Sonata No. 2 in A Major (1804), i, meas. 17–22 [11-9]

*   Rossini, Gioachino (*continued*), String Sonata No. 5 in E♭ Major (1804), i, meas. 131–39

*   Rubinstein, Anton, Piano Concerto No. 4 in D Minor, Op. 70 (1864), ii, meas. 13–16

°   ———, Piano Concerto No. 4 in D Minor, Op. 70 (1864), ii, meas. 65–72 [11-43]

*   Ruge, Filipo, Symphony in D Major, Brook III, p. 42 (1757), i, meas. 83

°*   ———, Symphony in D Major, Brook III, p. 49 (1757), iii, meas. 44–47 [8-27]

*   Saint-Georges, Chevalier de, Symphonie concertante in G Major, Op. 13, Brook III, p. 149 (1782), i, meas. 37–42

*   ———, Symphonie concertante in G Major, Op. 13, Brook III, pp. 151–52 (1782), i, meas. 95–100

°*   Sammartini, Giovanni Battista, Symphony in D Major, Jenkins/Churgin No. 14 (1739), i, meas. 29–36 [7-10]

°*   ———, Symphony in G Major, Jenkins/Churgin No. 39 (1740), i, meas. 4–5 [7-24c]

°*   Scarlatti, Domenico, *Narciso* (1720), Overture, i, meas. 98–100 [7-1]

°*   Schneider, Franz, Symphony in C Major, Freeman d514 (1777) (also attributed to Haydn, Hob. I:C11), iii, Trio, meas. 9–12 [12-3]

°*   Schubert, Franz, Symphony No. 1 in D Major, D82 (1813), i, meas. 1–8 [11-n.2]

    ———, Symphony No. 1 in D Major, D82 (1813), ii, meas. 34–37 [4-n.3]

°*   ———, Symphony No. 5 in B♭ Major, D485 (1816), i, meas. 5–12 [5-20, 11-n.2]

°*   ———, Piano Quintet in A Major, "The Trout," D667 (1819), v, meas. 195–98 [9-17]

°*   ———, Wanderer Fantasy, D760 (1822), meas. 161–65 [11-20a]

°   ———, "Das Wandern," *Die schöne Müllerin,* No. 1 (1823), meas. 5–6 [11-20b]

°*   Schumann, Robert, Symphony No. 1 in B♭ Major, "Spring" (1841), ii, meas. 55–58 [11-34a]

*   ———, Symphony No. 2 in C Major (1845), iv, meas. 221–26

°*   ———, Symphony No. 2 in C Major (1845), iv, meas. 237–41 [11-34b]

°*   ———, Symphony No. 3 in E♭ Major, "Rhenish" (1850), v, meas. 27–30 [11-33]

°*   ———, Symphony No. 3 in E♭ Major, "Rhenish" (1850), v, meas. 47–48 [11-32]

*   ———, Symphony No. 4 in D Minor (1841), iii, meas. 25–28

°   ———, Piano Sonata, Op. 11 (1832–35), Scherzo, meas. 1–8 [5-10]

°   ———, Faschingsschwank aus Wien, No. 1 (1839–40), meas. 1–8 [5-24]

°   ———, *Liederkreis,* Op. 39 (1840), No. 9, "Wehmut," meas. 14–17 [2-12, 2-13, 2-15, 2-19, 11-35a]

    Shostakovich, Dmitri, 24 Preludes and Fugues, Op. 87[1] (1951), Prelude 7, meas. 19 [4-6]

*   Sohier, Charles-Joseph Balthazar (L'Aîné), Symphony in F Minor, Op. 2, No. 6, Brook II, p. 666 (1751), i, meas. 2–3

°* Spohr, Ludwig, Violin Concerto No. 8 in A Minor (1816), i, meas. 1–10 [11-11]

°* Vandenbroeck, Othon-Joseph, Symphony in E♭ Major, Brook II, p. 717 (1795), i, meas. 1–4 [11-2]

°* Vanhal, Johann Baptist, Symphony in C Major, Bryan C9 (1772), i, meas. 1–4 [9-1b]

° ———, Symphony in C Major, Bryan C9 (1772), i, meas. 14–17 [9-2]

°* ———, Symphony in C Major, Bryan C11 (1775), iv, "l'Allegrezza," meas. 1–4 after a minor mode introduction [9-18]

* ———, Symphony in D Minor, Bryan D2 (1777), ii, meas. 45–48

°* ———, Symphony in F Major, Bryan F5 (1771), i, meas. 1–4 [9-24]

* ———, String Quartet No. 3 in C Major, Bryan C1 (1773), i, meas. 20–21

°* ———, String Quartet No. 5 in A Major, Bryan A4 (1784), iv, meas. 1–2 [10-5a, 11-15]

°* ———, String Quartet No. 5 in A Major, Bryan A4 (1784), iv, meas. 80–83 [10-5b]

°* Veracini, Francesco Maria, Violin Sonata, Op. 1 (1721), No. 6, iii, Pastorale, meas. 1–4 [7-7]

°* ———, Violin Sonata, Op. 1 (1721), No. 2, iii, Siciliana, meas. 5–6 [7-24b]

°* ———, Violin Sonata, Op. 1 (1721), No. 4, iv, meas. 2–3 [7-24a]

°* ———, Sonate Accademiche, Op. 2 (1744), No. 3, i, meas. 1–7 [10-43]

* ———, Sonate Accademiche, Op. 2 (1744), No. 3, i, meas. 9–11

* Vogler, (Abbé) Georg Joseph, Piano Concerto in C Major (1778), i, meas. 1–4

* Wagenseil, Georg Christoph, Symphony in D Major, DTÖ (1746), ii, meas. 17–18

* ———, Symphony in E Major, WV 393 (1759), ii, meas. 18–20

° Wagner, Richard, *Die Feen* (1833), Overture, meas. 9–16 after Piu allegro [11-27]

°* ———, Symphony in C Major (1832), ii, meas. 15–17 [11-28]

°* Weber, Carl Maria von, Clarinet Concerto in E♭ Major, Op. 74 (1811), i, meas. 54–58 [11-21]

* ———, Clarinet Concerto in E♭ Major, Op. 74 (1811), i, meas. 137–40

°* Werner, Gregor Joseph, *Symphoniae sex senaeque sonatae* (1735), Symphony No. 2, iii, meas. 1–4 [7-13]

°* ———, *Symphoniae sex senaeque sonatae* (1735), Symphony No. 4, i, meas. 1–4 [7-11]

°* ———, *Symphoniae sex senaeque sonatae* (1735), Symphony No. 5, iii, meas. 1–4 [7-12]

°* ———, *Symphoniae sex senaeque sonatae* (1735), Symphony No. 6, iii, meas. 5–8 [7-16]

NOTES

Preface

1. Fred Lerdahl and Ray Jackendoff, *A Generative Theory of Tonal Music* (Cambridge, Mass.: MIT Press, 1983), pp. 288–89.

Chapter 1: What is a Schema?

1. Ulrich Neisser, *Cognition and Reality: Principles and Implications of Cognitive Psychology* (San Francisco: W. H. Freeman, 1976), p. 54.
2. Frederick C. Bartlett, *Remembering: A Study in Experimental and Social Psychology* (New York: Cambridge University Press, 1932), p. 201.
3. Selby H. Evans, "A Brief Statement of Schema Theory," *Psychonomic Science* 8, no. 2 (1967): 87.
4. Stephen K. Reed, *Psychological Processes in Pattern Recognition* (New York: Academic Press, 1973), p. 26.
5. Joseph P. Becker, "A Model for the Encoding of Experiential Information," in *Computer Models of Thought and Language,* ed. Roger C. Schank and Kenneth Mark Colby (San Francisco: W. H. Freeman, 1973), p. 396.
6. David E. Rumelhart, "Schemata: The Building Blocks of Cognition," in *Theoretical Issues in Reading Comprehension,* ed. Rand J. Spiro, Bertram C. Bruce, and William F. Brewer (Hillsdale, N.J.: Lawrence Erlbaum Associates, 1980), p. 41.
7. Jean Matter Mandler, "Categorical and Schematic Organization in Memory," in *Memory Organization and Structure,* ed. C. Richard Puff (New York: Academic Press, 1979), p. 263. See also Jean Matter Mandler, *Stories, Scripts, and Scenes: Aspects of Schema Theory* (Hillsdale, N.J.: Lawrence Erlbaum Associates, 1984).
8. Rumelhart, "Schemata," pp. 40–41.
9. Eleanor Gibson, *Principles of Perceptual Learning and Development* (New York: Appleton-Century-Crofts, 1969). Reproduced in Reed, *Psychological Processes,* p. 12.
10. See, for example, Carol L. Krumhansl and Mary A. Castellano, "Dynamic Processes in Music Perception," *Memory & Cognition* 11 (1983): 325–34; and Thomas H. Stoffer, "Representation of Phrase Structure in the Perception of Music," *Music Perception* 3 (1985): 191–220.
11. Burton S. Rosner and Leonard B. Meyer, "Melodic Processes and the Perception of Music," in *The Psychology of Music,* ed. Diana Deutsch (New York: Academic Press, 1982), pp. 317–41.
12. Roger C. Schank and Robert P. Abelson, *Scripts, Plans, Goals and Understanding: An Inquiry into Human Knowledge Structures* (Hillsdale, N.J.: Lawrence Erlbaum Associates, 1977).
13. Ibid., p. 41.

14. Ibid., pp. 70, 77, 99.
15. Rosner and Meyer, "Melodic Processes," p. 327.

Chapter 2: A New Look at Musical Structure

1. George Mandler, "Organization, Memory, and Mental Structures," in *Memory Organization and Structure,* ed. C. Richard Puff (New York: Academic Press, 1979), pp. 307–9.
2. Mandler is more conservative than George A. Miller about the number of elements that basic mental structures accommodate. Miller, in his famous article "The Magical Number Seven, Plus or Minus Two: Some Limits on Our Capacity for Processing Information" (*Psychological Review* 63 [1956]: 81–97), held that the brain typically relates five to nine elements in a "chunk," i.e., a mental structure.
3. Michael Friendly, "Methods for Finding Graphic Representations of Associative Memory Structures," in *Memory Organization and Structure,* p. 107.
4. Harold Powers calls this the "fried-egg school of analysis" (a remark made at the 1982 annual convention of the Society for Ethnomusicology).
5. Friendly, "Methods," p. 125.
6. Among humanists, Hegel is frequently the source. For scientists, see Clifford Grobstein, "Hierarchical Order and Neogenesis," pp. 29–47, and Howard H. Pattee, "The Physical Basis and Origin of Hierarchical Control," pp. 71–108, in *Hierarchy Theory: The Challenge of Complex Systems,* ed. Howard H. Pattee (New York: George Braziller, 1973).
7. Mary Louise Serafine, in her article "Cognition in Music" (*Cognition* 14 [1983]: 119–83), even questions whether isolated pitches are the best psychological representation of music at an immediate, low level of structure.
8. Heinrich Schenker, *Free Composition (Der freie Satz),* trans. and ed. Ernst Oster (New York: Longman, 1979), pp. 4–5. *Der freie Satz* first appeared in 1935, the year of Schenker's death.
9. Felix Salzer, *Structural Hearing: Tonal Coherence in Music,* 2 vols. (New York: Dover Publications, 1962), 2: 79.
10. Joel Lester, *Harmony in Tonal Music,* 2 vols. (New York: Alfred A. Knopf, 1982), 1:176.
11. See Leonard B. Meyer, "Exploiting Limits: Creation, Archetypes, and Style Change," *Daedalus* 109, no. 2 (1980): 177–201; and Leonard G. Ratner, *Classic Music: Expression, Form, and Style* (New York: Schirmer Books, 1980).
12. Fred Lerdahl and Ray Jackendoff, "Toward a Formal Theory of Tonal Music," *Journal of Music Theory* 21 (1977): 154–55.
13. Ibid., pp. 155–56.
14. Cf. Joseph Kerman, "How We Got into Analysis, and How to Get Out," *Critical Inquiry* 7 (1980): 311–31.
15. Schank and Abelson, *Scripts, Plans, Goals and Understanding,* p. 41.
16. Ibid., pp. 70, 77, 99.
17. "Gap-fill" is a term used by Leonard Meyer, referring to the scalar filling in of an initial melodic leap. See Leonard B. Meyer, *Explaining Music: Essays and Explorations* (Chicago: University of Chicago Press, 1973), p. 8.
18. "Reversal before closure" is a Meyerian "plan." In the context of a linear descent, Schumann's reversal before closure is very similar to this earlier phrase by J. B. Bréval (Symphonie concertante in F Major, Op. 38 [?1795], iii, Presto, meas. 73–77):

19. Charles L. Cudworth, "Cadence galante: The Story of a Cliché," *The Monthly Musical Record* 79 (1949): 176. Cudworth's work is discussed by Daniel Heartz, s.v. "Galant," in *The New Grove Dictionary of Music and Musicians,* ed. Stanley Sadie (London: Macmillan Publishers, 1980).
20. Heartz, "Galant."

Chapter 3: Style Structures and Musical Archetypes

1. John R. Anderson, *Cognitive Psychology and Its Implications* (San Francisco: W. H. Freeman, 1980), p. 128.
2. In this context, "parametric entities" are musical patterns restricted to one of three dimensions—pitch succession, durational proportion, or harmonic stability.
3. Eugene Narmour, *Beyond Schenkerism: The Need for Alternatives in Music Analysis* (Chicago: University of Chicago Press, 1977), p. 164.
4. See especially chapter 11, "Idiostructure, Style Form, and Style Structure."
5. Narmour, *Beyond Schenkerism,* p. 173.
6. Ibid.
7. Ibid., p. 164.
8. Ibid., p. 174.
9. Ibid.
10. Ibid., pp. 174ff.
11. Ibid., p. 175.
12. Ibid., pp. 173–74.
13. Ibid., p. 164.
14. Ibid., pp. 177ff.
15. Ibid., p. 170. See also Leonard B. Meyer, *Explaining Music: Essays and Explorations* (Chicago: University of Chicago Press, 1973), pp. 6–7.
16. Estimations of the temporal characteristics of short-term memory vary greatly, not only because short-term memory can be defined in many ways but also because individuals have differing abilities. My use of "short-term memory" conforms in most respects to what is termed the "psychological present" in W. Jay Dowling and Dane L. Harwood, *Music Cognition* (Orlando, Fla.: Academic Press, 1986), pp. 179–81.
17. Northrop Frye, *Anatomy of Criticism* (Princeton, N.J.: Princeton University Press, 1957).
18. Meyer, *Explaining Music,* p. 213.
19. Ibid., p. 214.
20. Ibid., pp. 213–14.
21. Ibid., p. 214.
22. Meyer, "Exploiting Limits," p. 204.
23. Rosner and Meyer, "Melodic Processes," p. 318.
24. Meyer, *Explaining Music,* p. 91.
25. Leonard B. Meyer, *Emotion and Meaning in Music* (Chicago: University of Chicago Press, 1956), pp. 85–86.
26. Ibid., p. 93.
27. Ibid., p. 92.
28. Ibid., pp. 85–86.
29. Ibid., p. 125.
30. Meyer, *Explaining Music,* p. 90.
31. Ibid., p. 174.
32. Ibid.
33. Ibid., p. 94. Meyer borrowed the notion of axial melodies from Narmour.
34. Ibid., p. 183.

35. Ibid.
36. Ibid., p. 191.
37. Ibid.
38. Ibid., pp. 213–26.
39. Ibid., p. 213.
40. Meyer, "Exploiting Limits," pp. 180, 201n.
41. Meyer, *Explaining Music,* p. 72.
42. Meyer, "Exploiting Limits," p. 201n.
43. Meyer, *Explaining Music,* p. 191.
44. Ibid., p. 213.
45. Meyer, "Exploiting Limits," p. 182.

Chapter 4: Defining the Changing-Note Archetype

1. For instance, Leonard G. Ratner lists 1–7...4–3 as a "structural melody" in his *Classic Music: Expression, Form, and Style* (New York: Schirmer Books [Macmillan], 1980), p. 89.
2. Meyer, *Explaining Music,* pp. 191–96; idem, "Grammatical Simplicity and Relational Richness: The Trio of Mozart's G Minor Symphony," *Critical Inquiry* 2 (1975): 693–761; idem, "Exploiting Limits," p. 202n; and Rosner and Meyer, "Melodic Processes," p. 325.
3. The 5–4...6–5 pattern is more characteristic of nineteenth- than eighteenth-century phrases. For example this phrase from Schubert's Symphony No. 1 in D Major, D82 (1813), ii, meas. 34–37:

4. Rumelhart, "Schemata," p. 34.
5. Endel Tulving, "Episodic and Semantic Memory," in *Organization of Memory,* ed. Endel Tulving and Wayne Donaldson (New York: Academic Press, 1972), pp. 381–403.
6. Jean M. Mandler, "Categorical and Schematic Organization," pp. 159–99.
7. Janet L. Lachman and Roy Lachman, "Theories of Memory Organization and Human Evolution," in *Memory Organization and Structure,* ed. C. Richard Puff (New York: Academic Press, 1979), p. 163. The authors have redrawn data from Allan M. Collins and Elizabeth F. Loftus, "A Spreading-Activation Theory of Semantic Processing," *Psychological Review* 82 (1975): 407–28.
8. Becker, "Encoding of Experiential Information," p. 410.
9. Ibid.

Chapter 5: Schematic Norms and Variations

1. Narmour's term "style structure" provides a useful alternative to such circumlocutions as "instantiation of a schema" or "actual example of a schematic category."
2. Doubts have been raised as to the authenticity of this piece (see the list of Haydn's works in *The New Grove Dictionary of Music and Musicians,* ed. Stanley Sadie [London: Macmillan Publishers, 1980]). For the present purpose, whether Haydn wrote the piece from which example 5-4a is taken does not really matter, for there is no question that it is indeed a bona fide eighteenth-century composition.
3. Default values are discussed in the first section of chapter 1.

4. In a few instances (e.g., example 5-28) the two schema events *are* the subphrases.

5. Schematic ambiguity may even be the point of this and other deceptively simple phrases by the mature Beethoven.

6. See, for example, chapter 5 of Anderson, *Cognitive Psychology.*

Chapter 6: A Schema Across Time

1. Henri Focillon, *La vie des formes* (Paris: Librairie Ernst Leroux, 1934); English ed., *The Life of Forms in Art,* trans. Charles Beecher Hogan and George Kubler (New Haven: Yale University Press, 1942).

2. The process of abstraction can involve more than averaging. For example, few if any of the round objects encountered in the world are "perfectly" round. Averaging the shapes of hundreds of apples, oranges, or bicycle wheels would not result in an exact circle. Yet the abstraction of *circle* may well be "perfect roundness." One explanation for this might be that innate aspects of human vision constrain and influence the abstraction of visual schemata in such a way as to lead to idealizations such as *circle, straight line,* and so on. It is also possible that auditory proclivities constrain and influence the abstraction of musical schemata. If there exist innate abilities to recognize basic musical forms and processes, then these abilities could be used to "normalize" (not just to average) the central tendencies of a schema. While this is a significant possibility that demands careful study, at present so little is known of what is innate in musical cognition that I have not ventured to assign a historical function to auditory proclivities.

Chapter 7: 1720–1754: Scattered Examples

1. 1720 is the date of the earliest example I have found of the 1–7...4–3 schema in concerted instrumental music; 1754 lies just prior to a sharp increase in the structure's population and typicality curves. In compiling the population statistics used in this study I have adopted the expedient of tallying the examples in five-year blocks, e.g. 1720–24, 1725–29, etc. Thus the date 1754 represents the end of the segment 1750–54.

2. Reinhard Strohm, *Italienische Opernarien des frühen Settecento (1720–1730)* (Cologne: Arno Volk Verlag, 1976).

3. Compare, for example, this excerpt from the Finale of Mozart's Symphony in C Major, KV 128 (1772), iii, meas. 12–13 (not a 1–7...4–3 structure but having a 1–2...7–1 bass).

4. See example 3-4, as well as Meyer, "Exploiting Limits," p. 182.

5. Other inferences are possible: Kirnberger may have been pedantically trying to regularize Bach's counterpoint by resolving the dissonant ④ earlier; nineteenth-century scholars may have then rejected Kirnberger's alteration because they wanted a pure *Urtext* and were only too glad to dismiss the authority of a minor composer who lacked "genius."

6. Meyer notes this theme in "Exploiting Limits," p. 205n.

7. Here "linkage" means only the use of a single connecting element and does not imply the broader *Knüpftechnik* as discussed by Heinrich Schenker, Arnold Schoenberg, and others.

Chapter 8: 1755–1769: Sharp Increases in Population and Typicality

1. "Symphony" is taken in the broadest sense to include overtures, sinfonie concertante, partitas, and those serenades arranged for performance as symphonies.

2. It is interesting to note that this structure is a radically altered version of a high-② complex first heard in the tonic in measures 7–9:

3. This is made clearer after hearing the aria's opening theme:

4. If, as I have suggested, the mental abstraction of a schema from various larger contexts can create a predisposition for composing more autonomous and typical structures, and if creating more typical 1–7…4–3 structures involves avoiding overlapping processes, then it seems probable that, to compensate for the suppression of this "connective tissue," composers needed to develop other means for creating musical continuity. That is, the increasing typicality of mid-level 1–7…4–3 style structures, in conjunction with changes in other mid-level structures, ought to have affected the organization of higher-level structures. In *Montezuma*, Graun was requested by his patron Frederick the Great to use the newer *cabaletta* aria form (a truncation of da capo form) recently introduced by Hasse. I am not suggesting that characteristic 1–7…4–3 style structures *caused* the development of the eighteenth-century *cabaletta*, but I do maintain that major changes in mid-level structures must have had some impact on structures at lower and higher levels.

Chapter 9: 1770–1779: The Peak

1. Anderson, *Cognitive Psychology*, p. 133.
2. *Webster's New World Dictionary*, 2d college ed., s.v. "prototype."
3. Charles Rosen discusses this phrase in *The Classical Style: Haydn, Mozart, Beethoven* (New York: W. W. Norton, 1972), pp. 90–91.
4. The "stretching of intervals" as a distinguishing feature of musical Romanticism has been suggested by Leonard B. Meyer. See his "Music and Ideology in the Nineteenth Century," *The Tanner Lectures on Human Values, Vol. VI: 1985*, ed. Sterling M. McMurrin (Salt Lake City: University of Utah Press, 1985).
5. Meyer discusses similar versions of this larger schema in "Exploiting Limits," p. 187.

Chapter 10: 1780–1794: New Complications

1. Both these added melodies avoid the B♭–A–G beginning of the second half of the "Batti, batti" theme. This descending third is a transposition down one step of the theme's beginning, and as such it forms another instance of the trend toward stepwise transposition of a 1–7…4–3 style structure's

conformant sections. The significance of this trend is that it breaks down one of the distinctions between 1–7...4–3 and 1–7...2–1 schemata. For instance, the following example from Haydn's Symphony No. 101 could just as easily and perhaps more naturally have been a 1–7...2–1 structure ([a] Haydn, Symphony No. 101 in D Major, "The Clock" [1793–94], i, Presto, meas. 81–84; [b] hypothetical 1–7...2–1 structure):

For both the "Batti, batti" theme and the Haydn example just mentioned this stepwise transposition allows an expressive upward leap to be made in the course of the second phrase half. In other words, schematic differentiation and typicality are traded for emotional affect.

2. The appoggiaturas indicated here are part of operatic performance tradition; they are present, for example, in the commercially available recording of this work, Philips 6707 029.

Chapter 11: 1795–1900: A Legacy

1. Meyer, "Exploiting Limits," pp. 190–201.
2. A distinction must be made between Schubert's earlier and later compositions. He did not favor the 1–7...4–3 style structure in his mature works but did employ it in his youth. An example from the "Trout" Quintet has already been cited (see example 9-17). Among still earlier works, the opening Allegro themes of both the First and Fifth Symphonies have 1–7...4–3 structures ([a] Schubert, Symphony No. 1 in D Major [1813], i, Allegro, meas. 1–8; [b] Schubert, Symphony No. 5 in B♭ Major [1816], i, meas. 5–12):

The progress Schubert was making away from highly closed forms is evident in comparing these themes. For example, whereas the First Symphony's theme ends with an authentic cadence, the Fifth Symphony's theme moves to a tonic six-four chord; and whereas the schema dyads in the First Symphony are direct, in the later work they are more indirect and less obvious.

3. Transcribed from a radio broadcast.
4. Transcribed from Nonesuch 71218; the key may be incorrect.
5. Psychologists have borrowed the word rehearsal from the performing arts. In studies of memory this term indicates a prompting or repetition of something to prevent its being forgotten.
6. Rey M. Longyear, *Nineteenth-Century Romanticism in Music* (Englewood Cliffs, N.J.: Prentice-Hall, 1969), p. 26.
7. Thomas Mann, *Doctor Faustus: The Life of the German Composer Adrian Leverkühn as Told by a Friend,* trans. H. T. Lowe-Porter (New York: Alfred A. Knopf, 1948), p. 53.
8. Adapted from Paul Mies, *Beethoven's Sketches: An Analysis of His Style Based on a Study of His Sketch-Books* (London, 1929; reprint ed., New York: Dover Publications, 1974), p. 15.
9. As quoted in Joseph de Marliave, *Beethoven's Quartets* (London, 1928; reprint ed., New York: Dover Publications, 1961), p. 305.
10. Deryck Cooke, *Gustav Mahler: An Introduction to His Music* (London: Cambridge University Press, 1980), p. 69.
11. Alma Mahler (Werfel), *Gustav Mahler: Memories and Letters* (Seattle: University of Washington Press, 1971), p. 24.
12. See, for example, Carl Dahlhaus, ed., *Studien zur Trivialmusik des 19. Jahrhunderts* (Regensburg, 1967); and Helga de la Motte-Haber, ed., *Das Triviale in Literatur, Musik, und bildender Kunst* (Frankfurt am Main, 1972).
13. Edward Garden, s.v. "Rubinstein, Anton," in *The New Grove Dictionary of Music and Musicians,* ed. Stanley Sadie (London: Macmillan Publishers, 1980).
14. As quoted in Edward T. Cone, ed., *Berlioz: Fantastic Symphony* (New York: W. W. Norton, 1971), pp. 219, 237.
15. Ibid., p. 242.
16. Ibid., p. 241.
17. Hans Dieter Zimmermann, *Schema-Literatur: ästhetische Norm und literarisches System* (Stuttgart: W. Kohlhammer, 1979).
18. Transcribed from Nonesuch H-71298.
19. George Bernard Shaw, *Shaw's Music,* vol. 2 (London: The Bodley Head, 1981), p. 441.
20. Ibid., p. 191.

Chapter 12: Conclusions

1. Cudworth, "Cadence galante," pp. 176–78.
2. Ibid., p. 178.
3. Ratner, *Classic Music,* p. 89.
4. Wayne Slawson, review of *The Psychology of Music,* ed. Diana Deutsch, *Music Theory Spectrum* 5 (1983): 124.
5. Lerdahl and Jackendoff, *A Generative Theory,* p. 288.
6. Peter Nowell, Ian Cross, and Robert West, eds., *Musical Structure and Cognition* (London: Academic Press, 1985); and Dowling and Harwood, *Music Cognition.*
7. James R. Meehan, "An Artificial Intelligence Approach to Tonal Music Theory," *Computer Music Journal* 4, no. 2 (1980): 64.
8. Jeff Todd Titon, "Talking about Music: Analysis, Synthesis, and Song-Producing Models," *Essays in Arts and Sciences* 6, no. 1 (1977): 56.

BIBLIOGRAPHY

Anderson, John R. *Cognitive Psychology and Its Implications*. San Francisco: W. H. Freeman, 1980.

Bartlett, Frederick C. *Remembering: A Study in Experimental and Social Psychology*. New York: Cambridge University Press, 1932.

Becker, Joseph P. "A Model for the Encoding of Experiential Information." In *Computer Models of Thought and Language*, edited by Roger C. Schank and Kenneth Mark Colby. San Francisco: W. H. Freeman, 1973.

Collins, Allan M., and Elizabeth F. Loftus. "A Spreading-Activation Theory of Semantic Processing." *Psychological Review* 82 (1975): 407–28.

Cone, Edward T., ed. *Berlioz: Fantastic Symphony*. New York: W. W. Norton, 1971.

Cooke, Deryck. *Gustav Mahler: An Introduction to His Music*. London: Cambridge University Press, 1980.

Cudworth, Charles L. "Cadence galante: The Story of a Cliché." *The Monthly Musical Record* 79 (1949): 176–78.

Dahlhaus, Carl. "Some Models of Unity in Musical Form." *Journal of Music Theory* 19 (1975): 2–30.

———, ed. *Studien zur Trivialmusik des 19. Jahrhunderts*. Regensburg, 1967.

Dowling, W. Jay, and Dane L. Harwood. *Music Cognition*. Orlando, Fla.: Academic Press, 1986.

Evans, Selby H. "A Brief Statement of Schema Theory." *Psychonomic Science* 8, no. 2 (1967): 87–88.

Focillon, Henri. *La vie des formes*. Paris: Librairie Ernst Leroux, 1934. [*The Life of Forms in Art*. Translated by Charles Beecher Hogan and George Kubler. New Haven: Yale University Press, 1942.]

Friendly, Michael. "Methods for Finding Graphic Representations of Associative Memory Structures." In *Memory Organization and Structure*, edited by C. Richard Puff. New York: Academic Press, 1979.

Frye, Northrop. *Anatomy of Criticism*. Princeton, N.J.: Princeton University Press, 1957.

Garden, Edward. "Rubinstein, Anton." In *The New Grove Dictionary of Music and Musicians*, edited by Stanley Sadie. London: Macmillan Publishers, 1980.

Gibson, Eleanor. *Principles of Perceptual Learning and Development*. New York: Appleton-Century-Crofts, 1969.

Grobstein, Clifford. "Hierarchical Order and Neogenesis." In *Hierarchy Theory: The Challenge of Complex Systems*, edited by Howard H. Pattee. New York: George Braziller, 1973.

Heartz, Daniel. "Galant." In *The New Grove Dictionary of Music and Musicians*, edited by Stanley Sadie. London: Macmillan Publishers, 1980.

Howell, Peter, Ian Cross, and Robert West, eds. *Musical Structure and Cognition*. London: Academic Press, 1985.

Kant, Immanuel. *The Critique of Pure Reason*. Great Books of the Western World. Vol. 42, *Kant*, translated by J.M.D. Meiklejohn. Chicago: Encyclopaedia Britannica, 1952.

Kerman, Joseph. "How We Got into Analysis, and How to Get Out." *Critical Inquiry* 7 (1980): 311–31.

Krumhansl, Carol L., and Mary A. Castellano.

"Dynamic Processes in Music Perception." *Memory & Cognition* 11 (1983): 325–34.

Lachman, Janet L., and Roy Lachman. "Theories of Memory Organization and Human Evolution." In *Memory Organization and Structure,* edited by C. Richard Puff. New York: Academic Press, 1979.

Lerdahl, Fred, and Ray Jackendoff. *A Generative Theory of Tonal Music.* Cambridge, Mass.: MIT Press, 1983.

———. "Toward a Formal Theory of Tonal Music." *Journal of Music Theory* 21 (1977): 111–72.

Lester, Joel. *Harmony in Tonal Music.* 2 vols. New York: Alfred A. Knopf, 1982.

Longyear, Rey M. *Nineteenth-Century Romanticism in Music.* Englewood Cliffs, N.J.: Prentice-Hall, 1969.

Mahler (Werfel), Alma. *Gustav Mahler: Memories and Letters.* Seattle: University of Washington Press, 1971.

Mandler, George. "Organization, Memory, and Mental Structures." In *Memory Organization and Structure,* edited by C. Richard Puff. New York: Academic Press, 1979.

Mandler, Jean Matter. "Categorical and Schematic Organization in Memory." In *Memory Organization and Structure,* edited by C. Richard Puff. New York: Academic Press, 1979.

———. *Stories, Scripts, and Scenes: Aspects of Schema Theory.* Hillsdale, N.J.: Lawrence Erlbaum Associates, 1984.

Marliave, Joseph de. *Beethoven's Quartets.* London, 1928. Reprint. New York: Dover Publications, 1961.

Meehan, James R. "An Artificial Intelligence Approach to Tonal Music Theory." *Computer Music Journal* 4, no. 2 (1980): 60–65.

Meyer, Leonard B. *Emotion and Meaning in Music.* Chicago: University of Chicago Press, 1956.

———. *Explaining Music: Essays and Explorations.* Chicago: University of Chicago Press, 1973.

———. "Exploiting Limits: Creation, Archetypes, and Style Change." *Daedalus* 109, no. 2 (1980): 177–205.

———. "Grammatical Simplicity and Relational Richness: The Trio of Mozart's G Minor Symphony." *Critical Inquiry* 2 (1975): 693–761.

———. "Music and Ideology in the Nineteenth Century." In *The Tanner Lectures on Human Values, Vol. VI: 1985,* edited by Sterling M. McMurrin. Salt Lake City: University of Utah Press, 1985.

———. "Toward a Theory of Style." In *The Concept of Style,* edited by Berel Lang. Philadelphia: University of Pennsylvania Press, 1979.

Mies, Paul. *Beethoven's Sketches: An Analysis of His Style Based on a Study of His Sketch-Books.* London, 1929. Reprint. New York: Dover Publications, 1974.

Miller, George A. "The Magical Number Seven, Plus or Minus Two: Some Limits on Our Capacity for Processing Information." *Psychological Review* 63 (1956): 81–97.

Momigny, Jérôme Joseph de. *La seule vraie théorie de la musique.* Paris, 1821. Reprint. Geneva: Minkoff, 1980.

Motte-Haber, Helga de la, ed. *Das Triviale in Literatur, Musik, und bildender Kunst.* Frankfurt am Main, 1972.

Narmour, Eugene. *Beyond Schenkerism: The Need for Alternatives in Music Analysis.* Chicago: University of Chicago Press, 1977.

Neisser, Ulrich. *Cognition and Reality: Principles and Implications of Cognitive Psychology.* San Francisco: W. H. Freeman, 1976.

Pattee, Howard H. "The Physical Basis and Origin of Hierarchical Control." In *Hierarchy Theory: The Challenge of Complex Systems,* edited by Howard H. Pattee. New York: George Braziller, 1973.

Puff, C. Richard, ed. *Memory Organization and Structure.* New York: Academic Press, 1979.

Ratner, Leonard G. *Classic Music: Expression, Form, and Style.* New York: Schirmer Books, 1980.

Reed, Stephen K. *Psychological Processes in Pattern Recognition.* New York: Academic Press, 1973.

Rosen, Charles. *The Classical Style: Haydn, Mozart, Beethoven.* New York: W. W. Norton, 1972.

Rosner, Burton S., and Leonard B. Meyer. "Melodic Processes and the Perception of Music." In *The Psychology of Music,* edited by Diana Deutsch. New York: Academic Press, 1982.

Rumelhart, David E. "Schemata: The Building Blocks of Cognition." In *Theoretical Issues in Reading Comprehension,* edited by Rand J. Spiro, Bertram C. Bruce, and William F.

Brewer. Hillsdale, N.J.: Lawrence Erlbaum Associates, 1980.

Salzer, Felix. *Structural Hearing: Tonal Coherence in Music.* 2 vols. New York: Dover Publications, 1962.

Schank, Roger C., and Robert P. Abelson. *Scripts, Plans, Goals and Understanding: An Inquiry into Human Knowledge Structures.* Hillsdale, N.J.: Lawrence Erlbaum Associates, 1977.

Schank, Roger C., and Kenneth Mark Colby, eds. *Computer Models of Thought and Language.* San Francisco: W. H. Freeman, 1973.

Schenker, Heinrich. *Free Composition (Der freie Satz).* Translated and edited by Ernst Oster. New York: Longman, 1979.

Serafine, Mary Louise. "Cognition in Music." *Cognition* 14 (1983): 119–83.

Shaw, George Bernard. *Shaw's Music.* Vol. 2. London: The Bodley Head, 1981.

Slawson, Wayne. Review of *The Psychology of Music,* edited by Diana Deutsch. *Music Theory Spectrum* 5 (1983): 121–26.

Stoffer, Thomas H. "Representation of Phrase Structure in the Perception of Music." *Music Perception* 3 (1985): 191–220.

Strohm, Reinhard. *Italienische Opernarien des frühen Settecento (1720–1730).* Cologne: Arno Volk Verlag, 1976.

Titon, Jeff Todd. "Talking about Music: Analysis, Synthesis, and Song-Producing Models." *Essays in Arts and Sciences* 6, no. 1 (1977): 53–57.

Tulving, Endel. "Episodic and Semantic Memory." In *Organization of Memory,* edited by Endel Tulving and Wayne Donaldson. New York: Academic Press, 1972.

Wolf, Eugene K. "Authenticity and Stylistic Evidence in the Early Symphony: A Conflict in Attribution between Richter and Stamitz." In *A Musical Offering: Essays in Honor of Martin Bernstein,* edited by Edward H. Clinkscale and Claire Brook. New York: Pendragon Press, 1977.

Zarlino, Gioseffo. *Istitutioni harmoniche.* Venice, 1558.

Zimmermann, Hans Dieter. *Schema-Literatur: ästhetische Norm und literarisches System.* Stuttgart: W. Kohlhammer, 1979.

INDEX

Page numbers in italics refer to the Appendix (a listing of individual musical examples referred to or presented in the text).